W9-DAR-880

Microsoft®
Certification
Success Guide

Other books by the author

The Ultimate OS/2® Programmer's Manual
John Mueller

Microsoft Macro Assembler 5.1: Programming in the 80386 Environment
John Mueller and Wallace Wang

The Clipper® Interface Handbook
John Mueller

The Ultimate DOS Programmer's Manual
John Mueller

Memory Management and Multitasking Beyond 640K
Lenny Bailes and John Mueller, Foreword by John C. Dvorak

The Ultimate DOS Programmer's Manual—2nd Edition
John Mueller

The Hands-On Guide to Network Management
John Mueller, CNE and Robert A. Williams, CNE, CNI

Novell Certification Handbook
John Mueller, CNE and Robert A. Williams, CNE, CNI

The Novell CNA/CNE Study Guide
John Mueller, CNE and Robert A. Williams, CNE, CNI

Microsoft®
Certification
Success Guide

John Paul Mueller

Windcrest®/ McGraw-Hill
New York   San Francisco   Washington, D.C.   Auckland   Bogotá
Caracas   Lisbon   London   Madrid   Mexico City   Milan
Montreal   New Delhi   San Juan   Singapore
Sydney   Tokyo   Toronto

pbk   1 2 3 4 5 6 7 8 9 DOH/DOH 9 9 8 7 6 5 4
hc   1 2 3 4 5 6 7 8 9 DOH/DOH 9 9 8 7 6 5 4

Library of Congress Cataloging-in-Publication Data
Mueller, John, 1958–
        Microsoft certification success guide / by John Mueller.
            p.   cm.
        Includes index.
        ISBN 0-07-043973-7
        1. Electronic data processing personnel—Certification.
        2. Microsoft software—Study and teaching. I. Title.
        QA76.3.M84   1994
        005.36—dc20   94-29630
                                                        CIP

Acquisitions editor: Brad Schepp
Editorial team: Robert Ostrander, Executive Editor
                Aaron Bittner, Book Editor
Production team: Katherine G. Brown, Director
                Susan E. Hansford, Coding
                Jan Fisher, Desktop Operator
                Nancy K. Mickley, Proofreader
                Jodi L. Tyler, Indexer
Design team: Jaclyn J. Boone, Designer   0439737
                Brian Allison, Associate Designer   WK2

Esther Darneal has always been more than just another family member to me. She has been confidant, friend, and everything else that a mother should be. I will always remember her love and kindness; it's the best part of human existence.

Contents

Appendices

Introduction

 ## What will this book do for you?

The Microsoft Certification Success Guide is the one source of information you need to prepare for, attain, and use any of the certifications offered by Microsoft. There are many network administrators, programmers, managers, and other professionals who need to get their certification, but are unaware of the requirements or unsure of whom to contact. This book provides you with all the answers you need to improve your job performance by getting a Microsoft certification.

Of course, improving job performance is one step toward many goals. For example, you may want a job with more responsibility, better pay, or greater advancement potential. The Microsoft Certification Success Guide helps you gain these goals by showing you how to present your certification to potential employers or clients. Learning how to present your certification is as important as getting it in the first place. In total, this book helps you ten specific ways. It helps you to:

❶ Learn the differences between the various certifications offered by Microsoft. This includes the relatively new Microsoft Certified Product Specialist, Microsoft Certified Systems Engineer, and Microsoft Certified Trainer certifications. Many users are unsure what level or type of certification they need. Especially unclear are the differences between Microsoft Certified Product Specialist and Microsoft Certified Systems Engineer. This book helps you understand the differences and plan for the level of certification that meets your needs.

❷ Enhance your career by getting a Microsoft certification today. Many people face a Microsoft certification as an extra responsibility they neither want nor need. The Microsoft Certification Success Guide helps you over this hurdle by showing you the benefits of such a certification. In many cases a positive attitude could mean the difference between getting and not getting certified.

❸ Plan for the certification process. It's unfortunate, but many people start certification training with no idea of what to expect or how to prepare for it. There are instances where the person has never even used a computer before, but now they have to learn to run a network. The Microsoft Certification Success Guide will help people prepare for certification by helping them understand the certification requirements. It also helps them create a checklist tailored to their needs. Writing down what you need to do is at least half the battle in planning for certification.

❹ Understand what support you can expect from Microsoft. Part of the benefit of getting certified is the support that Microsoft provides for these people. While the documentation provided with the certification package outlines some of the benefits, a mere list is not enough. The Microsoft Certification Success Guide helps people understand what they can do with these additional support items.

❺ Plan for continuing education requirements. Many people approach a Microsoft certification as they would a high school education. Once it's over, they peacefully go back to their old routine, never acknowledging the need to continue their education. Fortunately, the Microsoft recertification requirements will quickly make these people aware of the need for continuing education. This book will help them prepare for it before they lose their certification due to lack of planning.

⑥ Find all your certification questions answered in one place. One of the big problems in getting a Microsoft certification is that the prospect spends many hours searching for answers to their questions. This problem isn't new or unique; colleges and universities face the same problem. Many authors have addressed the issues of getting from point A to point B in these institutions. For example, just look at all the books that tell you how to get a GED or take an SAT test; both are requirements for getting into a college or university. Currently there is no guide for people who want to become a Microsoft Certified Product Specialist (or attain any other Microsoft certification for that matter); this book answers that need.

⑦ Get your certification quickly and easily. The Microsoft Certification Success Guide provides tips and hints that reduce the chance of failure when taking a test. This could shave days or even weeks from the certification process. Add to this the time saved researching the certification itself and you could end up saving a month or more in the certification cycle.

⑧ Learn what courses are available. Many people miss opportunities to learn something they really wanted to know about a Microsoft product simply because they don't know what courses are available. The Microsoft Certification Success Guide provides a list of classes provided by Microsoft. All you need to do is decide which courses you want to take (as long as they meet certification requirements), sign up, and take the courses.

⑨ Get answers to your questions quickly and easily. The Microsoft Certification Success Guide provides a list of important phone numbers that you can call whenever you need help with a problem. Instead of writing these numbers on scraps of paper that get lost whenever you really need them, using this guide can really help you get help quickly. In addition, instead of playing telephone tag with the one person you thought could help only to find out they can't, this book helps you find the right person the first time.

⑩ Find sources of additional information. There is no one book solution to every problem. Rather than strand you without the resources you need, this book provides a list of places you can go for additional help. This resource is very important to both the novice and the expert reader.

 # Understand why you need certification

Many people don't understand what a Microsoft certification is or why they need it. This includes employers as well as clients. Even if you understand why the certification is important, presenting these facts to an employer or client may prove difficult. The Microsoft Certification Success Guide provides you with a full description of each of the certifications and why they are important. This not only increases your own knowledge, but helps you explain it to potential clients and employers as well. Knowing this information could mean the difference between getting a job or losing it to someone less qualified than you. It also helps you get the level of compensation you deserve for having a certification.

 # Get all the information needed to attain your certification

Ever try to get through all the layers of bureaucracy required to get any kind of license or certification? Anyone who has had this frustrating and time-consuming experience will tell you that any help you can get will literally cut weeks from the process. The Microsoft Certification Success Guide helps you through the mire of red tape and false leads so you can get your certification fast. Consider it your road map to bigger and better things.

 # Create your own certification map

Every person needs to look at different aspects of the certification process. This book helps you tailor a certification map that meets your specific needs. Rather than use a generic map that someone else created to meet their needs, you can forge your own road through the certification jungle. Of course, forging your own path takes more time and effort, but it pays in the long run because you'll know how to use your certification better.

This book helps you see what roadblocks you'll face and how to avoid them. It also helps you create your certification map faster and more accurately. Mistakes cost time; let this book help you prevent certification mistakes that could add weeks or even months to your certification effort. The check lists and other organizational aids help you get organized quickly.

 Learn how to use your certification to enhance job opportunities

The bottom line in getting certified is enhanced job opportunities. This allows you to get a job with higher pay and to perform more interesting work. Why make every day a boring trudge to the same old work? This book shows you how to use that certification to make life interesting and your work more profitable.

CHAPTER 1

Getting started

E VERYONE needs to learn the basics before they start a new task. Getting a Microsoft certification isn't any different. This chapter explains what types of certification Microsoft offers, what differentiates them from other certifications, and the criteria for getting the certification. We will also discuss all the duties and responsibilities associated with the various certifications. We even include a procedure for creating your own certification checklist; a must for anyone serious about attaining this useful and beneficial credential.

Microsoft uses a very basic scheme for its certification process. You must complete one or more tests within each area to gain your certification. Microsoft offers a course that covers each required exam. You can choose whether or not you take the course. However, taking the course does improve your chances of passing the exam.

What complicates this process is that Microsoft also offers a variety of courses that are not related to a basic certification. These courses help managers and consultants achieve business goals or gain new insights into the world of computing. This book lists all the available Microsoft courses in appendix C. This chapter shows you which course offerings pertain to your certification.

Microsoft offers two major classes of certification: Microsoft Certified Product Specialist (MCPS) and Microsoft Certified Systems Engineer (MCSE). Both certifications lend you credibility and valuable knowledge. As you understand what each certification requires, you will be able to select the one that is right for your knowledge and experience level.

Deciding which certification you need

The sheer number of certifications available today make it nearly impossible for the average person to figure out exactly what he or she wants by simply reading the vendor literature. There are several questions that you must answer before you pick the certification program you want to pursue. For one thing, why are you getting certified? Second, you need to determine your needs. A third question might include the number or type of supplementary courses you plan to take. Finally, you must determine the needs of your clients (if you are a consultant) or your company (if you are an employee).

Let's look at the first question. If you really don't know much about networks, then the question of whether you need certification is very easy. You need the training to get your work done; getting certified is one way to get this training. The number of unskilled personnel who need to deal with networks is on the increase today. It is this influx of new faces, more than anything else, that drives the certification effort today.

On the other hand, suppose you are already the network administrator for a company or successful in your consulting business. The big question you need to ask yourself is whether you even need certification. After all, you can perform your job adequately right now without the aid of any type of official recognition. This is a typical response to the certification process by a fully trained technician. Technically, the person saying it is quite right. Just like anything else in life, it's the knowledge that you possess that counts. However, you have to provide proof of that knowledge to a potential employer or client. The best way to do so is to get certified. A "sheepskin" can mean the difference between getting the job or having to look elsewhere.

Now that I have the disclaimers out of the way, I can get to the meat of the subject. What you really need to ask yourself is this, "Do I want to earn more money?" The answer to that question provides the bottom line response to the question of whether you need to get certified. You need to consider your needs before you consider anything else. Certification brings with it all kinds of responsibilities

and rights. It also helps you build a much stronger career path. Chapters 2, 6, and 8 answer this question in a lot greater detail. All that you really need to figure out right now is the type of certification that's right for you.

The third question is a lot more difficult to answer. The supplementary (or elective) courses that you choose depend on a lot of different criteria. These criteria include: personal experiences, personal goals, your company and client needs, general interests, and continuing education requirements. Of course, there are probably other criteria you can add to this list as well. Whatever the motivation, make sure you choose your elective courses carefully. Take the time to plan your certification path. You may even find that you want to take some courses that are not part of the certification path. Microsoft certainly offers a wide variety of courses that can enhance the career path of any individual. Don't let your certification blind you to other possibilities.

The fourth question is very easy. You need to get the job done; it's pretty simple to understand why. With this in mind, you have to take the time to consider the needs of your company or clients. It's their needs that motivate you to get certified. The money you earn by working for them will supply the gold at the end of the certification rainbow.

The following two sections help you understand the two major Microsoft certifications. As previously stated, Microsoft offers a wide variety of courses. Many of these courses will help you build your knowledge base and may even result in a few new jobs if you're a consultant. However, not all of those courses pertain to Microsoft's certification program. The section on creating a certification checklist will help you over this hurdle as well. Make sure you fully understand all the nuances of attaining your certification before you actually begin the process.

 # Microsoft Certified Product Specialist

The Microsoft Certified Product Specialist (MCPS) could come from any of a number of backgrounds. This is a person skilled in a particular desktop operating system environment. They may also

work with a particular application. An MCPS may or may not provide consulting services to a company. They may be a manager for a department, or the technician assigned to help new users learn the basics of computing. As you can see, there is no typical MCPS.

Whatever your background, every product specialist shares several things in common. These are the things that define your title; they make you special in the computing community. The following list provides you with an idea of some of these similarities. Every MCPS must be:

> ➤ Completely trained in the operating system of choice. This means more than just knowing the simple commands. It means that you are fully trained to use the environment to its fullest.

> ➤ Completely trained in one or more products. As with the operating system, this means that you know how to use the product to solve problems. It also means that you know many of the nuances of using the product.

> ➤ Fully aware of all the updates available for a product. This means that you know the current version number of your product specialty. It includes any bug fix updates. You should know where to obtain the updates. Microsoft commonly places these updates on CompuServe or sells them through local retailers. (In some cases they take both courses.)

> ➤ Good at working with people. In most cases an MCPS helps other people find solutions to problems. This means that you will work with people who do not possess your level of knowledge. You must exhibit a certain amount of patience and the ability to teach others the things that you worked so hard to learn.

> ➤ Ready to assist a Microsoft Certified Systems Engineer (MCSE) in day-to-day network maintenance and training activities. You may find that you become responsible for helping the company MCSE in training individuals. This frees the MCSE to perform network specific duties in other parts of the company.

Microsoft currently supports two operating system choices and four product choices. The operating systems include: Windows and Windows NT. The product selections include: Microsoft Excel, Microsoft Word, Microsoft Mail, and Microsoft Project. Figure 1-1 shows the MCPS certification routes that you can pursue.

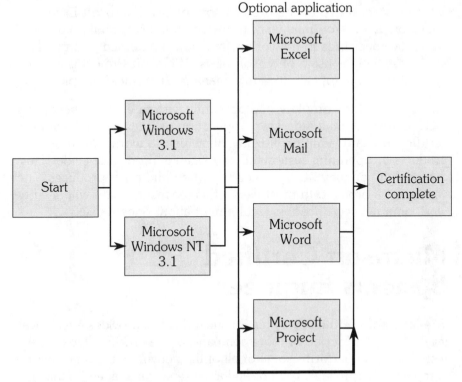

Figure 1-1

Sample MSCPS certification checklist.

As you can see from the diagram, the first choice you need to make is what operating system you will specialize in. Consultants should choose Microsoft Windows, because it is the operating system of choice for most companies right now. Employees should choose the operating system used by their employer.

Once you complete this requirement, you can choose one or more products to specialize in. You do not have to complete a desktop application exam to get your certification. This is an elective requirement that enhances the certification you receive. Some MCPSs may choose to become desktop operating system specialists. Your choice of products largely depends on the products used by your company or clients. It doesn't pay to specialize in a product that no one uses. You may, however, want to select more than one product. This is especially true of a consultant. It is very likely that your clients

will own at least two of the products on the list: Microsoft Excel and Microsoft Word. You may want to include Microsoft Mail if your company specializes in network installations and at least some of those installations use a Microsoft basis. Microsoft Project is a product that will appeal more to a manager than most people.

You only need to complete one operating system exam to become an MCPS. You can take a desktop application exam to enhance your certification. Any additional exams allow you to work with those products or operating systems. Every exam is product specific. This means that you may need to recertify when Microsoft produces a new version of a product. In most cases, this means that you will need to work on a new certification requirement about once a year.

Microsoft Certified Systems Engineer

The Microsoft Certified Systems Engineer (MCSE) provides a technical level of support for one or more companies. The MCSE is typically a technician who performs some or all of the network maintenance for a company. You probably will not find any users or managers in this category. This certification is for the technician or consultant who lives and breathes computers on a daily basis. If you don't know your way around both the hardware and software installed on the typical computer, then you may want to consider becoming an MCPS instead.

Whether you work for a company or operate as an independent consultant, every MCSE shares several things in common. These are the things that define your title; they make you special in the computing community. The following list provides you with an idea of some of these similarities. An MCSE must be:

> ➤ Completely trained in three different operating systems including: Microsoft Windows, Microsoft Windows NT, and Microsoft Windows NT Advanced Server. You also get to choose between two other operating system requirements: Networking with Microsoft Windows or Networking with Microsoft Windows for Workgroups. This means more than just knowing the simple commands. It means that you are fully trained to use the environment to its fullest.

➤ Completely trained in one or more network operating systems. This means that you know more than just how to log in and out of a network. An MCSE knows the network inside-out.

➤ Completely trained in one or more advanced systems products. As with the operating system, this means that you know how to use the product to solve problems. It also means that you know many of the nuances of using the product.

➤ Fully aware of all the updates available for a product. This means that you know the current version number of your product specialty. It includes any bug fix updates. You should know where to obtain the updates. Microsoft commonly places these updates on CompuServe or sells them through local retailers. (In some cases they take both courses.)

➤ Good at working with people. In most cases an MCSE helps other people find solutions to problems. This means that you will work with people who do not possess your level of knowledge. You must exhibit a certain amount of patience and the ability to teach others the things that you worked so hard to learn.

➤ Good at network problem resolution. The MCSE needs to know both hardware and software. They need to know how to install NICs and standard boards like video adapters. The MCSE must also know about different types of cable and how to use them.

Microsoft currently supports five operating system choices and seven product choices. The operating systems include: Microsoft Windows, Microsoft Windows NT, Microsoft Windows NT Advanced Server, Networking with Microsoft Windows, and Networking with Microsoft Windows for Workgroups. The product selections include: Microsoft SQL Server Database Administration for OS/2, Microsoft SQL Server Administration for Windows NT, Microsoft Mail Enterprise, Microsoft LAN Manager Network Administration, Microsoft LAN Manager Advanced Network Administration, Microsoft SQL Server Database Implementation, and TCP/IP for Microsoft Windows NT. Figure 1-2 shows the MCSE certification routes that you can pursue.

As you can see from the diagram, the first thing you need to do is pass the three required operating system exams. Once you complete this task, you can choose between Networking with Microsoft Windows or

Figure 1-2

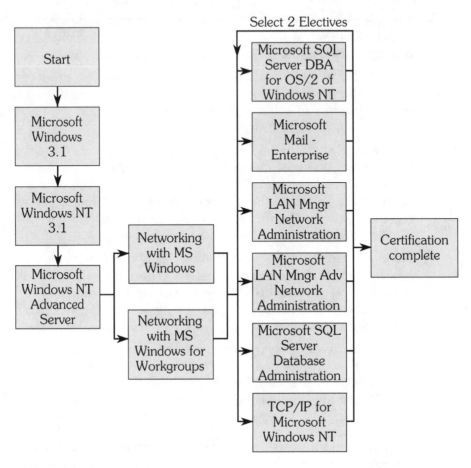

Sample MSCSE certification checklist.

Networking with Microsoft Windows for Workgroups. The choice here is fairly simple for a consultant. If most of your clients own small networks that you could manage using Windows for Workgroups, that probably makes the best choice. Otherwise, choose Networking with Microsoft Windows. Employees of companies should make the choice based on their company's needs. In most cases this means that you will choose the Networking with Microsoft Windows option.

Once you complete your four operating system exams, you need to choose two of the electives. The choices here are a little less clear

than the operating system choices. You need to make a decision based on your client or company needs. For example, if you are a consultant who specializes in database management systems, then you may want to look at taking the two SQL Server specific exams. Note that you must choose between OS/2 or Windows NT. Microsoft will not allow you to take both as your two electives. Of course, you could take both in conjunction with another elective.

Company employees may find it advantageous to concentrate on the network itself. For example, if your company uses TCP/IP, then you may want to take the TCP/IP for Microsoft Windows NT elective exam. You will certainly want to take the Microsoft LAN Manager Network Administration and Advanced Network Administration exams if your company makes use of that product. Make sure you match the exams you take with the needs of your company. You may even want to spend some time with management to consider the issue before you make the leap.

Microsoft currently offers a fast track for MCSEs. The fast track allows you to complete the exams faster and at a reduced cost. Fast track trainees receive a free copy of Windows NT Advanced Server and a training voucher good for one of the courses. In addition, CNEs, ECNEs, CBSs, and CBEs do not have to take the Networking with Microsoft Windows 3.1 exam. There are other considerations for this program as well. Make sure you call to find out the particulars of the current program if you qualify.

⇨ Microsoft Certified Trainer

The Microsoft Certified Trainer (MCT) provides training services for a Microsoft SP ATC. In other words, this is one of the very first people that most CP candidates meet on the road to certification. As Microsoft's training representative, the MCT must meet a higher standard than the other certificate holders. This doesn't mean that the MCT takes special courses; quite the contrary. The MCT takes the same courses and exams as any other CP. The difference comes after the candidate finishes these initial requirements. If you enjoy working with people and like to help others meet their certification goals, then you might want to become an MCT.

Every MCT works for a Microsoft SP ATC. This is one of the requirements for getting your certification. There are many other things that MCTs share in common. The following list provides you with an idea of some of these similarities. MCTs must be:

➤ Completely trained in the operating system(s) of choice (if you decide to pursue operating systems as a specialty). This means more than just knowing the simple commands. It means that you are fully trained to use the environment to its fullest. You must certify on each operating system that you want to teach.

➤ Completely trained in one or more products (if you decide to specialize in Microsoft products). As with the operating system, this means that you know how to use the product to solve problems. It also means that you know many of the nuances of using the product. As with the operating system requirements, you must certify on every product that you want to teach.

➤ Fully aware of all the updates available for a product. This means that you know the current version number of your product specialty. It includes any bug fix updates. You should know where to obtain the updates. Microsoft commonly places these updates on CompuServe, or sells them through local retailers. As an MCT, you will know a lot more about the future of Microsoft's products than the other CPs. You will attend special seminars and other events to keep up-to-date on the product. As an instructor, you will also receive a lot of feedback from the people you teach. This gives you a real advantage over many other people in the field.

➤ Good at working with people. In most cases an MCT helps other people find solutions to problems. Students will come through your door looking for solutions, in addition to the certification materials you teach. This means that you will always work with people who do not possess your level of knowledge. You must exhibit a phenomenal amount of patience and the ability to teach others the things that you worked so hard to learn.

➤ Completely trained in one or more network operating systems (if you choose to pursue this route). If you want to teach others about networks, then you need to know about them too. This means that you know more than just how to log in and out of a network. An MCT knows the network inside-out.

➤ Good at network problem resolution (only if you teach network related topics). The MCT needs to know both hardware and software. They need to know how to install NICs and standard boards like a video adapter. The MCT must also know about different types of cable and how to use them. Of course, just knowing this information isn't enough; you need to know how to communicate this information to others.

➤ Fully qualified instructors. They know how to communicate with others. The certification process adds the required Microsoft specific knowledge. Finally, the Microsoft Trainer Preparation Course helps you get ready to present this information to a class. Every MCT shares this experience.

Microsoft currently supports five operating system choices and eleven product choices for MCTs. There is also a plethora of other courses you can choose to teach (see appendix C). The operating systems include: Microsoft Windows, Microsoft Windows NT, Microsoft Windows NT Advanced Server, Networking with Microsoft Windows, and Networking with Microsoft Windows for Workgroups. The product selections include: Microsoft Excel, Microsoft Word, Microsoft Mail, Microsoft Project, Microsoft SQL Server Database Administration for OS/2, Microsoft SQL Server Administration for Windows NT, Microsoft Mail Enterprise, Microsoft LAN Manager Network Administration, Microsoft LAN Manager Advanced Network Administration, Microsoft SQL Server Database Implementation, and TCP/IP for Microsoft Windows NT. Figure 1-3 shows the MCT certification routes that you can pursue.

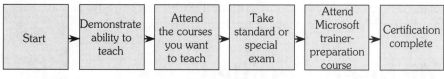

Figure 1-3

Sample EMSCSE certification checklist.

As you can see from the diagram, the certification process begins with a look at your teaching qualifications. I'll examine this topic in more detail in the next chapter. Essentially, you need some type of physical proof that you can teach before you begin the certification

process. Chapter 2 discusses a number of methods that you can use to provide this proof to Microsoft.

The second thing you need to do is attend the courses that you want to teach. If there are no established classes, then you will attend a course taught by a Microsoft employee. Some people refer to these courses as "factory" schools. There is no better way to learn how to teach a course than to watch other people do it. Unlike the other certifications, you must attend the courses to become an MCT. This means that you will attend one course for each specialty you want to pursue.

The third requirement is to take the required exams. Just like every other certification candidate, you must prove that you completely understand how to use and maintain the Microsoft product or operating system. Some courses do not provide a standard exam. Microsoft provides a special exam just for MCTs in this case. You always have to take an exam to prove your technical proficiency.

The fourth requirement is to take the Microsoft Trainer-Preparation Course. This is a special course designed to help MCTs prepare for their roles as instructors. It includes things like how to set up your classroom, how to deliver the material, lab presentation techniques, and a variety of other instructor related topics. As you can see, this course helps you provide the best level of training to the students that you'll teach.

There is a final requirement that doesn't appear in our diagram, but is very important. MCTs must maintain a higher standard of education than any other CP. This means that the MCT will spend more time maintaining their certification. In addition, you must maintain your level of instruction. Microsoft constantly monitors the quality of instruction that MCTs provide to their students.

Microsoft Certified Developer Specialist

The Microsoft Certified Developer (MCD)[1] certification program is under development right now. Microsoft has started writing exams for

---

[1]This name will probably change before the program is introduced. Microsoft also refers to this program as Microsoft Certified Solution Developer and Certification for Developers.

products like Visual BASIC and Access. Whether or not you can actually participate in this program yet was up-in-the-air at the time of publication. However, the program will appear sometime in the near future. If you are a programmer, developer, or other support specialist who wants to show your clients that you care a little more about your output than someone else, then you may want to pursue this certification program.

Creating a certification checklist

Now that you have a basic idea of what each certification entails, you can create a checklist. This checklist will help you organize your thoughts and actions to help safeguard against missing or forgetting any of the requirements. Often, as we start to pursue a goal or certification we lose sight of what it is that we really want to accomplish and why. The use of the checklist along with understanding why we want or need the certification (covered in-depth in chapter 2) will help you maintain the proper focus to succeed.

The checklist that you create should have information about the certification that you will pursue, courses, and related exams. This includes dates of training courses, course numbers, dates of the exams, and exam numbers. Other pieces of information included in the checklist are: telephone numbers of your contacts at Microsoft, the Microsoft Solution Provider Authorized Training Centers (Microsoft SP ATC) facility where you attend classes, the Drake registration office, and the Drake testing office. You may also want to include addresses of the above mentioned locations, an area for reference material, and an area for any notes.

There are two very important contacts mentioned in the previous paragraph. First, the Microsoft SP ATC is a training center that provides Microsoft-certified training. The difference between someone who teaches Microsoft and a Microsoft SP ATC is much like the difference between a nonaccredited and an accredited college or university. You may learn something from either source of information, but people tend to view your credentials with less enthusiasm if you don't use a Microsoft SP ATC. Some people will

disregard your Microsoft training altogether if you don't receive your training from a Microsoft SP ATC. The reason is obvious; you receive training from a known good source if you use a Microsoft SP ATC. The level of training is dubious at best from any other source.

The second contact is the Drake Testing Center. This is a company that provides testing for a wide range of certifications; everyone from CPAs to Registered Nurses goes to Drake to take exams. The person sitting next to you during an exam may not even know very much about computers; he or she may fly planes for a living. Drake testing centers appear in a wide variety of locations. You can find them in dedicated test centers or borrowing space at a training facility like a college or university. You may even find one at your local Microsoft SP ATC.

The Drake Testing Center always uses someone who is certified by them to administer the examinations you take. This person makes certain that you do not have an opportunity to cheat on the examination, that you have any required testing materials, and that your test environment is as quiet and comfortable as possible. You are required to follow any instructions the administrator may provide, and the administrator is the only one you can talk to during the examination.

One thing that these test center administrators do not do is handle your examination. Drake downloads the examinations from the test center on a daily basis and sends them to the appropriate places. The computer automatically grades the examinations after you take them. As you can see, your examination is untouched by any human hands but your own. If you fail, there is little chance that you will convince anyone that there was any problem except a lack of study on your part. If you do notice a flaw in your examination, make sure you point it out to the test center administrator immediately. The administrator can provide feedback to Microsoft and may help you if you narrowly missed passing your examination. Reporting the problem will also reduce the risk of someone else stumbling over the same problem. As a result, you will also want to report the problem to your contact at Microsoft.

Now that you understand what you want to do and whom you need to contact, it's time to start a checklist. The following sample checklists will give you an idea of what you may want to include in your checklist. If you decide to use the checklists in this book, use a highlighter to mark which courses and exams you are going to use in obtaining your required credits. Be sure to add in any information that will help you reach your goals.

The checklist for the MCPS certification usually is not as detailed as the ones for the MCSE and MCT certifications. The example in Fig. 1-4 lists the basic information.

MCPS Certification Checklist

Figure 1-4

Item Description	Date
Understand the Responsibility of an MCPS	_____
Complete Goals Worksheet	_____

Operating System Exam Description (Choose One)	Exam Number	Exam Pass Date
Microsoft Windows	70-30	_____
Microsoft Windows NT	70-40	_____

Product Exam Description (Choose One)	Exam Number	Exam Pass Date
Microsoft Word for Windows	70-33	_____
Microsoft Excel	70-31	_____
Microsoft Project	70-32	_____
Microsoft Mail for PC Networks - Desktop	70-35	_____

Figure 1-4   *Continued.*

Other Information:

Phone Number: _____

Date of Exams: _____

_____

Location of Test Center: _____

Date Paper Work Sent to Microsoft: _____

Reference materials: (Books, Software, etc.): _____

_____

Misc.: _____

_____

_____

Notice that the first two items tell when you understand the responsibility of an MCPS and when you complete the goals worksheet. This is the preplanning section, which demonstrates that you know what you are doing and why. The next two areas define the exam description, exam date, and exam pass date. Note that there is one operating system and one product requirement. Simply select one item from each section. This is what you need to do to fulfill the requirements of MCPS. As you pass the exams, fill in the dates. In the last section of the checklist, we provide a space for information like the phone numbers for the testing center and for Microsoft. The form includes other areas for dates of exams and the locations of test centers. When filling in the test center location, make sure you include street address, cross streets, and any special directions about how to get to the test center. The next line documents when you sent your paperwork to Microsoft. Also provided is space for any references that may help you study or prepare for the exams and a space for any other comments or ideas that you may find important. Filling out each area of the checklist ensures that you complete each step necessary to become certified.

The MCSE and MCT checklists are a little more involved than the one for the MCPS. Both certifications have a list of required and elective credits that you must keep track of. Notice that this form contains additional information designed to keep you on the right path. For example, in addition to the preplanning section, I include all of the required and elective courses. This allows you to see all of the possible selections in one place. The sample checklist in Fig. 1-5 for the MCSE is more involved.

MCSE Checklist

Figure 1-5

Item Description				Date
Understand the Responsibility of an MCSE				_____
Complete Goals Worksheet				_____

Operating System	Course Number	Course Date	Exam Number	Exam Pass Date
Microsoft Windows	278	_____	70-30	_____
Microsoft Windows NT	211	_____	70-40	_____
Microsoft Windows NT Advanced Server	237	_____	70-41	_____

Operating System Electives (Choose One)

Networking with Microsoft Windows	321 and (344 class-room or 319 self-study)	_____	70-47	_____

Figure 1-5   *Continued.*

Networking with Microsoft Windows for Workgroups	321 and (178 class-room or 324 self-study)	_____	70-46	_____

Electives

Microsoft SQL Server Database Administration for OS/2	214	_____	70-20	_____
Microsoft SQL Server Database Implementation	158	_____	70-21	_____
Microsoft SQL Server Database Administration for Windows NT	213) (complete) or 286 (update)	_____	70-22	_____
Microsoft SQL Server Database Administration for Windows NT Upgrade Exam	213 (complete) or 286 (update)	_____	70-23	_____
Microsoft Mail for PC Networks - Enterprise	341	_____	70-37	_____
Microsoft TCP/IP for Microsoft Windows NT	236	_____	N/A	_____
Microsoft LAN Manager 2.1 Network Administration	235	_____	70-10	_____
Microsoft LAN Manager 2.1 Advanced Network Administration	239 and 146	_____	70-11	_____

Microsoft SP ATC/Course Information:

MSSPATC Name: _____

Phone Number: _____

Contact Name: _____

Location: _____

Course Start Times: _____

Comments: _____
_____

Testing Information:

Phone Number: _____

Date of Exams: _____
_____

Location of Test Center: _____

Microsoft Information:

Date Called Microsoft to Order MCSE application: _____

Date Paper Work and Picture Sent to Microsoft: _____

Reference materials: (Books, Software, etc.): _____
_____

Other: _____
_____

The information contained in this checklist documents the preplanning responsibilities and goals, as well as the certification courses and exams. The checklist is divided into areas that help you know which are required and which are electives. I also added the course/exam name along with the corresponding numbers for easy reference. A note area allows you to keep track of any notes or

comments that you may want to make about the subject. At the end of the checklist is a section for the phone numbers, addresses, contact names, and reference material. I even supplied some space for any additional information that may assist you in your quest.

The MCT checklist in Fig. 1-6 keeps the needs of the MCT in mind. Notice that it is a little more freeform and complicated than the other forms presented in this chapter. This reflects the nature of the MCT training. Of course, this means that you will need to spend a little more time customizing this form.

Figure 1-6

MCT Checklist

Item Description	Date
Understand the Responsibility of an MCT	_____
Complete Goals Worksheet	_____
Demonstrate Instructional Skills	_____
Attend All Required Courses (See the list in the next section.)	_____
Take All Required Exams (See the list in the next section.)	_____
Attend Microsoft Trainer-Preparation Course	_____

Operating System	Course Number	Course Date	Exam Number	Exam Pass Date
Microsoft Windows	278	_____	70-30	_____
Microsoft Windows NT	211	_____	70-40	_____
Microsoft Windows NT Advanced Server	237	_____	70-41	_____
Networking with Microsoft Windows	321 and (344 classroom or 319 self-study)	_____	70-47	_____

Networking with Microsoft Windows for Workgroups	321 and (178 classroom or 324 self-study)	_____	70-46	_____

Products

Microsoft SQL Server Database Administration for OS/2	214	_____	70-20	_____
Microsoft SQL Server Database Implementation	158	_____	70-21	_____
Microsoft SQL Server Database Administration for Windows NT	213 (complete) or 286 (update)	_____	70-22	_____
Microsoft SQL Server Database Administration for Windows NT Upgrade Exam	213 (complete) or 286 (update)	_____	70-23	_____
Microsoft Mail for PC Networks - Enterprise	341	_____	70-37	_____
Microsoft TCP/IP for Microsoft Windows NT	236	_____	N/A	_____
Microsoft LAN Manager 2.1 Network Administration	235	_____	70-10	_____
Microsoft LAN Manager 2.1 Advanced Network Administration	239 and 146	_____	70-11	_____
Microsoft Word for Windows	N/A	_____	70-33	_____
Microsoft Excel	N/A	_____	70-31	_____

Figure 1-6

Continued.

Microsoft Project	N/A	_____	70-32	_____
Microsoft Mail for PC Networks - Desktop	341	_____	70-35	_____

Microsoft SP ATC/Course Information:

Microsoft SP ATC Name: _____

Phone Number: _____

Contact Name: _____

Location: _____

Course Start Times: _____

Comments: _____
_____

Testing Information:

Phone Number: _____

Date of Exams: _____

Location of Test Center: _____

Microsoft Information:

Date Called Microsoft to Order MCT application: _____

Date Paper Work and Picture Sent to Microsoft: _____

Reference materials: (Books, Software, etc.): _____
_____

Other: _____
_____

As with the MCSE checklist, this one contains a lot of preplanning requirement entries. It also provides the requisite note area that allows you to keep track of any notes or comments that you may want to make about the subject. At the end of the checklist is a section for the phone numbers, addresses, contact names, and reference material. I even supplied some space for any additional information that may assist you in your quest.

I have provided you some ideas for creating your own checklist. Table 1-1 provides you with the reference list of all the courses and exams that Microsoft offers.[2] The list includes each course name and number, exam number, and credit value. I provided space at the end of the list so you can add any new courses and exams that Microsoft adds after this book goes to print.

				Table 1-1
Course/Exam List				
Course title	**Course #**	**Course length**	**Exam #**	**Alternate training**
Microsoft Windows 3.1	278	5 days	70-30	Upgrading to Microsoft Windows video training support for professionals
Microsoft Windows NT 3.1	211	5 days	70-40	Supporting Microsoft Windows NT: self-study training kit
Microsoft Windows NT Advanced Server 3.1	237	5 days	70-41	N/A
Microsoft Word for Windows 2.0	None	N/A	70-33	On-line documentation and Word manuals, third-party books

[2]Courses and exams are being added and removed as technology and products evolve. To find the latest course and exam offerings, use the fax-back number or the Education number located in appendix A.

Table 1-1   **Continued**

Course title	Course #	Course length	Exam #	Alternate training
Microsoft Excel 4.0	None	N/A	70-31	On-line documentation and Excel manuals, third-party books
Microsoft Project 3.0	None	N/A	70-32	On-line documentation and Project manuals, third-party books
Microsoft Mail for PC Networks 3.2 - Desktop	285	3 days	70-35	N/A
Microsoft Windows for Workgroups 3.1	178	5 days	70-45	Moving to Microsoft Windows for Workgroups: video training for support professionals
Networking with Microsoft Windows for Workgroups 3.1	???	? days	70-??	N/A
Networking with Microsoft Windows 3.1	???	? days	70-??	N/A
Microsoft SQL Server 4.2 Database Administration for OS/2	214	4 days	70-20	N/A
Microsoft SQL Server 4.2 Database Implementation	158	5 days	70-21	N/A
Microsoft SQL Server 4.2 Database Administration for Windows NT	213 or 286	5 days 2 days	70-22	N/A
Microsoft SQL Server 4.2 Database Administration for Windows NT, Upgrade Exam	213 or 286	5 days 2 days	70-23	N/A
Microsoft Mail 3.2 for PC Networks - Enterprise	???	5 days	70-37	N/A

Microsoft TCP/IP for Microsoft Windows NT	???	? days	70-??	N/A
Microsoft LAN Manager 2.1 Network Administration	235	5 days	70-10	N/A
Microsoft LAN Manager 2.1 Advanced Network Administration	239 and 146	3 days 2 days	70-11	N/A

CHAPTER 2

Understanding the certification process

T HE first chapter provided you with a better understanding of what each certification will help you accomplish. However, this is the company view of the certification. It only answers part of the question, "What can the certification do for my current company?" This is great for your employer, but it doesn't help you understand how to accomplish this feat, or why you should even attempt it. Everyone wants more from an educational experience than to simply fulfill a company requirement. Fortunately, Microsoft certification can help you in a more personal way. It can pave the way to new jobs with higher pay and more interesting work. Instead of helping the boss juggle paperwork all day, you can run your own department in a larger company if you have the right certification. Even if you're self-employed, a certification can help you increase your clientele and allow you to charge a higher hourly rate. In many cases a certification provides the basis for starting a networking business.

This chapter helps you concentrate on how the certification helps you. It answers questions like "Why is certification important?" and "How do I attain my personal goals as well as the company's goals?" Once you understand these concepts, you can take a detailed look at the certification requirements. This will help you complete the certification checklist you started in chapter 1.

This chapter also helps you schedule the time required to complete the certification. Believe it or not, the major reason that many people fail to get certified is a lack of time. Certification requires a personal

investment just like any other educational experience. You must schedule time to take the classes, study, and take the exams. What is more important, you must schedule time for continuing education. Many people attend classes, but cut a few because they don't quite have the time required to attend. Then they try to take the exams without studying. Finally, because they are totally unprepared to take the exams, they get frustrated after the first few questions, then rush through the rest. This is a sure way to fail. Even the people who do get certified can lose that certification if they don't attend to continuing education requirements. Certification, more than anything else, means that you are willing to devote the time required to maintain a specific level of education and competency. The guidelines in this chapter help reduce the probability of such an occurrence.

Why do you need certification?

There are many people who look at certification as simply another "sheepskin" to hang on the wall. Certification is a lot more than simply some classroom study and a few exams. It is a commitment by you to maintain a specific level of training in order to perform a set of very specific tasks. It also involves the personal satisfaction of knowing that you have the skills to perform that job to the standards set by the industry.

Discovering exactly what certification will do for you is a big part of completing the requirements successfully. You need to keep these goals in mind as you choose classes and prepare for exams. Having a goal in view also helps when you take the exams and set the time aside to maintain your proficiency. Figure 2-1 provides you with some ideas of how to create your own goals worksheet. You can use this worksheet to help you throughout the certification process.

As you can see, the form is very straightforward. It contains blanks for your name, the certification you intend to pursue, and the date you plan to attain it. Make sure you keep both the Certification and Anticipated Date of Completion fields up-to-date as you progress. Explanations of the Goals area fields appear in the following sections. You should couple this form with the Certification Checklist found in chapter 1.

Figure 2-1

Microsoft Certification Goals Worksheet

Name: _____

Certification: _____

Anticipated Date of Completion: _____

Goals:

Profession Recognition: _____
_____
_____

Network Skills: _____
_____
_____
_____

Industry Trend: _____
_____
_____
_____

Microsoft Support: _____
_____
_____
_____

Other: _____
_____
_____

The following paragraphs examine the reasons for certification in detail. Make sure you list the reasons that fit your situation on your Goals Worksheet. Listing the reasons you are doing something at the beginning of a project often helps you complete it. These reasons help you to focus on the goals you set at the start of the certification process and emphasize the personal need to complete them.

Professional recognition

There are many people stuck in "dead end" jobs that would prefer to do something else. Many administrative assistants or other support personnel would prefer a job with a little excitement, rather than the same old work every day. A Microsoft certification can help you reach that goal. Even if you do have a fairly interesting job, a Microsoft certification can provide the variety that makes work interesting. Instead of spending all day every day shuffling papers, you could spend part of that time working with the network or teaching someone to use an application. You could become the resident expert, thus enhancing your promotion potential as well as your self-esteem.

Another group of people who really need Microsoft certification to gain professional recognition are consultants. How many times has a client asked why they should use you rather than Joe or Mary down the street? Have you had to lower your per-hour charge just to get the job? Wouldn't it be nice to have a reason that you could show in no uncertain terms to the client? These are all reasons why a consultant would want professional recognition—not only to increase personal satisfaction and gain a reputation from your peers, but to gain the respect of your clients as well.

As you can see, professional recognition goes a long way toward making every day an adventure rather than an exercise in boredom. A Microsoft certification is a good way of getting the professional recognition you need to gain this goal. Of course, these are only two ways that professional recognition can help. Now is the time for you to think about how professional recognition will help you. Make sure you write it down on your Goals Worksheet.

Network/product skills

This is one area that you may or may not feel concerns you. Perhaps you have had some hands-on experience with a network before, and you keep up with the latest news in the trade journals. You may already think you know everything you could about Word for

Windows or Excel. No matter what you think your level of experience is, certification training is always the best method for gaining network and application program skills. Even if you don't learn anything by going through the process, you will at least hone the skills you already possess.

While on-the-job training is a viable way of gaining some information, it does not give you the full effect of certification training. When you go through network or application program classes, the instructor provides you with information based on the input of hundreds or even thousands of other people. There is no way to gain this type of information in the vacuum of OJT. Even if you could gain the book knowledge, certification training provides you with at least one other valuable asset. You get to test this input in a laboratory environment. Your company won't let you test the networking knowledge you gain on the company LAN, but you can test it at a training center. They won't pay someone to test a word processor, but they will pay for someone to use it for work-related purposes. Certification training ensures that you really know how specific networking conditions normally look and how to fully install all the features of the Microsoft network products. It ensures that the product specialist really does know every way of getting the last ounce of functionality from an application program.

Skills include both knowledge from books and practical experience from hands-on training. You will likely spend as much time using your new skills as you will learning them. The instructor is there to help you fully comprehend what the manuals contain. How often have you read the manuals, only to feel like you didn't know any more when you finished than when you started? In many cases you understand what the manuals say, but fail to implement the procedures correctly. Learning from an instructor through certification training gives you the feeling of knowing Netware, not simply taking your best guess about what you think will happen.

Because every trainee begins with a different level of knowledge, it is important that you gauge what you know with what you expect to learn. This is one of the goals that will help you keep on track. Once you determine what you expect to gain from the certification process regarding network or application program skills, then you need to

write it down. Keep this goal in mind as you take each of your courses. Also use it as a guide for helping you study. Concentrate on your weak areas before taking the exam.

⇨ Industry trend

A weak (but viable) reason to get certified is that it is an industry trend. Many companies do not want to trust the valuable information on their network to someone who doesn't possess the proper training. Likewise, they will most certainly hire a certified professional before someone who merely claims to know how to use an application. References are nice, but a certificate is just as good, if not better, in many cases. (Of course, having both the certificate and references is the best situation of all.) Having an MCPS, MCSE, or MCT certificate will open many employment opportunities for you. Of course, having both experience and a certification is almost a sure winner at the negotiation table. As you can see, having the proper credentials always works to your benefit.

This is probably a good time for you to write down some of the ways that you can use your certification once you get it. Make sure you look at the various trade papers[1] that will show how industry trends will help you in gaining the type of employment you want. You could write these trends down or even take clippings from the trade papers to use for future reference.

Clippings from trade magazines and newspapers are especially important for consultants. They provide an extra level of credibility when you bid on a large networking or application training job. Remember that the client is more apt to listen to what industry has to say than simply take your word that certification is a good and necessary requirement for selecting someone to install a network or train their staff.

⇨ Microsoft support

Microsoft provides an added layer of support for people who get certified to use their products. After all, it only makes good business

---

[1]See appendix B (Sources of Additional Information) for ideas on what trade papers you should read to find out what's going on in the networking industry.

sense for them to do so. There are several mechanisms that Microsoft uses to accomplish this.

➤ Special assistance on the Microsoft product support line. Not because Microsoft offers a special service, but because the support technicians know that you are fully qualified to use a particular product. This means they can rule out a lot of the novice-related problem areas.

➤ Several forums on CompuServe where you can discuss new advances in networking and application program technology, or get a little help with an especially thorny problem. You can also use this forum to download new versions of drivers and programs.

➤ Use of the Microsoft Certified Professional logo for your price sheets, advertising pamphlets, business cards, and resume. Only a certified person may use this logo.

➤ A prepaid trial membership to TechNet. MCPSs get it for three months, while MCSEs get it for a year.

As you can see, Microsoft's commitment to the certificate holder is just as great as the commitment you must have to get certified. The ability to receive special support from a company also works to both an employer's and a client's benefit. If these people know that you can provide them with better-than-average support because of your relationship with Microsoft, it could work to your advantage in getting the job. You need to keep this support in mind as part of the method you use to sell your skills to a potential employer or client.

⇨ Other reasons

By now your head is buzzing with other ideas about how certification can help you. Make sure you write them down while they are fresh in your memory. These ideas can prove to make the difference between failing and passing as time progresses. In addition, personalizing your goals list may provide the edge you need to gain an advantage over the competition.

What if you decide to bid on a job that another certified person has already bid on? Telling your client how your approach to networking

or training differs from the competition can make the difference between getting the job or giving it to your competitor. You need to base part of this reasoning on how you approach your certification.

How about a job opportunity where more than one certified person has applied? Telling a potential employer how you see your certification may make them take notice. Make sure you let people know that you took the time and effort to get the most out of your valuable certification training. Give them a reason to view you as someone who is willing to put a little more effort into doing the job right.

What are the certification requirements?

Now that you have a better idea of *why* you would want to get certified, we need to take a detailed look at *how* you can get it. The following paragraphs provide you with a detailed look at the certification requirements for each level of certification.

 MCPS

The MCPS certification deals with the desktop. You are the desktop operating system and application support guru of the corporate world when you attain this certification. This certification essentially tells the world that you know how to use a particular operating system and application set to the fullest extent possible.

The certification requirements consist of one desktop operating system exam. This exam looks at your operating system skills. You may also qualify to work with a desktop application by completing an application-specific elective exam. This second exam looks at your ability to use a particular application. There are two operating systems, Microsoft Windows and Microsoft Windows NT, that you can choose for your specialty. In addition, you can choose from one of four applications: Microsoft Word, Microsoft Excel, Microsoft Mail (desktop), or Microsoft Project. The requirements for this program appear in Fig. 2-2.

Figure 2-2

MCPS Certification at a Glance

1. Take the time to go through your Microsoft Windows or Microsoft Windows NT manuals. Highlight any topics that refer to features that you do not use on a daily basis. You may even want to use two colors: one for "never use" and another for "seldom use." These highlighted areas represent weak areas in your field of study. Make sure you take the time to fully study them before you take the exam. Use a hands-on approach to try to use the features whenever possible. Use the same approach when studying for your application-specific exam.

2. Take the appropriate course. Chapter 1 provides you with a detailed description of the course number for each exam. You will want to spend a little time considering which elective courses to take. For example, you may want to take the Microsoft Excel exam if spreadsheets are a major thrust of your business or the company where you work. Make sure you don't confuse yourself by taking more than one class at a time. Take a class, then follow it immediately by taking the exam. This way, the material you learned in class is fresh in your mind during the exam.

3. Study the student manuals provided during the class. Make sure you study any weak areas in your knowledge skills. Check any notes you may have for information that does not appear in the manuals. Studying one student manual at a time may help reduce your confusion level when taking the associated exam.

4. Schedule your exam by calling (800) 755-EXAM. Make sure you double-check the exam number found in chapter 1. After all, you don't want to qualify for the wrong certification (or worse yet, waste money taking the wrong exam and failing it).

5. Drake will automatically submit your test results to Microsoft. You can call (800) 636-7544 (USA) or (800) 563-9048 (Canada) to find out about the status of your certification.

6. Wait for your first CP package to arrive. Sign the contract and send it back in to Microsoft. Make sure you check on the status of this paperwork. It must arrive at Microsoft for you to get your certification papers.

7. Subscribe to one or more trade journals that allow you to keep up on industry events and advances in network technology. Examples of trade journals for this level of certification include *PC Magazine* and *PC Week*. Both periodicals include application-specific sections on a regular basis. If

you have a specialty area, you may want to pursue a magazine that covers that ground. For example, if you mainly work with database management systems, you may want to get a periodical like *Data Based Advisor* for the database-specific networking tips.

8. Watch your mailbox for your certification papers and any other Microsoft-sponsored information.

9. Check with various printers about the cost of adding your new certification sticker to your resume, price lists, or advertisements. When your certification papers arrive, make sure you add the Microsoft Certified Professional logo to show that you've completed the required certification.

As you can see from Fig. 2-2, the certification process for MCPS is fairly simple. Of course, the first step is to take the appropriate courses. Many people feel that going to these courses is unnecessary. However, even if you have previous experience with the application with which you want to certify, you will need to know the Microsoft way of using the product. Your instructor will have insights and know many techniques for using the product that you may not know about. Microsoft will test you for this information whether or not you attended a course. Of course, this information is based on the experiences of thousands of users; it usually represents the most correct and efficient method for using the application to its fullest.

The next step is to study for the exam. I recommend that you avoid cluttering your mind with information from too many sources. Take time to study your class notes and the student manuals thoroughly. This represents the best possible method for passing the exams. Make sure you spend extra time studying areas you are weak in. You might want to have someone else quiz you on various aspects of the material contained in the application manuals. Make sure you spend plenty of time testing your knowledge of the techniques you learn by trying them out on your computer.

Once you know enough about the operating system or application, schedule your exams. If you are a morning person, schedule the exams in the morning. Likewise, if you are an afternoon person, schedule your exams in the afternoon. Always schedule the exams when you are most alert. Remember, you only have your brain to work with when it comes time to take the exams. There are no books

allowed in the examination room. You might want to consider the day of the week as well. Some people schedule their exams on a Monday, when they feel most rushed. Don't fall into this mistake. Schedule your exams for a day when you really have time to take them.

Immediately after you take your exams, Drake will submit the test results to Microsoft. This will get the certification ball rolling. Of course, it doesn't really end there. Take a proactive approach to your certification. You will probably need to call Microsoft from time to time to check on the progress of your certification paperwork.

At some time after you complete all the certification requirements, you should receive your first certification package from Microsoft. This envelope will contain several important pieces of information and at least one piece of paperwork that you must complete. The first thing that you'll want to look at is the Microsoft Certified Professional Transcript. You will receive one of these every time you pass an exam. This tells you what exams Microsoft gave you credit for. Make sure it matches the checklist you completed in chapter 1. The second item of interest is the guidelines document for using your logo. Read this, then pick up the Microsoft Certified Professional Program and Logo Agreement. Take the time to read the entire contract and make sure you know what it says. Sign the contract and send it back to Microsoft. This is the last step you need to take before you get your certification papers.

While you wait for your certification papers to arrive, you might want to go to your local bookstore and browse the shelves for books and periodicals that pertain to your operating system and application program specialty. Make sure you get material you can understand. It doesn't matter how well the book or periodical explains the topic if you can't grasp what it means. B. Dalton's Software Etc. and Waldenbooks both provide well-stocked periodical stands. If you don't have one of these stores in your area, look for a technical bookstore. *PC Magazine* and *PC Week* both contain a wide variety of material that a product specialist needs to know. For example, they both contain product reviews along with their application program solution sections. Periodicals may include Microsoft-supplied information as well. You might want to maintain a subscription to any of Microsoft's CD-ROM subscription services like Microsoft TechNet or Microsoft Developer

Network. (See appendix B for ideas on what trade papers you should read to find out what's going on in the computing industry.)

MCPSs that run their own business will also want to check on the cost for placing the Microsoft Certified Professional logo on price lists and advertisements. Even if you have to spend a little money, the recognition you receive from placing this logo on your forms will really increase business. No one will know that you went through all the training required to receive this valuable certification unless you advertise it. Make sure you get all the value you can out of the certification process.

MCPSs that are going to work for a company might want to place the Microsoft Certified Professional logo on their resume. A logo of this type can really help differentiate your resume from all others in the stack. It can make the difference between a potential employer actually reading your entire resume or tossing it after looking at the first few lines. The logo will definitely attract the attention of anyone who looks at your resume; use it to your benefit.

 MCSE

The MCSE certification deals with the world of enterprise networking. Think of it as a larger world than the one dealt with by the MCPS. You are the network support guru of the corporate world when you attain this certification. This certification essentially tells the world that you know how to use a total of three operating systems and application set to the fullest extent possible.

The certification requirements consist of six exams. The first three required exams are those for Microsoft Windows, Microsoft Windows NT, and Microsoft Windows NT Advanced Server. You must pass the exams before you can get certified. Therefore, it really pays to get past this area first. These exams look at your operating system knowledge. The fourth exam looks at your networking skills at the desktop. You may choose either the Networking with Microsoft Windows or the Networking with Microsoft Windows for Workgroups exam. The fifth and sixth exams look at your ability to use a particular network-related application. There are seven different

applications you can choose from: Microsoft SQL Server Database for OS/2, Microsoft SQL Server Database for Windows NT, Microsoft Mail—Enterprise, Microsoft LAN Manager Network Administration, Microsoft LAN Manager Advanced Network Administration, Microsoft SQL Server Database Implementation, and TPC/IP for Microsoft Windows NT. You cannot choose both Microsoft SQL Server Database for OS/2 and Microsoft SQL Server Database for Windows NT. If you choose one, you cannot choose the other. The requirements for this program appear in Fig. 2-3.

Figure 2-3

MCSE Certification at a Glance

1. Take the time to go through your Microsoft Windows, Microsoft Windows NT, and Microsoft Windows NT Advanced Server manuals. Highlight any topics that refer to features that you do not use on a daily basis. You may even want to use two colors: one for "never use" and another for "seldom use." These highlighted areas represent weak areas in your field of study. Make sure you take the time to fully study them before you take the exam. Use a hands-on approach to try to use the features whenever possible. Use the same approach when studying for your application specific exam.

2. Take the appropriate courses. Chapter 1 provides a complete listing of the courses you can take. Make sure you take all the required courses and exams. You will want to spend a little time considering which elective courses to take. For example, you may want to take the Microsoft SQL Server Database Implementation exam if database management is a major thrust of your business or the company where you work. Make sure you don't confuse yourself by taking more than one class at a time. Take a class, then follow it immediately by taking the exam. This way, the material you learned in class is fresh in your mind during the exam.

3. Study the student manuals provided during the class. Make sure you study any weak areas in your knowledge skills. Check any notes you may have for information that does not appear in the manuals. Studying one student manual at a time may help reduce your confusion level when taking the associated exam.

4. Schedule your exams by calling (800) 755-EXAM. Take the appropriate exams for both the required and optional courses you attended. Make sure you leave enough time between exams to allow for study. Don't rush the exams.

5. Drake will automatically submit your test results to Microsoft. You can call (800) 636-7544 (USA) or (800) 563-9048 (Canada) to find out about the status of your certification.

6. Wait for your first CP package to arrive. Sign the contract and send it back in to Microsoft. Make sure you check on the status of this paperwork. It must arrive at Microsoft for you to get your certification papers.

7. You probably already subscribe to one or more trade journals like *PC Magazine* or *PC Week*. Make sure you also subscribe to one more network-specific trade journals that allow you to keep up on industry events and advances in network technology. Examples of trade journals for this level of certification include *LAN Times*. This magazine provides a much more intense view of networking than more generic magazines like *PC Magazine* do. If you have a specialty area, you may want to pursue a magazine that leans toward that bias. For example, if you mainly work with database management systems, you may want to get a periodical like *Data Based Advisor* for the database-specific networking tips.

8. Watch your mailbox for your certification papers and any other Microsoft-sponsored information.

9. Check with various printers about pricing for adding your new certification sticker to your resume, price lists, or advertisements. When your certification papers arrive, make sure you add the Microsoft Certified Professional logo to show that you've completed the required certification.

As you can see from Fig. 2-3, the certification process for MCSE is about the same as for MCPS. The big differences are the number of exams you need to take and the view of the computing world that you take. Of course, the first step is to take the appropriate courses. Many people feel that going to these courses is unnecessary. However, even if you have previous experience with the application you want to certify with, you will need to know the Microsoft way of managing a network and using network applications. Your instructor will have insights and know many techniques for using the product that you may not know about. Microsoft will test you for this information whether or not you attended a course. Of course, this information is based on the experiences of thousands of users; it usually represents the most correct and efficient method of managing a network with the least amount of problems. You can actually make your network run a lot smoother and more efficiently by taking these courses to gain the knowledge you need.

The next step is to study for the exam. We recommend that you avoid cluttering your mind with information from too many sources. Take time to study your class notes and the student manuals thoroughly. This represents the best possible method for passing the exams. Make sure you spend extra time studying areas you are weak in. You might want to have someone else quiz you on various aspects of the material contained in the application manuals. Make sure you spend plenty of time testing your knowledge of the techniques you learn by trying them out on your computer.

Once you know enough about the operating system, networking at the desktop, or advanced systems application, schedule your exams. If you are a morning person, schedule the exams in the morning. Likewise, if you are an afternoon person, schedule your exams in the afternoon. Always schedule the exams when you are most alert. Remember, you only have your brain to work with when it comes time to take the exams. There are no books allowed in the examination room. You might want to consider the day of the week as well. Some people schedule their exams on a Monday, when they feel most rushed. Don't fall into this mistake. Schedule your exams for a day when you really have time to take them.

Immediately after you take your exams, Drake will submit the test results to Microsoft. This will get the certification ball rolling. Of course, it doesn't really end there. Take a proactive approach to your certification. You will probably need to call Microsoft from time to time to check on the progress of your certification paperwork.

At some time after you complete all the certification requirements, you should receive your first certification package from Microsoft. This envelope will contain several important pieces of information and at least one piece of paperwork that you must complete. The first thing that you'll want to look at is the Microsoft Certified Professional Transcript. You will receive one of these every time you pass an exam. This tells you what exams Microsoft gave you credit for. Make sure it matches the checklist you completed in chapter 1. The second item of interest is the guidelines document for using your logo. Read this, then pick up the Microsoft Certified Professional Program and Logo Agreement. Take the time to read the entire contract and make sure you know what it says. Sign the contract and send it back to

Microsoft. This is the last step you need to take before you get your certification papers.

While you wait for your certification papers to arrive, you might want to go to your local technical bookstore and browse the shelves for books and periodicals that pertain to your networking specialties. Don't be too surprised if this material is scarce. You may need to scour the trade magazines looking for adequate material. Don't discount the card decks that various magazines send your way. Some of them contain advertisements for advanced books. Talk with your peers as well. User group meetings usually make a good place to ask about books and magazines on a particular topic.

Make sure you get material you can understand. It doesn't matter how well the book or periodical explains the topic if you can't grasp what it means. B. Dalton's Software Etc. and Waldenbooks both provide well-stocked periodical stands, but most of this information is very generic in nature. You will probably want to look for a technical bookstore in your area even if one of these bookstores is nearby. You may want to check out your local university or college as well.

PC Magazine and *PC Week* both contain a wide variety of material that a system engineer needs to know. For example, they both contain product reviews along with their application program solution sections. This is a good place to start, but you need to go further. Get the heavy-duty magazines as well. *PC Magazine* will address your network user needs. Magazines like *LAN Times* will address your personal knowledge needs. Periodicals may include Microsoft-supplied information as well. You might want to maintain a subscription to any of Microsoft's CD-ROM subscription services like Microsoft TechNet or Microsoft Developer Network. (See appendix B for ideas on what trade papers you should read to find out what's going on in the computing industry.)

MCSEs that run their own business will also want to check on the cost for placing the Microsoft Certified Professional logo on price lists and advertisements. Even if you have to spend a little money, the recognition you receive from placing this logo on your forms will really increase business. No one will know that you went through all the training required to receive this valuable certification unless you

advertise it. Make sure you get all the value you can out of the certification process.

MCSEs that are going to work for a company might want to place the Microsoft Certified Professional logo on their resume. A logo of this type can really help differentiate your resume from all others in the stack. It can make the difference between a potential employer actually reading your entire resume or tossing it after looking at the first few lines. The logo will definitely attract the attention of anyone who looks at your resume; use it to your benefit.

 # MCT

The MCT certification deals with the world of training. You are the first person that many candidates will meet and a source of knowledge they will draw upon for years to come. Your certification tells the world that you have met rigid standards both technically and in your instruction techniques. The candidate knows that you can not only perform the work that you are trying to teach, but that you will present it in the best way possible. Of course, this is a huge responsibility and many people may think that it's an unattainable goal. While the goal of becoming certified as an MCT is certainly difficult, it is very fulfilling as well. An instructor needs to present the best image possible. The MCT certification process assures that only the very best become certified.

The certification requirements consist of a number of prerequisites, course requirements, and finishing touches. There are two prerequisites. You must be an employee of a Microsoft SP ATC and you have to prove your ability to teach. You can choose any number of courses to teach. These courses include elements of the CP program and managerial or alternative education courses. Appendix C provides you with a complete list. The operating system courses include: Microsoft Windows, Microsoft Windows NT, Microsoft Windows NT Advanced Server, Networking with Microsoft Windows, and Networking with Microsoft Windows for Workgroups. There are eleven different applications you can choose from: Microsoft Word, Microsoft Excel, Microsoft Mail (desktop), Microsoft Project, Microsoft SQL Server Database for OS/2, Microsoft SQL Server Database for Windows NT, Microsoft Mail

Enterprise, Microsoft LAN Manager Network Administration, Microsoft LAN Manager Advanced Network Administration, Microsoft SQL Server Database Implementation, and TPC/IP for Microsoft Windows NT. An MCT must take all the courses that he or she wants to teach. Once you take the exams for the courses you want to teach, you can take the Microsoft Trainer-Preparation Course. The requirements for this program appear in Fig. 2-4.

MCT Certification at a Glance

Figure 2-4

Note

Do not even start this process unless you are an employee of a Microsoft SP ATC or other approved organization. Microsoft will not accept applications from other sources.

1. Be sure you meet all the prerequisites to begin the certification process. This includes being an employee of a Microsoft SP ATC. You must also demonstrate your training skills. There are four ways that you can use to demonstrate this ability. First, you could go to the three-day Instructional Techniques Workshop offered by Feisen, Kaye, and Associates (you can call them at (613) 829-3412 or (818) 768-4816). Attending an in-house or public instructional skills course may provide sufficient proof. You must provide the course description and proof of completion with your application. Experiential knowledge is sufficient if you provide 2 letters of recommendation and 10 names/telephone numbers of students you taught in the last two months. Provide proof that you are already a certified instructor through another hardware or software vendor. This route also requires that you provide the names and telephone numbers of 10 students that you taught in the last two months. Once you meet these two criteria, submit your application to Microsoft.

2. Take the time to go through all the manuals of products or operating systems that you want to teach. Highlight any topics that refer to features that you do not use on a daily basis. You may even want to use two colors: one for "never use" and another for "seldom use." These highlighted areas represent weak areas in your field of study. Make sure you take the time to fully study them before you take the course. This will not only help you ask intelligent questions in class, but improve your exam scores as well. Use a hands-on approach to try to use the features whenever possible.

Figure 2-4   *Continued.*

3. Take the appropriate courses. Chapter 1 provides a complete listing of the courses you can take. Make sure you take all the required courses and exams. Microsoft requires you to take every course that you want to teach. Make sure you don't confuse yourself by taking more than one class at a time. Take a class, then follow it immediately by taking the exam. This way, the material you learned in class is fresh in your mind during the exam.

4. Study the student manuals provided during the class. Make sure you study any weak areas in your knowledge skills. Check any notes you may have for information that does not appear in the manuals. Studying one student manual at a time may help reduce your confusion level when taking the associated exam.

5. Schedule your exams by calling (800) 755-EXAM. Take the appropriate exams for both the required and optional courses you attended. Make sure you leave enough time between exams to allow for study. Don't rush the exams.

6. Drake will automatically submit your test results to Microsoft. You can call (800) 636-7544 (USA) or (800) 563-9048 (Canada) to find out about the status of your certification.

7. Attend the Microsoft Trainer-Preparation Course. This is an MCT-specific requirement that helps you get ready for class. Make sure you take notes on everything you learn; it could mean the difference between success and failure.

8. Wait for your first CP package to arrive. Sign the contract and send it back in to Microsoft. Make sure you check on the status of this paperwork. It must arrive at Microsoft for you to get your certification papers.

9. You probably already subscribe to one or more trade journals, like *PC Magazine* or *PC Week*. Make sure you also subscribe to one more specific trade journals that provide information on your areas of expertise. For example, if you mainly work with database management systems, you may want to get a periodical like *Data Based Advisor* for the database-specific networking tips.

10. Watch your mailbox for your certification papers and any other Microsoft-sponsored information.

11. Check with various printers about pricing for adding your new certification sticker to your resume, price lists, or advertisements. When your certification papers arrive, make sure you add the Microsoft Certified Professional logo to show that you've completed the required certification.

As you can see from Fig. 2-4, the certification process for MCT is very different from the MCPS and MCSE requirements. The big difference is the view of the computing world that you take. You are an instructor, not a worker in industry. Of course, the first step is to ensure you meet all the required prerequisites. Then you take the appropriate courses. Unlike the other certification programs, MCT certification requires you to take the courses.

The next step is to study for the exam. I recommend that you avoid cluttering your mind with information from too many sources. Take time to study your class notes and the student manuals thoroughly. This represents the best possible method for passing the exams. Make sure you spend extra time studying areas you are weak in. You might want to have someone else quiz you on various aspects of the material contained in the application manuals. Make sure you spend plenty of time testing your knowledge of the techniques you learn by trying them out on your computer.

Once you know enough about the operating system, networking at the desktop, network application, or other course requirements, schedule your exams. If you are a morning person, schedule the exams in the morning. Likewise, if you are an afternoon person, schedule your exams in the afternoon. Always schedule the exams when you are most alert. Remember, you only have your brain to work with when it comes time to take the exams. There are no books allowed in the examination room. You might want to consider the day of the week as well. Some people schedule their exams on a Monday, when they feel most rushed. Don't fall into this mistake. Schedule your exams for a day when you really have time to take them.

Immediately after you take your exams, Drake will submit the test results to Microsoft. This will get the certification ball rolling. Of course, it doesn't really end there. Take a proactive approach to your certification. You will probably need to call Microsoft from time to time to check on the progress of your certification paperwork.

Once you complete the courses and exams, you need to take the Microsoft Trainer-Preparation Course. This course is only taught at Microsoft by Microsoft personnel. It's specifically designed to help you learn the Microsoft methods of presenting information and

setting up a classroom. You look at things like course flow, the design and objectives of each course you want to teach, and a variety of other instructor-related tasks.

At some time after you complete all the certification requirements, you should receive your first certification package from Microsoft. This envelope will contain several important pieces of information and at least one piece of paperwork that you must complete. The first thing that you'll want to look at is the Microsoft Certified Professional Transcript. You will receive one of these every time you pass an exam. This tells you what exams Microsoft gave you credit for. Make sure it matches the checklist you completed in chapter 1. The second item of interest is the guidelines document for using your logo. Read this, then pick up the Microsoft Certified Professional Program and Logo Agreement. Take the time to read the entire contract and make sure you know what it says. Sign the contract and send it back to Microsoft. This is the last step you need to take before you get your certification papers.

While you wait for your certification papers to arrive, you might want to go to your local technical bookstore and browse the shelves for books and periodicals that pertain to your networking specialties. Don't be too surprised if this material is scarce. You may need to scour the trade magazines looking for adequate material. Don't discount the card decks that various magazines send your way. Some of them contain advertisements for advanced books. Talk with your peers as well. User group meetings usually make a good place to ask about books and magazines on a particular topic.

Make sure you get material you can understand. It doesn't matter how well the book or periodical explains the topic if you can't grasp what it means. B. Dalton's Software Etc. and Waldenbooks both provide well-stocked periodical stands, but most of this information is very generic in nature. You will probably want to look for a technical bookstore in your area even if one of these bookstores is nearby. You may want to check out your local university or college as well.

PC Magazine and *PC Week* both contain a wide variety of material that a system engineer needs to know. For example, they both contain product reviews along with their application program solution sections. This is a good place to start, but you need to go further. Get the heavy duty magazines as well. *PC Magazine* will address your network user needs. Magazines like *LAN Times* will address your personal knowledge needs. Periodicals may include Microsoft-supplied information, too. You might want to maintain a subscription to any of Microsoft's CD-ROM subscription services like Microsoft TechNet or Microsoft Developer Network. (See appendix B for ideas on what trade papers you should read to find out what's going on in the computing industry.)

MCTs that are going to work for a different company might want to place the Microsoft Certified Professional logo on their resume. A logo of this type can really help differentiate your resume from all others in the stack. It can make the difference between a potential employer actually reading your entire resume or tossing it after looking at the first few lines. The logo will definitely attract the attention of anyone who looks at your resume; use it to your benefit.

 MCD

Microsoft has not yet fully developed the requirements for the MCD certification as of this writing. However, you should be able to participate in it in the near future. The course descriptions in appendix C of this manual should give you some idea of what the certification program will require. Call the Microsoft Sales Information Center at (800) 636-7544 (United States) or (800) 563-9048 (Canada) for details on this exciting new program. Make sure your client knows that you're the best programmer for the job. Get your MCD certification today.

 How long does certification take?

Some people look at the time required to gain certification as the number of hours spent in class and the time required to take exams. Nothing could be further from the truth. The certification process is ongoing and requires a commitment if you want to maintain it. There are paperwork and continuing education requirements that you must

consider in addition to the more obvious requirements. The following paragraphs will provide you with the information you need to take all these factors into account.

⇨ Training

The time you spend in training depends on the certification you plan to achieve. In most cases the courses are two to five days long. Chapter 1 contains a table that tells you the exact length of each class. To obtain the total time required to complete the training requirements for certification, simply add the length of each class you intend to take.

The important consideration for this time requirement is not really the length of each class, but coordinating the class time. It helps to talk with your local Microsoft SP ATC representative to get a listing of course availability and dates. Simply mark out the days for each course on a calendar to plan for the time you need to spend in training.

There is another way to look at the training time investment. It is very unlikely that time will allow you to schedule more than one class per week. As a result, you can simply count the number of classes you need to take, and count it as the number of weeks you need to set aside for training. Of course, you will still have some time each week to get work done at your job or business.

⇨ Testing

As a practical rule, no one can tell you exactly how long testing will take. The problem is that while the exam times are a constant, study time is not. Taking an exam before you study for it is likely to produce very frustrating results. You need to plan sufficient study time or you will fail the exam.

A general rule of thumb that you can follow is to plan at least two hours of study per day for the same number of days it took you to

complete a course. For example, if you had a four-day course, then you should plan eight hours of study time. Of course, you will not want to try to get all your studying done in one day. Plan for a maximum of three hours per day. Any more study time during one day will reduce the effectiveness of your study time.

Make sure you include at least one hour plus travel time to take the exam itself. For example, if it takes about 20 minutes to travel from your office to the testing center, plan on at least 1 hour and 40 minutes for the exam. Remember that you need to get to the testing center at least 15 minutes early. As a result, you may want to add this additional time to your estimate as well.

⇨ Paperwork

Paperwork is the bane of everyone everywhere. We get it dumped on our desk and into our laps. It's the glue that holds our businesses together and the bond that makes business work. Fortunately, Microsoft requires a minimum of paperwork from you during the certification process. All you need to do is take your exams. Drake automatically forwards your test results to Microsoft. Once Microsoft receives all the test scores required for a particular certification, you should automatically receive your first CP package. Simply check the contents for accuracy and sign the enclosed contract. Send the contract back to Microsoft. You will want to check to make sure they receive it. Make sure you copy down the name of the person you talked to in case there are problems with the paperwork later.

The biggest paperwork requirement for your Microsoft certification is personal records. Without records you will never know where you are or where you are going. Even worse, you won't have any idea at all of the significance of what you accomplished by completing your certification. Human memory being what it is, paperwork is the only way to make sure you remember what takes place during the certification process. You need to maintain your personal paperwork to keep the goal of certification in view. The forms in this book are paperwork, but they will help you achieve this goal.

Of course, you will need to spend more time getting your logo put on business forms and price lists. This is yet another form of paperwork. You cannot avoid the results of getting a certification, the good or the bad. The time spent with this paperwork will, of course, pay handsome dividends later. It helps to keep that result in sight as you struggle through the paperwork maze.

Continuing education

How much time is too much or too little for continuing your education? It really varies by individual requirements. You must consider what you plan to learn about, what your current level of education is, and what the requirements of your company/clients are. A good rule of thumb is at least one hour training time per day for MCSEs without any special requirements like database management tasks. An MCPS can probably get by with about half that investment, while an MCT probably requires quite a bit more.

Make sure you spend enough time both reading and practicing so that you feel comfortable with the level of your skills. Trying to learn at least one new item per day is probably a good idea. Make sure you spend a little time trying out new ideas with the network or application program itself. Perhaps a different directory arrangement or a new menuing system will help improve overall system efficiency. MCPSs may want to try to improve their macro programming skills or work out a new way of creating mail merge documents. You may even want to spend a little time trying out new add-on products for both the network and your application programs. Some companies will provide you with an evaluation copy of their product so you can try it out. Investing in yourself is good for both you and the company. Besides, you will never maintain your certification if you do not take the time required to train.

CHAPTER 3

Learning the trade

BY this point, you should have in mind the certification that best suits your experience and knowledge. You may want to become an MCPS because you like to train people, or you may simply need to support users of a Microsoft application in the corporate environment. This is the course to choose if you spend most of your time working with users and application programs. To reach the next level in your pursuit of this certification, it's very important to understand which applications you want to specialize in using and teaching. It is also very important to understand the needs of the users you will teach or support. You may even want to take a poll of their needs.

The MCSE certification applies more to people who like to work with networks. This is a natural course if you already have other network-related certifications, like Novell's CNE. You may even decide to get both certifications if you are a consultant. Whatever the case, to reach the next level of certification you may need to expand your understanding of the theories and practical experience of some aspect of networking.

You can increase your experience levels in a variety of ways. It may come as on-the-job training (OJT), the reading of trade magazines, attending seminars or lectures, or by the hands-on trial and error method. Other ways to get the experience you need for advancement may come from a formal education. This formal education could come in different ways, such as attending Microsoft courses, vendor training from companies like Compaq or 3Com (for MCSEs), or obtaining a degree from a college or university. Most organizations will prefer that you have a certification like the MCSE before they let you maintain the network, but if you want to advance into a higher position or into management, the company will require you to have a college degree. This includes degrees in information

science, computer science, or even computer technology. The same facts hold true for the MCPS. You may start out by getting your certification and some OJT supporting users, but will probably want some type of college degree (or at least a training certificate) to advance. You will almost always find that the degree buys you more recognition than a certificate, but either will do as a starting point.

In chapter 2 I covered the requirements for becoming certified by Microsoft as a networking or an application program expert. In this chapter, I will explore different ways to learn the trade. This will address the type of training that's required for your particular situation, or even whether it's necessary. If training is in your future, what level of training will you need? It is very important to get the proper level of training so you can advance your career as easily as possible. Finally, I will cover how to get the most from what you learn.

Is training really required?

Is training required? YES! The level and amount of training depends on your current educational level. I'm not talking about simple book learning here, but a combination of experience and training. If you want to advance in this industry (and I assume that you do, or you would not have picked up this book or considered becoming certified by Microsoft as a networking or application program expert), you will need more training. It is the type and level of training that you need to determine.

There are always people who claim to be experts who do not need any training. They usually base this claim on the amount of time they have spent at their current job and the credentials they attained in the past. That may be true for a particular area, but no one knows everything there is to know about networking (or computers in general). The same idea holds true for application programs, even though they are less complex than a network. People who believe that they are experts in everything are only fooling themselves. They are cheating themselves out of really learning, growing, and becoming all that they can be in this business. The fact is that as technology changes, so do the things you need to know. Yesterday's experience and training is not enough; you need to know about the

specifics of your network or application today. Of course, that experience and past training *does* help you to get up to speed faster. That's why you need to determine your educational needs based on what you know today.

Chapter 1 told you about the requirements and responsibilities of the different certifications. You have also completed the goals worksheet from chapter 2, so you know exactly what certification you want to attain and what it means to you. The certification process has been outlined as well, so you know what to expect and what you are trying to accomplish with your education. Armed with this information, you can now decide whether you require a formal education to attain your certification.

To decide if you need additional education, take a look at the job duties you perform. If you are trying to advance in a company, look at the job description of your next likely position. If your education and experience meet the criteria, then you may not need to do any special learning of the trade. What you do need to do is get books and trade journals that tell you about the current state of the network or application you want to specialize in. Add to that knowledge by getting some hands-on experience. You need to practice what you learn through these books and magazines. If you are not totally confident that you know what is required for the certification and job that you are applying for, then you need some form of formal education in addition to these less formal learning methods. It is essential that you take the time to learn about your training needs before you start the actual certification process. Any other course of action only wastes time and makes it a lot less likely that you'll succeed.

⇨ Deciding what level of training you need

Now that you know that training is essential, you have to decide precisely what level of training you need. It is a matter of economic importance that you don't invest in too much training; that would greatly increase the cost of your certification with no visible performance benefit. On the other hand, not getting the training you

require will only prove frustrating, and may even prevent you from getting certified. There is a balance between these two extremes that you need to find. The level of training you require depends on a number of factors, including how comfortable you feel with the subject matter. You may only need a few hours of review with a study manual, or you may need to spend a few years developing the skill required to reach your goal.

The MCPS needs a good foundation of experience with application programs and how users interact with them. If you don't have a lot of experience in this area, you will need to spend some time taking courses to get an overview of the application, reading books to learn the intricacies of the product, applying your new knowledge by using the application, and then teaching other people what you know to get the experiential knowledge. You may find that you know how to work with users really well, but don't have a clue about the application. This means you could potentially skip the last step or greatly reduce your time there. What about the expert user? You may find that you know the application well, but if you can't express this knowledge to someone else, then you really need to spend some time learning.

If your goal is to become an MCSE and you have been working with networking products for some time, chances are good that you will pass the exam if you attend the Microsoft courses at a Microsoft SP ATC and spend some time studying the material. The MCSE must know all the elective application requirements as well as the four operating system requirements. It is important that you determine which classes you need to take before you start the certification process. You will not pass the exams without a firm grasp of both operating systems and applications. Many candidates feel that if they know the network, then they have everything they need. Nothing could be further from the truth. An MCSE needs to know the network, the applications that run on it, and how to explain network policies and procedures to the users of that network. You should follow a set of steps similar to the ones for the MCPS in the previous paragraph.

This is not to say that it is impossible to attain your certification without formal training. There are many people that have become certified by simply studying the student manuals they borrowed from

someone else. This is book-level knowledge that will not serve you or your clients very well. Once these people get out into the workplace, it becomes apparent that they are not qualified to service or administer a network, or train someone else to use an application. These are the people that give the certification a bad name by doing their work so poorly that the person who hired them wonders what good certification does. Luckily, these people get weeded out of the marketplace in a short time; clients and employers hear of their bad reputation and refuse to have anything to do with them. It doesn't take long for their reputation to get passed around.

To help you decide what levels of training you actually need, you need to know which certification you want and at what level your skills are. Use the skill level chart in Fig. 3-1 to determine your current skill level. Simply check the box that reflects your current level of understanding for a particular subject. This chart, along with your goals worksheet from chapter 2, will help to pinpoint your level of expertise. The key to making these worksheets and charts work is being truthful with yourself. We all want to believe that we have more expertise or knowledge than we really have. Remember that only you will see this chart. No one else needs to know how you rank yourself. When ranking yourself in the skill's chart, choose the lower level of the skill ranking if you have any doubts about your skill. This will help you to strengthen any weak areas that you may have, and reinforce the subject matter at hand.

Skill Level Ranking Chart

Figure 3-1

Skills	Level High									Low
	10	9	8	7	6	5	4	3	2	1
Microsoft Windows										
Microsoft Windows NT										
Microsoft Windows NT Advanced Server										

Figure 3-1 *Continued.*

Skills	Level High									Low
	10	9	8	7	6	5	4	3	2	1
Microsoft Word for Windows										
Microsoft Excel										
Microsoft Project										
Microsoft Mail for PC Networks - Desktop										
Microsoft Mail for PC Networks - Enterprise										
Microsoft Windows for Workgroups										
Networking with Microsoft Windows for Workgroups										
Networking with Microsoft Windows										
Microsoft SQL Server Database Administration for OS/2										
Microsoft SQL Server Database Implementation										
Microsoft SQL Server Database Administration for Windows NT										
Microsoft TCP/IP for Microsoft Windows NT										
Microsoft LAN Manager Network Administration										
Microsoft LAN Manager Advanced Network Administration										

Others:

Prepared	Areas Needing Improvement
_____	_____
_____	_____
_____	_____
_____	_____
_____	_____
_____	_____
_____	_____
_____	_____

Of course, you may find it difficult or even possible to provide a truthful answer about your skill level. Microsoft provides a handy aid for determining your skill level. You can use the Microsoft Certification Professional Assessment Exams[1] to determine your skill level. The exams replicate the exams you will see at Drake. They are, however, not exact duplicates. You could pass these exams with flying colors and not pass the actual exam. The reason is simple: the real exams draw upon a huge base of questions. There is no way that you will see the same exam twice. As a result, questions you do well on in the sample exam probably won't appear on the real test.

[1]You can either call Microsoft to get this disk, or download it from CompuServe. Simply GO MSWIN and download the CP_ASM.ZIP file.

The skill chart can be separated into four areas. The first area lists the skills that an expert in Microsoft networks or application programs must know and use in the field. This is only a general sampling of the different skills. You may find that within a skill you know some of the subtopics very well, and that your knowledge of other subtopics needs improvement. If you rank yourself very high on the chart for a particular skill, you will normally find this to be the case. Remember the key is to be honest with yourself. Extra space is available at the bottom of the skill list so that you can add any additional skills you think are necessary. If you are a manager and are helping your employees become certified, you will want to include any unique or special requirements specific to your company or that you feel are necessary for certification.

The second section within the chart is the ranking area. This is the section where you will rank yourself on a scale of 1 to 10. The rankings are listed from high to low with 10 being a high ranking, and a 1 being a low ranking. Remember to be honest when ranking yourself; this is for your eyes only, and will be a study index. If you over-rank yourself, you may be missing out on studying an area that you are weak in. When selecting your ranking, place a check mark under the appropriate skill level. If you feel that you are between levels, place your check to the low side of the scale.

At the bottom of the skills chart is the third section. The section has the label "Areas Needing Improvement." In this area, write down the specific areas in which you need to improve. This will be both general topics from the skills section and specific subtopics from within the general skills. Be specific when filling this area out, as it will be the basis for determining what to study. These notes will identify your weak points, and then knowing what they are, you will be able to focus on acquiring the right information. If you feel that you need more room to document your improvement areas, continue them on another piece of paper. Do not shortchange yourself by failing to include all of your improvement areas. These are your weak areas, and to become not only certified but a professional networking person you must target your weak points, then concentrate your efforts on these topics.

The fourth and final section can be found to the left of "Areas Needing Improvement." Fill this section with a date when you feel that you know the subject matter included in your weak areas. Keeping track of your milestones is important; it provides you with a feeling of accomplishment. By recording the date that you feel comfortable with your weak points, you will feel at ease to move on to another topic.

Compare your goals worksheet and the skills chart to determine the level of training you require. For example, if your goal is to become an MCSE and you have been working as a network administrator, then you know the administration side of Microsoft network products, but may have never installed or configured a file server. Instead of spending a lot of time working with commands and other parts of the administrative side of the picture, you may want to try setting up the network software on a spare machine. You won't actually use this server for anything, but the experience will help you pass your exam. This route will be much more productive in reaching the goals you set than taking every course or studying everything about Microsoft network products. You may find that no courses are necessary, but that some light review of the manuals is all you need. (You may want to find someone with a copy of the student manuals and study the manuals as well. This improves your chances of passing the exams.)

The same strategy holds true for the MCPS certification. The worksheets may show that you know how to work well with users, but lack the hands-on application experience required to pass the exam. In this case, it would probably help to get one or two books on the application and work through the examples on your machine. Alternatively, you may find that you need to concentrate on specific product areas rather than the product as a whole. You may need to take the Microsoft courses first before you can address this area. Make sure you take the time to figure out where these weak points occur. Of course, you will want to make use of the formal education route if you have no experience with a particular application or network product.

When you feel that you have completed studying and preparing yourself for the exams, re-evaluate yourself again with the skills chart and the Microsoft Certification Professional Assessment Exams. This time, use a different color pen when ranking yourself, so you can compare your skill level now as opposed to the first time you

completed the chart. If you find that you are still not happy about your ranking, find the areas that need improving and concentrate on those areas. Use the sample exam as a gauge for finding specific study areas that require improvement. Repeat this process until you feel as if you know the topics cold. As you continue to find your weak points, take whatever steps are necessary to become trained.

Obtaining the required financing

Financing your training is an important step in the certification process. Training is extremely expensive; don't fool yourself about the cost. An average class in Southern California will set you back $1,900. The courses range from $1,700 to $2,250 depending on the locality. For example, this same course may only cost $2,000 in Alabama or it may cost more, but that's not the point. The point is that you will have to pay for it before you actually start class. Most training centers charge the same fee for every Microsoft course, but this may vary from place to place. You will definitely want to take the time to shop around. Make sure you factor in hidden costs like transportation to the class site when you make your determination of where to study.

There are other unwelcome surprises when it comes to computing the costs for other items needed for your certification. For example, each exam will cost you $100. It is very unlikely that you will pass all the exams on the first attempt. In fact, there is a 70% to 80% failure rate on the Microsoft exams. Most of this is due to a lack of study, but an informal poll of people who had gotten their certification shows a failure rate of 1 in 4 tests (for every three tests they passed, they failed one). With this in mind, you should probably add a minimum of one retake to your cost analysis. This means that if you want to become an MCPS, you need to add $200 to the cost analysis for testing if you only plan to certify for one product. Add another $100 for each additional product. If you decide to certify on three or more products, then it is a good idea to add two retakes or $200 to the cost. Every MCSE candidate should consider adding $800 to their analysis if they plan to go the standard route. Drake offers a special package that will reduce your costs. Make sure you call Drake to find out what the special package offers. Their current package is for

CNEs who plan to get their MCSE certification. You can get a package of 5 tests for $400. Make sure you add $200 to this amount for retakes. This brings the cost of the special package to $600.

Don't shortchange your cost computations. For example, every book you decide to buy costs about $25. Most people buy one or two books for each subject they want to study, but you'll want to factor in a number that reflects your study habits. This may seem like a small cost, but by the time you add five or six books to the picture, it can really add up.

Everyone can get financial support, but finding the correct source takes time and effort. Before you begin the actual process of funding your education, take time to figure out how much financing you need. The following points summarize the things you need to take into consideration.

- ➢ Training costs
- ➢ Testing costs
- ➢ Travel expenses
- ➢ Lost work time
- ➢ Miscellaneous expenses

The first step is to add up all the costs of classes and testing. Make sure you add a little extra for failed tests in your estimate. Even though you probably won't fail an examination if you prepare properly, it's best to plan for a failure just in case. You need this money, in addition to your normal paycheck and a little bit of extra money for emergencies and miscellaneous expenses. Failure to plan ahead will certainly cost you your certification.

Also take time to consider hidden costs. For example, you need to factor in additional travel expenses if the test and training centers are further away than your usual place of work. In some cases you may need to take time off from work to attend class. Some companies will not allow you to miss work to attend class; others will ask you to make up the time by working extra hours later. If your company will not pay you during this time, you need to factor in the amount you

would need to pay your bills. As an alternative, you could always take vacation time. Try to think about all the possible sources of trouble and alternatives you can exercise. As you can see, there is a lot to consider in the financial arena before you even begin the process of getting the financing.

There are a number of ways to get the money you need for certification training. The sources you use really depend on a number of factors, including whom the training will benefit and for what length of time you need to pay the training costs. Of course, the most important factor is the technique you plan to use to get the aid. Do you go to your company or simply rely on your own resources? The technique you use greatly affects your chances of success. Figure 3-2 provides you with some ideas on techniques you can use to get this financial aid. As you can see, there are at least three different techniques that you can use to finance your training.

Some people save for the training before they actually begin, that way there are no costs to burden them after they graduate. Consultants or people who plan to start their own business often use this technique. Trying to pay for your education and get a business going at the same time usually doesn't work very well. However, most people take a learn-now-pay-later approach to the whole process.

Company sponsorship is the method that most people use to get certification training. Convincing your company to sponsor you to become an MCSE is relatively easy if they just installed a LAN or the network administrator recently left the company. The need for someone to manage the LAN is usually pretty obvious by the time all the hardware and software gets installed. An MCPS candidate may want to wait until the latest update of an application. For example, what happens when the company decides to update a word processor? You can use this window of opportunity to get a little training. The company will see the need for training while everyone is busy learning that new word processor. It may not be a very important consideration six months later when all the employees know how to use that word processor. Of course, convincing them that you're the right person for the job might prove a little more difficult. This is a situation where you need to provide proof that you can not only do the job, but do it better than anyone else in the company.

Figure 3-2

Some people save the money they need for education, then begin to go to school. While this method does mean a delay in getting your training, it reduces the after-training expenses you'll encounter. This is ideal for consultants.

A common source of money for training is company sponsorship. You convince your company that it is in their best interest to supply the money required for training. This usually involves some type of payback period.

One option that many people don't consider is combining support from a number of sources. For example, you could get your company to support half the cost, a loan to support a quarter of the cost, and savings to support the rest.

Getting financial aid.

There are other forms of sponsorship as well. For example, you might get a state or federal government agency that promotes work programs to sponsor your training. Almost all of these opportunities are offered to someone who is currently out of work. Contact your local welfare or unemployment office for more information on these programs. You may also want to contact organizations like NOW (National Organization of Women) to find out about special programs in the workplace. Other forms of sponsorship cover everything from veterans programs to scholarships and grants. For example, many veterans fail to use their Montgomery GI Bill benefits. You can find out about these opportunities at your local VA office. Some life insurance companies offer scholarships to their members. Contact your insurance agent to find out if your company is one of them. As you can see, this form of sponsorship is going to take some research on your part.

There is always a group of people who can't get total financial support from one source. These are the people who usually need to work a little harder to get anything done in their company, or they might be part of a small business that can't afford the total cost of training. In these cases, you might need to spend time putting together a package deal. One or more sources help you get the training you need and reap the benefits of that training. To use this technique you spend time getting part of the support from one source, then use that source as a means to get other people to join in. For example, what if you are part of a small company? The company may recognize the need to obtain the services of a trained network administrator, but may not have the financial resources to pay for the training. If you could put part of your own money into the support fund (or get a scholarship or other form of financial support), the company might provide the other part.

As you can see, there are a lot of sources you can tap for financial support during your training. The technique you use to gain financial support determines which sources you try to tap. One person that I know of tapped family members as investors in his company. They helped him pay the cost of his education. In return, he paid them back what they invested plus a dividend based on the increase in business that the certification supplied. There are also student loans and scholarships that you can use. Some of these sources will not be available to you simply because you don't qualify for one reason or another. Make sure you don't waste time trying to tap a financial source that you can't possibly use.

Figure 3-3 shows you just some of the sources that you can use to acquire the capital required for certification training and testing. These six sources represent the ones that people most commonly use. The following paragraphs describe all these options in detail. Use your imagination and detective skills to track down other sources of potential financial support you can use. Some jobs offer more potential sources of financial support than others do. Remember, only a lack of research and motivation can prevent you from finding the financial support you need.

Figure 3-3

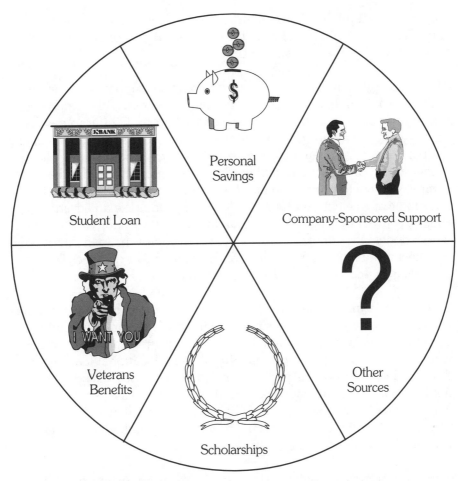

Personal Savings

Company-Sponsored Support

Student Loan

Veterans Benefits

Scholarships

Other Sources

Sources of financial support.

Company-sponsored support

Getting financial support from a company is the most common method that people use. You usually need to provide proof that the company needs the services that your training will provide and that you are the best person for the job. In most cases, you must show a willingness to repay the company by promising to work for them for a specified period of time after you complete the training. There are also instances where you will have to repay the company any monies

they expended if you fail to meet your goal. These are all the considerations you need to take into account if you plan to go this route to getting financial support.

At this point you may think that getting company support is an all-or-nothing proposition. There are a lot of different possibilities when you attempt to get support from your company. You could offer to pay for half of your training (or get financial assistance from another source) and ask the company to pay the other half. This shows that you are willing to invest in your own future and makes it a lot more likely that the company will help provide financial assistance. Some companies also offer interest-free education loans. Essentially, you take an advance against your salary to pay for the training. Every week (or whatever your pay period is) the company takes a small portion of the loan out of your paycheck. The interest-free nature of this loan makes it especially appealing to people on a lower income scale.

Some people think that getting company support is only for full-time employees. There are many situations in which a company might consider providing educational benefits to a part-time employee as well. For example, you might qualify for the educational loan benefit described in the previous paragraph. Other scenarios include going full-time for a specific payback period or, in rare cases, showing that you will provide a very great benefit to the company with the training you get. Never limit your horizons to what you think you can get. Remember, all the company can do is say "no."

Getting a proposal together is one of the most important parts of this method of getting financial support. You need to prove two things. First, if you are an MCSE, you need to provide proof that the company needs the services of a network administrator for their LAN. Likewise, if you are an MCPS, you need to provide proof that the company can benefit from the training or other product-related services that you offer. Second, you need to prove that you are the only person (or the most qualified person) to fill that role.

There are quite a few tools in this book that help you get started on this proposal. The Microsoft Certification Goals Worksheet in chapter 2 (Fig. 2-1) helps you determine what you plan to achieve from this training. A goals worksheet can also show management that you are

serious about obtaining the training. It can also provide you with reasons that the company needs a network administrator. The Skill Level Ranking Chart in Fig. 3-1 can not only show personal weak and strong areas, but provide a basis for showing why you are the best candidate for the job. Much of the material in chapter 6 can also help you get the information needed to create a convincing proposal.

Figure 3-4 provides a sample outline you can use to get started on your proposal if you want to become an MCSE. Figure 3-5 shows a similar outline for the MCPS. Of course, you'll need to modify either of these outlines to meet any company specific requirements or to meet your own personal needs. Make sure you don't go to management empty-handed. Even if you don't write a formal proposal, you can at least get together all the answers to questions they are likely to ask. Make sure you are prepared to provide them with the best possible reasons to help you achieve your goals and provide you with the financial support you need.

Introduction   Figure 3-4

    A Description of the Proposal

    A Synopsis of any Relevant Company Rules, Regulations, or Benefits

    Definitions of Terms and Acronyms

How Will This Training Benefit the Company?

    Demonstrated Need for a Network Administrator

    Cost/Benefits Analysis

    Resident LAN Expert Available at All Times

What am I Willing to Provide the Company in Exchange for the Training?

Why am I the Best Person for the Job?

    Existing Skills

    Existing Training

    Training Goals

    Personality Traits

    Other Considerations

Conclusion

Sample company financial aid proposal outline.

Figure 3-5   Introduction

    A Description of the Proposal

    A Synopsis of any Relevant Company Rules, Regulations, or Benefits

    Definitions of Terms and Acronyms

How Will This Training Benefit the Company?

    Demonstrated Need for a User Assistant or Trainer

    Cost/Benefits Analysis

    Improved User Productivity

    Reduced Need for Outside Services

        Macro Programming

        Style Sheet Creation

        Programming in Word BASIC

        Other Services

What am I Willing to Provide the Company in Exchange for the Training?

Why am I the Best Person for the Job?

    Existing Skills

    Existing Training

    Training Goals

    Personality Traits

    Other Considerations

Conclusion

MCPS proposal outline.

As you can see, there are a number of things that you need to put in the proposal. The MCPS and MCSE versions of the outline are similar; however, the content of these sections will vary a great deal because of the different orientations of these two certifications. It is very important to make this section specific to *your* certification and *your* qualifications. The introduction allows you to quickly summarize the reasons that you put the proposal together. Make sure you include any relevant company rules or guidelines. You also need to define any nonstandard terms you use within this section. Likewise, the conclusion summarizes the contents of the proposal. It won't contain a repeat of the information the proposal contains; it will simply summarize the high points of your proposal. A manager should get a good idea of what you are trying to say by simply reading the

introduction and conclusion of the proposal. Then, if the manager wants more details, he or she can read the contents of the proposal.

There are three main areas in the body of this outline; your outline may include more. The first thing you need to do is concentrate on the needs of the company. Show management that you are thinking of the company first, yourself second. The MCSE needs to show how an in-house network administrator can benefit the company. The first part of the section tells the company about the need to have a network administrator or trainer available. Of course, one of the first questions that comes to mind is "why not use an outside consultant to perform this work?" You need to demonstrate the need to keep a staff administrator. One way to do this appears in the second part of this section. Showing management that it is actually cheaper to maintain a staff network administrator is one way to prove your point. There are also intangible benefits that you can cite. For example, one intangible benefit is the security in knowing that no one outside the company has access to vital data. This information appears in the third part of this section. These same ideas hold true for the MCPS. The first section tells how you can help users during the entire workday. An outside consultant cannot offer this service unless they remain at your company (an expensive proposition in most cases). You can also show how you can provide some of the same nonuser services that a consultant would. For example, you can show the need for creating macros for a spreadsheet or style sheets of a word processor.

The second area of the proposal tells management what you are willing to exchange for the financial support. Of course, what you offer is up to you. The standard items include a promise to stay with the company for a specific amount of time and other concessions. This is something that the MCPS will probably want to concentrate on. The MCSE may want to offer something like the additional hours to implement a new security plan or upgrade the LAN using your new knowledge. Make sure you let management know that you are willing to negotiate. If you offer something they don't want and make it obvious that you are not willing to negotiate, then your proposal will fail even if management is interested in getting a trained network administrator or trainer on staff. Don't kill your chances of becoming certified by being inflexible or unimaginative.

The third area of the proposal must concentrate on you. Tell management why you are the best person for the job. This is the place where you can brag about your capabilities a little bit (don't brag too much, though). Initially you can concentrate on tangible evidence like your current job skills and training. Then, let management know about your training goals. Showing them the tangible parts of your plan makes it obvious that you want to succeed in your certification goals. Finally, you can tell them about the intangible benefits you can offer the company. For example, are you good at working with people? Make sure you offer management some evidence of this intangible skill. Does your work record demonstrate that you're a hard worker? Make sure you let management know about this, too.

As you can see, writing a financial support proposal requires an investment in time and effort. The results are well worth the effort though. Getting your certification can open new doors of opportunity that you might not get otherwise. In addition, some of the work you need to do for the proposal is a direct result of the work you would need to do for certification anyway. Many of the pieces of information that you need to convince management to provide you with financial support already appear in other areas of this book. You can also use them for other certification goals.

 # Student loans

There are many sources you can tap for student loans, even though most people look no further than their local bank. Of course, the number and type of sources vary by region of the country and your personal situation. Remember that guy who tapped his family for a student loan in the previous section? You can tap anyone or any institution that has money. So, the first objective is to find out where you can get a student loan. The following paragraphs provide some pointers you can use in this area.

> In most cases your local college or university can supply you with this information. Just look in the student catalogs or other brochures provided by them. The writers of these books pack them with great ideas for finding financial aid. (Obviously the

college or university wants to make it as easy as possible for someone to attend; you're simply using this source of information for another purpose.)

➤ You should also check with friends. You might be surprised at the bits of information you find out this way. For example, a friend might have read about a new student aid program in the newspaper that you missed. There is no way that you can know everything going on in your community; friends can help fill in the gaps.

➤ Life insurance companies and other financial planning institutions also make good places to check for this type of information. Some life insurance companies actually sponsor student loans and grants for their clients. While few banks sponsor grants, most provide some type of student loan program.

Once you determine where you can get a student loan, you need to find out the criteria for getting the loan. For example, any student loan will require that you provide evidence of income. A government loan may require that you fall below a specific income level while a bank loan may require that you exceed a specific income level. The one loan that may require the least financial information is a student loan provided by an insurance company or fraternal organization. In most cases, you secure this type of loan with your insurance policy or other tangible asset.

You need to take other things into consideration with a student loan as well. For example, what type of payback period does the institution offer and how high is the interest? By shopping around you can usually optimize these features to your benefit. Especially important is the interest rate. Even waiting a few days can change the amount of interest you pay on the loan. A check on the stability of the bank or other lending institution is important too, because most loans contain a clause that forces you to pay back the entire loan in one lump sum should the lending institution request it. Consider any stipulations that the lender may have about the loan. For example, some lenders may require that you provide proof of schooling in the form of a graduation certificate. You need to find out everything you can about the institution, what types of loans they offer, and what you can expect from them in the way of payment plans.

Of course, you also need to consider what you can afford. Unfortunately, some people find that they get into more debt than they can repay (as witnessed by the number of government student loans that remain unpaid). Make sure you aren't taking out too large a loan for your education. If you don't plan ahead, you may find yourself living on peanut butter and jelly sandwiches for a long time before you get the loan repaid. Even worse, you may end up filing for bankruptcy. There is a good rule of thumb to follow. Never take out a student loan with monthly payments more than 15% of your current income. If you can delay repaying the loan until you graduate, then you can probably take out a loan of no more than 10% of your anticipated income. Of course, these percentages assume that you are close to debt free when you get the loan. Reduce the amount you can borrow by any outstanding loans or credit card payments. When in doubt, always plan on a lower, rather than an optimum, income after you get your certification. A little planning goes a long way toward ensuring you achieve your goals without worrying about money all the time.

Now comes the important part of the process. Once you decide on a particular lender, get all the paperwork filled out. They usually require a lot of financial information. For example, a potential lender will want to know where you work and live in addition to what you make. They will always ask for other credit references. A lender may even ask for some personal information. The best idea is to get a copy of the loan paper and fill it out at home if possible. That way you will have all the required information at your fingertips. After you get the form filled out, take it back to the lender. Always sign the loan in front of the lender's representative (normally a bank or other officer). Take any required documentation with you as well. For example, some lenders require that you bring in a pay stub or other proof of income. They may require that you bring in a birth certificate and other forms of identification as well. Make sure you ask the lender about these requirements when you get the loan forms.

⇨ Scholarships

The number and variety of scholarships available to you are probably limited when compared with other forms of education. Unlike your local college or university, it is doubtful that your local Microsoft SP

ATC will have any type of scholarship plan available. Most of these scholarships are tied to a specific institution of learning. A scholarship gets created when someone endows the university or college with the money required to fund it.

Don't let the paucity of scholarships deter you from exploring this avenue of financial aid. Fortunately, there are a few other places to get a scholarship that could help in this situation. For example, many life insurance companies and fraternal organizations provide scholarships. Some of these scholarships are aimed at technical schooling rather than more traditional subjects. Your local church or other organization may have scholarships available as well. In many cases there are very few stipulations placed on these scholarships by the people setting up the fund. A check with the leaders of these organizations may reveal a scholarship that very few people know about.

Unfortunately, most of these scholarships are fairly small. Most of them will pay for one or perhaps two of the courses you require for certification. If you do go this route, plan on supplementing your scholarship fund with money from personal savings or other sources. In many cases a scholarship offers just the right amount of additional funding to get company support for your educational needs. This is especially true of smaller companies that want the services of a network administrator but lack the funds for training. As you can see, even if the scholarship is small, it can make the difference between getting and not getting your education.

Don't forget to check into student grants as well. This form of scholarship is extremely limited, but worth checking into. In most cases a grant is limited in the way you can spend the money. For example, a grant may stipulate that you can only use the money to pay for the course, not books or other supplementary expenses. A grant usually requires some type of nonfinancial payback as well. In this way, a grant is like a loan where the payback is in the form of services rather than money. For example, the company providing the grant may expect you to provide feedback in the form of a paper or other helpful information. In the case of an insurance company, they may expect you to provide some type of personal recommendation for sales purposes.

Once you do get a scholarship or grant, make sure you understand all the qualifications. For example, many scholarships require that you pass the course before you receive payment from the scholarship fund. You need to supply proof that you passed the course in the form of a graduation or other type of certificate. If this is true, you will have to pay for your certification course from a savings account, then reimburse the account once you receive the scholarship money. (Most Microsoft SP ATCs require you to pay for your classes in advance.) Grants usually provide the money up front.

Some scholarships and grants have other types of requirements, such as when the person who started them has restricted their use to specific types of education. Make sure you understand all these requirements before you use the money you expect to receive from the scholarship. In some cases, failure to observe a specific requirement could result in a loss of scholarship or grant monies.

 # Veterans' benefits

It's amazing how few veterans actually use their GI benefits to further their education, especially when you consider the time they spent in the service to get these benefits. In many cases the perception is that the veteran educational benefits are only for college, not for technical or vocational training. However, there are many forms of technical/vocational training that qualify for these educational benefits as well. Because the plan that you are eligible for varies by the date you entered the service, check with your local VA office for your exact benefits. Remember that some VA plans require that you make payments into a fund from your military pay. The government provides matching funds, essentially doubling every payment you make. If you fall into this category and did not make payments while in the service, you may not qualify for educational benefits now. If you are currently in the service, make sure you understand your benefits before you get out. The following paragraphs provide you with some basic guidelines for using your VA benefits.

There are a few things that you will need to prepare for if you use veterans' benefits. First, there is the usual amount of ever-changing

government paperwork to fill out if you go this route. Make sure you talk to your local VA representative well in advance to get all the required paperwork. Unlike most college financial aid reps, your Microsoft SP ATC representative will probably not know how to get the required paperwork started. You will probably need to take care of this requirement yourself. Spend some time learning how to fill the paperwork out correctly. The government will not recognize your request if you submit incorrectly completed paperwork. Also, make sure you check that the certification training qualifies for VA benefits, because the requirements for these programs change on an almost continual basis. (As of this writing, they do qualify.)

Once you determine that you qualify, the training qualifies, and that you have all the paperwork filled out correctly, make sure your local Microsoft SP ATC will accept government payment. Some Microsoft SP ATCs require payment in advance of the course. If not, then you will need to work out some type of arrangement with the Microsoft SP ATC; the government pays only after you successfully complete the course. Unfortunately, they also pay the educational institution directly, making it more difficult to work something out. The government will not issue the check to you. In addition, you will have to supply the government with proof of completion before they will make the payment. It is important to understand that there is both starting and ending paperwork that you need to turn in to the VA. You may need to spend some time working with the Microsoft SP ATC on this issue. Of course, the big benefit of this plan is a guaranteed payment to the Microsoft SP ATC. This may help you get a post class payment approved.

⇨ Personal savings

All the previous methods of getting financial aid had one thing in common: someone else paid the bills for your training. Of course, this is the best way to pay for your training, but it doesn't always work out that way. If you do plan to pay for all or part of your training using your own financial resources, make sure you have enough to complete your training before you even start. This is a good rule of thumb, because it is all too common for someone to

start certification training, only to drop out later due to a lack of funds. In fact, the best plan is to make sure you have all your bills covered, plus a little for emergencies, plus the total amount required for certification classes and testing. Remember, paying for the classes isn't the end of your financial responsibility. You also need to set aside the money required for testing and continuing education.

There are other sources of personal income that you can tap besides your savings account. For example, some people have paid up life insurance policies that they can borrow against. In many cases, the money contained in these policies can pay for the entire schooling process. The interest on such a loan is usually pretty small—almost always below the rate that you'll get from a bank or other financial institution. For example, while the prime lending rate was 9½%, the average bank loan was running 12%, and the average credit card was running 18% in California, people were able to take a loan on their life insurance for a mere 6¼%. Of course, your life insurance company's policies will probably vary from this average, so it pays to check with them in advance. In many cases you can borrow up to half the face value of an insurance policy. If the face value is $5,000, you can probably borrow up to $2,500. Never depend on the "cash value" printed on the policy. Always call the insurance company to see what you can borrow (and even if they allow you to do so). In essence, an insurance loan is one where you borrow from yourself.

You can also take money out of an IRA or other long-term savings account if you're willing to pay the penalties and don't want to wait until you have the money saved in your regular savings account. Of course, you need to spend some time with your bank working out the details of this solution. The penalties and other legal considerations vary by bank and savings plan. On average, you will have to pay the bank a 10% penalty for early withdrawal. In addition, you will have to pay the federal and state income taxes on this money.

One final solution to get the last bit of support you need is to pay for part of your classes using a credit card. Many people will pay for all their classes using a credit card, then pay off the credit card company through their monthly bill. Of course, to pay for the entire cost of certification classes and testing using a credit card, you need a fairly high line of credit. The big disadvantage to this method is the high

interest rate you'll pay for your training. Most credit card interest rates run from 15% to 21%, making this one of the most expensive methods of paying for your schooling. On the other hand, you may need to get the training immediately to take advantage of an opportunity. You need to weigh the cost of the lost opportunity against the potential cost in interest.

Other programs

There are other payment programs that you can try to use. For example, some states and the federal government have job training plans for minorities (in addition to student loans or other forms of assistance you must repay). If you qualify for one of these plans, then the money you receive may pay for all or part of your schooling costs. As with the veterans' benefits mentioned earlier, there is usually a lot of paperwork involved with this approach. Make sure you know all the requirements before you start signing up for class. In most cases you'll need to combine the money you get from these programs with some type of other financial aid package. For example, your company may help pay for part of the cost if you can get government support for the other part. In fact, the personnel office of your company is a good place to begin your search for appropriate aid programs.

You might be able to get grants from corporations or other organizations in exchange for some type of consideration. For example, a consultant might get a grant from a company in exchange for free maintenance service for a specific amount of time. Of course, it takes time and effort to ferret out these sources of financial aid. You might want to consider this as a final option if all the other plans in this section of the book fail to produce results.

Who do you talk to about training?

You realize the need for training of some sort. So to whom do you talk about obtaining the proper training? The proper training is essential to obtaining the level of expertise needed to complete your

goal of certification. The level of certification you wish to acquire along with the level of experience and knowledge you currently have will help you to decide the type of training needed. Thus far, I have helped you understand what your skill levels and knowledge levels are; I will now look at where and how to obtain that training.

Training comes in many different ways and from many different sources. The type of training that will best suit your needs will depend on your personal work and study habits. In many cases the best form of training will be to obtain your training from job experience. This is referred to as on-the-job training or OJT. In other cases the best means of training will be to attend a structured course. Other types of training include third-party lectures, books, magazines, videotapes, audio tapes, self-study manuals, instructor-led classes, and of course the trial and error method.

Hands-on training

The on-the-job training (OJT) method of education is a time-honored way of obtaining information. Some people refer to OJT as the school of hard knocks. It is the most time-consuming method of learning the information needed for certification, but few people will find a more permanent way to remember that information. While this type of training will supply you with the most hands-on, real-world way of performing a task, the amount of time you must invest before you have enough information to become certified may be measured in years. You learn as you work. The OJT method of learning is inexpensive and very good for the slow learner. If you don't have a time limit hanging over your head, OJT is superior to just about any other method of learning. The whole process comes down to a simple phrase: quality over quantity. OJT provides long-lasting, real-world results that will certainly help you advance.

This is not to say that if you do not have OJT you cannot pass the certification, or if you are working for an organization that you will not become certified for a long time. Remember that Microsoft is testing your knowledge, not your ability to do the job fast or how long you will remember the information. These other two factors will affect

how valuable your certification is to you as an individual. A consultant who can work faster than someone else will get more jobs done in a day. The trainer who can remember information better will teach the class with fewer interruptions.

The best place to acquire on-the-job training would be, of course, in a job that's related to your educational requirements. This may not be a very easy task for many people. Many times, before you can get hired by a company, you must have the same skills that you are trying to learn. If this is the case, you may have to work out an arrangement with the prospective employer to work as an entry-level person or to work at a reduced rate. Other times you may be able to work out an arrangement to help and assist in the projects free of charge in return for the hands-on experience. While this is not putting any money into your pocket, you will be getting the necessary training that you are looking for. Consider it a payment toward your education.

When you start to look for places of employment, either on a training basis or for permanent placement, remember that you are not locked into a long-term permanent job. If at some point in time you find that you are not learning what you need to learn, or that you are not happy where you are, you can always find another job that will give you what you are looking for. Just because you are trying to get some education or are currently certified, you do not have to stay at a place you are not happy with. If you are not happy or comfortable with your situation, you will not be as apt to learn what you need to know as quickly as if you really enjoyed the job.

So where and how do you start to look for this job? The first place to start should be to check your personal resources. These are people that may be in a position that can help you. They may include family members, friends, neighbors, or people you work with. Often these people will not be able to directly help you, but they may know of someone that may know someone that will be able to help you. You will then have a warm lead and a name that you can use as a possible reference and as an ice-breaker. The more people you let know what you are doing and what you are looking for, the better your chances are of getting that warm lead. The more personal contact you have with a prospective employer, the higher your chances are of obtaining a position.

Another area to turn to for a prospective employer for on-the-job training would be the "help wanted" section of the newspaper. This source of leads will point you to employers that have the need for some type of assistance. You will find that this is usually a tougher way to land a position than finding a warm personal lead. There will normally be many people that apply for the same position, and often some of the applicants are better qualified or overqualified for the position. This will make it very difficult for you to get very far. You may need to find some type of angle to make your services more attractive. This may include working at a lower pay rate, or signing on with this company for a long time.

Other sources to look at for on-the-job training would be job services, job counselors, employment agencies, and head-hunter services. These are all good places to contact for opportunities. You will more than likely find that they will want or need someone with some type of experience, and you are again caught in the loop of not being able to find a job without experience, and not being able to get experience without a job. The final way to find the OJT you need would be to knock on doors. Look in the phone book for computer and Microsoft dealers in your area and then just visit them. The in-person approach will normally yield the best results. You are presenting yourself to the possible employer so that they can see what you are like. They can talk face to face with you and get to know you. You will also be able to present your situation to them in a way that you cannot do over the phone. Remember, you must create a reason why they should help you. You must create an incentive for the company to hire you.

→ Instructor-led training

The fastest way to get the training you need and bring yourself up to speed is to enroll in a professional education program. The instructor at the Microsoft SP ATC has already been through the school of hard knocks (referred to as OJT in the previous section). He or she can help you get your certification quickly and with the fewest number of disasters possible. You will also get a more rounded education, an overview of the subject. This means that you will gain an equal knowledge of every aspect of your specialty. OJT, on the other hand, suffers from the very repetitiveness that makes it such an effective teacher; you will find that you know some areas better than others and this will definitely affect your certification exam results. The instructor will normally present you with a series of lectures along with oral or written question-and-answer periods, lab exercises, and hands-on experience.

Another benefit of an instructor-led course at your local Microsoft SP ATC is the manuals you receive in class. These student manuals are an invaluable source of information. Many people keep them handy even after they get their certification, because the manuals contain such a wealth of information. In addition, the manuals provide you with a good idea of what and how to study for the exam.

Even though a professional education has many benefits, there are a few pitfalls as well. You will learn the Microsoft way of doing things, not the real-world perspective that you gain from OJT. This form of training provides you with book knowledge, not experience. You will need to gain that later. Remember, these courses are fast-paced. They try to cram what the instructor learned in a few months into your head in a few days. If you are a slow learner, then you may find the instructor-led courses inadequate. (The instructor will take some additional time to help you learn, but there are only so many hours allocated to the process.)

Instructor-led courses are available from a variety of different sources. These sources include Microsoft Solution Provider Authorized Training Centers (Microsoft SP ATCs), colleges, universities, vendors, and different third-party educational facilities. Each of these different educational facilities provides a vast assortment of services. The services offered by these institutes range from the very general to the very specific. The lengths of classes also range from just a few hours to four or more years. The cost of the different educational services will range from nothing to thousands of dollars.

Because the educational facilities will vary in class size, materials offered, length, cost, and types of services, you will need to consult with them for your needs. To locate the different institutes in your area, check the phone book, talk to your local chamber of commerce, and check with the local computer dealers. Often the local computer

dealers will be able to tell you where the best place in town is to get training. Because they are in the trade and see many of the qualified people working in the industry, they will know which institute has the best reputation in the industry.

The best place to obtain the required information for the Microsoft certifications would be from a Microsoft Solution Provider, Microsoft Subsidiary, or Microsoft itself by calling (800) 426-9400 (USA) or (800) 563-9048 (Canada). Microsoft makes excellent training available for their certifications as well as their line of products. While Microsoft does offer some training for the MCT directly, most of the training comes from the Microsoft Solution Provider Authorized Training Centers (Microsoft SP ATCs).[2] Microsoft requires the centers to teach their courses at a strict level of quality. Microsoft inspects the centers for proper hardware and software, as well as the general overall condition of the facility. Each center must use Microsoft Certified Trainers (MCTs) to teach the courses. The instructors have passed a series of competency exams and have attended special courses designed to make sure that they meet the Microsoft standards for teaching the course.

The Microsoft SP ATCs are distributed worldwide, with the largest concentration being in the United States. Some of the Microsoft SP ATCs are quite large, with upwards of 10 classrooms in one location. There are also a few Microsoft SP ATC companies that have education centers in different parts of the country. The centers are all basically the same, because Microsoft authorizes each one and each center must meet the Microsoft guidelines. What distinguishes the different centers from each other is the quality of the instructors. While each instructor is Microsoft-certified, many of the instructors teach only what is in the Microsoft course manuals. While this is the base information required for the Microsoft certifications, it may not always lend itself to real-world experiences. The "extras" that the better instructors include usually come from years in the field practicing what they teach. We have all had the instructor or professor that really knows the book material that they are teaching, but ask them a question that is not part of the manual and they

[2]The name of these training centers may change to Microsoft Solution Provider Authorized Technical Education Centers in the future.

haven't a clue. When selecting the education center that you want to attend, be sure to ask for references from past students. Talk to these people and get a feel about how the instructor handled the class, subject matter, and questions that weren't covered by the course material. You will find that most of the instructors will get good reviews.

Other items that separate the Microsoft SP ATCs will be the courses that they offer. Many of the classes require the latest in computer technology and some of the smaller Microsoft SP ATCs cannot cost justify the expense of the equipment. These centers are left teaching only the basic core classes. This is okay for the basic certifications but if you want to become an MCSE then you will have to find a Microsoft SP ATC center that teaches the advanced classes. The amount and frequency of courses are also an issue. If the class that you want to attend is offered only quarterly you may have to wait a few months before attending the class. Some of the larger Microsoft SP ATCs offer most of the core classes on a monthly rotation and the advanced classes on a four to six week rotation.

Whether you attend a large or small Microsoft SP ATC, you will receive quality training from some of the most credible institutes around. Microsoft has long been recognized by the industry for their proactive approach to training their dealers, users, and technicians. You can always count on the course materials written for their software to be current with what's on the market.[3] To get a list of Microsoft SP ATCs in your area you can call Microsoft directly at (800) SOL-PROV USA or (800) 563-9048 (Canada). Appendix A contains a list of numbers for Microsoft subsidiaries in other countries. Any subsidiary should be able to help you. Once you do reach Microsoft, they will provide you with a list of Microsoft SP ATC centers in your area. You can also use the Microsoft FastTips service to obtain information. There are four numbers you can use: Desktop Applications (800) 936-4100, Personal Operating Systems (800) 936-4200, Development (800) 936-4300, and Advanced Systems (800) 936-4400. The Microsoft Download Service (206) 936-6735 (USA) or (905) 507-3022 (Canada) is a BBS you can use to obtain information or download the latest patches for your software.

---

[3]With advancements in the industry made almost daily, the course materials are kept as current as possible.

 # Self-study training

Microsoft as well as other sources offers self-study programs. Table 1-1 lists the names of the self-study courses available for various programs. Your Microsoft representative can probably recommend a few other ideas for self-study as well. The self-study programs are good for self-starter people that have both the time and attitude to study on their own. By using the self-study programs offered by Microsoft and the Microsoft SP ATCs, you can save yourself a few dollars.

Microsoft usually supplies the self-study courses in one of three forms: manuals, videotapes, or computer-based training (CBT). They do not supply you with any instructor input when using the self-study program. Of course, the advantage of using tapes is that you can play the tapes over and over again until you fully comprehend what you need to know. The disadvantage is that there is nowhere you can turn if the tapes do not answer every question you have. While you could turn to other people in your company, or peers in a user's group, it is not quite the same as having the instructor-led training. Which method you use is up to you. Some people can get all they need from the self-study method.

The self-study programs are an excellent way to get some form of training, hands-on experience, and knowledge needed to attain the Microsoft certification. It will save you money, because you won't have to attend the more expensive instructor-led courses. If you decide to participate in the self-study program and make it work for you, be sure that you are 100% dedicated to reaching your goal. The biggest disadvantage to the self-study program is the amount of individual work it takes to prepare yourself. You will not have the luxury of having a structured class and an instructor that will lead you by the hand through each chapter of the manuals. You will have to devote at least two hours a day to studying the Microsoft manuals and researching any questions that you have about the subject matter.

To find out more about the self-study courseware, contact your local Microsoft SP ATC, your local computer dealer, or call Microsoft. The courses available will vary from education center to education center, so be sure to thoroughly investigate what each has to offer.

Other types of training

Often the standard approach to training, such as on-the-job training or attending classes, does not always fit into our schedules. For this reason, alternative forms of education are very popular. The alternative forms of education may include books, audio tapes, videotapes, and computer-based training (CBT) programs. These are all excellent sources of information that will help to augment your training process.

From the experienced computer technician down to the beginner, a bookcase with a wide variety of computer books will be a necessity. This library will prove to be a great asset in your quest for advancement in the computer industry. With a well-rounded library, you will be able to reference the topics and subjects that you may not know very well. You will find that your library will grow immensely in a short time. Many of the books that you get will have just a few pages on the subject that concerns you right now, but will provide a source of reference on other material in the future.

There are many books about the Microsoft application programs and operating systems in bookstores now; the MCSE elective materials are a little more elusive. Many of these books are very general in nature, with the same material included in books supplied by Microsoft. They are usually someone's interpretation of the subject. In some cases they are often more concise than the Microsoft books. Most of the operating system books go into great detail on how to install the operating system and how to manage the system once it has been installed. The application program books tend to concentrate on the specifics of using the application; some also help you with installation details. If you attended the Microsoft courses, you will find this to be a repeat of the information that the instructor presented in class. On the other hand, these Microsoft-specific books are very helpful in teaching you about their products if you lack on-the-job experience. If you are new to the world of Microsoft products (an unlikely scenario), you will find that these books will help supplement your knowledge.

There is another good reason to buy some of these general Microsoft books for your library. The Microsoft classes focus on the current application programs and operating systems. This is acceptable for learning about the latest systems that are being sold, but you will find that in many businesses they still have old versions of the operating systems, and even more use old versions of the application programs. The old versions of these products provide the business with everything that they need. There is no reason for them to spend the money on a new product if the old one meets their needs. In their minds, a new version of the product will not provide them with anything worthwhile.

As a Microsoft expert, you will need to know about the early versions of these products and how they work. You should know the different commands and the different terminology that was a part of old versions of the various products. There are many differences in the versions of Word for Windows, for example. Version 1.0 is different from Word for Windows 2.0 and Word for Windows 6.0. This is one reason why books written about the different operating systems and application programs will be an asset to your library. It is sometimes difficult, if not impossible, to get books from Microsoft on these past products.

If you want to become an MCSE, don't ignore the general networking books. Many of these books have a lot of practical information about how to administer your network.[4] While these books may not provide Microsoft-specific information, they will help you gain a better understanding of networks in general. Even if you don't use this information immediately, you will find it essential later. The same hold true to a lesser degree for the application programs that the MCPS specializes in. For example, there are general books on desktop publishing that the MCPS who specializes in Word for Windows will find handy.

To find books on the Microsoft operating systems, networks in general, or application programs, you do not need to go very far. Most bookstores carry at least a few. The large bookstore chains normally carry a good line of Microsoft books written by many

[4]See "Hands-On Guide to Network Management" by John Mueller and Robert Williams (Windcrest book number 4418, ISBN 0-8306-4440-7) for more information about network administration in general.

different authors. Computer stores will usually carry one or two different ones as well. You will find that in many of the larger cities there will be technical bookstores that specialize in computer books. These stores will carry most of the books written about Microsoft products. You can normally find a list of the bookstores in your area by looking in the yellow pages of your phone book. Another good source on where to find computer books is contacting the Microsoft instructors from your area. They normally stay current with information on different computer related topics. They also visit the more technical bookstores on an ongoing basis to help themselves stay current with technology. You will also find that most of the more technical bookstores will supply you with a list of titles to which they have access, and will ship books anywhere in the world.

Besides books, another great source of training material is the use of audio and videotapes. Both Microsoft and third-party companies make tapes that are basically the Microsoft courses. These tapes will supply you with a great deal of information about the Microsoft products but are usually fairly expensive. While the cost makes them out of reach for most individuals, they are good for companies that need to train a few people in their organization. This allows them to buy one tape and then let all of their employees use it. This is a lot more cost-effective than sending all of their employees to a certification class. A note here for companies that may plan to do this: send one person to the certification course, or have a person that knows the Microsoft product in question. You will find that the tapes present a lot of material to you, but they will not be able to answer the questions that arise from watching the tape.

Microsoft offers a vast array of videotapes on different product topics. The tapes include both basic and advanced topics. Microsoft has had the tapes professionally done, and continues updating them as new products are released. You can order the tapes from Microsoft or from your Microsoft dealers. To get a list of tapes offered by Microsoft, call the Microsoft sales department or your Microsoft dealer. You can also download the Microsoft Education and Certification Roadmap from CompuServe. Just GO MSWIN or MSEDCERT and download the ENCMAP.ZIP file. Microsoft updates the roadmap as new products become available; the entire product receives quarterly updates.

Microsoft also offers a computer-based training (CBT) program that will help you to train for the certifications as well as to simply get a better understanding of the products they offer. The CBTs are computer programs that offer information that you read, followed by exercises that require input from the reader (sort of a mini-exam that you can use to test your knowledge). These are good programs that will help you understand the workings of a particular Microsoft product, but will usually stimulate many other questions not addressed by the program. The programs are also quite expensive for the individual, but are very attractive to companies that need to train more than one person. To get a list of available CBTs and the part numbers, call your Microsoft sales department or contact your Microsoft authorized dealer.

 # Getting the most from your training

As you have seen, there are many different approaches to training to become a certified Microsoft expert and for general knowledge of the computer industry. It is normal to feel a bit overwhelmed because of the vast amount of information that you will receive in preparation for your certification exams. The best advice to help you attain your certification: stay focused. By using the goals worksheet presented in chapter 2 and the information presented here in chapter 3, you will be able to formulate what your goals are and how to attain them. Keep your goals worksheet with you all the time and look at it often. This will keep you focused.

To get the most from your training, you will also want to take the training one step at a time. It becomes very easy to get caught up in the frenzy of trying to learn as much as you can, as fast as you can. Take one topic at a time and work with it until you feel as if you know the subject matter. Don't try to learn all the other related subtopics that are part of the main topic. You will find that *every* topic or subject will have many other related subtopics, and each one of them has many other topics and subtopics as well. Soon you will find that the subject that you had originally started to study is now replaced by a new topic and you have not learned anything more about the

original item of study. Take one item at a time and stick with it until you are finished.

Another good way to get the most from your training is to take many notes. If you are in a class you will want to take brief notes. Do not take notes on everything the instructor is saying. If you are doing this, you will find that you miss many things that the instructor says. You may not even catch enough of the discussion to be able to ask questions. Try to write just the key words that are being used, then, after the class is over (or at a break period) you can fill in some of the other information. Usually just the key words will start a thought process that will replay the lecture in your mind. Now at this point, you can write down as much information as you would like. You will have the time and be able to concentrate on how to convert the information from a thought to a written idea.

When reading the books and manuals you study, use a highlighter and sticky notes for references. Many people highlight sections of the text that they know; what you should be highlighting are the parts that you don't know, or the parts that you will need additional help on. Once you highlight the text, use the sticky note to mark the page for future use.

You will find that one of the best ways to study the course manuals is to break the process down into three parts. First, quickly read the material in a summary fashion. Don't spend much time reading the material; you only want to get familiar with the content of the book. For example, you may want to scan the headings and the first sentence of each paragraph. This will help you understand the author's intent in writing the book. Second, get a note pad, your sticky notes, and your highlighter. Then reread the manuals, making notes and highlighting the important information as well as the information that is new to you, or that you do not understand. The third step will be to study your notes and marked pages, and then research any areas that you do not understand.

Using this process will take a little more time than other techniques that you could use to study, but you will find that you will retain a lot more information; there is something special about converting the information from a thought in your mind to letters on a piece of

paper. The final step in this process will be different for each of you. Many times you will want to reread the manual and your notes again. If you feel as if you know the materials, consider taking the exams. You will have to make that decision when you get to that point, and it may change with each manual you read.

The secret to making this work (and passing the exams) will be to find the style, type of training, and studying technique that best stimulates your mind. This may take some time, and you may have to change the way you approach it to account for differences in difficulty between courses. Be aware of what techniques work for you, and which techniques produce the best results.

When doing your studying, you will find that short bursts of studying will produce better results than long periods of intense concentration. Remember the long all night "cram" sessions preparing for high school and college exams? All this did was put your mind in a state of exhaustion; more likely than not, you didn't retain any of the information you studied. You will be able to concentrate longer and remember better if have a rested mind. You will find too that your exam scores will be higher if you take the test when you are rested and alert.

When doing your studying, hit it hard for ten to fifteen minutes, then take a short break. Your actual study time will vary from day to day. It also varies from person to person. The best rule of thumb is to study until your mind starts to wander. The moment your mind starts to wander, you aren't getting any real work done; it's time to take a break. Get up and walk around, get a drink of water or a breath of fresh air. You will find that your concentration will be much higher and your retention will also be better. If you just study for hours on end, your concentration is usually high at the start and near the end. Most of the information in-between becomes diluted. The short burst prevents your mind from getting overwhelmed and tired.

Other study techniques include the use of flash cards, posters, and recording your notes on a cassette tape. All methods are proven ways to study and improve your knowledge base. When using the flash cards, use 3×5 cards with a question on one side and a complete answer on the other. You can use these while stuck in traffic,

watching TV, or just about any time. You can also give them to a friend and have them ask you the questions. The posters are similar to the flash cards. Get a package of poster paper and a large dark marker. On the posters, write just a few key words, then hang the posters around your house and office. The key words that you put on the poster should start a thought process that gets you thinking about some subject. The flash cards and the posters will not only help you in studying for the exams by using them over and over, but the process of making them also reinforces the concepts in your mind.

The use of cassette tapes is another way to get the most from your training. By recording your notes on a cassette, you can play the tapes over and over at any time. They are especially useful while you are driving; just plug them into your tape player. You will find that, by listening to your notes in your own voice, your mind will retain more. You will also be able to reuse the tapes for different classes and different manuals. Use the tape recorder to also record notes while in class. It then becomes possible to replay the course lectures at your convenience, and at your own pace. Often you will find that you missed something the instructor was talking about. This is especially true if the material is new to you. As you are thinking about what is being presented, the instructor moves onto another subject and you miss some part of what is then being said.

All the mentioned training techniques will help you to reach your goal of certification if you apply them. By staying focused on your goals, selecting a training program that's acceptable, and then applying the proper study techniques and refining them to your style, you will find yourself prepared for the exams.

CHAPTER 4

Taking the tests

T AKING tests is the least favorite part of any training experience; they seem to evoke the worst feelings from all of us. While general exams are difficult, professional examinations are more difficult than just about any other examination you can take. With most general exams you have a wide range of study aids available. If nothing else, you usually have a group of fellow students to talk with. Professional exams usually don't offer these aids; usually, only a small group of people interested in something more than just a general knowledge of the world around them takes these types of exams. Microsoft's examinations are no different. Not only is there a lack of third-party study aids, but each exam is totally different. Therefore, you can't even rely on the input from fellow students to help very much.

In addition, the emotional pressure of a professional exam is a lot greater than that caused by a general exam. Of course, the reason that emotions run the gamut from agony to ecstasy is easy to understand. The stakes are high; a career is up for grabs. Every professional exam you take has the potential of helping your career if you pass it, or reducing your potential if you don't.

Learning to take an exam is just like any other skill; you gain the knowledge to perform the task, practice until you become proficient, then demonstrate your ability. To become a proficient test taker you learn how to study, how to think when taking the exam, and how to prepare yourself emotionally. This chapter takes a look at all these elements and more. It helps you prepare for the Microsoft exams not only at the knowledge level, but at the emotional level as well.

There is another event you have to prepare for as well. Even if you go through all the training courses, study hard, and take the proper approach to testing, there is a good chance you will fail at least one

examination. After all, if there wasn't a chance of failure, would anyone really want to get certified? The potential for failure helps differentiate between those who really want the professional recognition that comes with certification and those who don't. Dealing with that failure is an important element of passing the exam the next time. Looking for places you made mistakes in the first attempt will help you prepare for the second attempt.

This chapter helps you cover the three areas of testing by telling you how to study and what to study. It also stresses the importance of taking the Microsoft viewpoint when answering questions. Most important of all, this chapter helps you over the ultimate hurdle, dealing with failure. The better prepared you are to take the test, the more devastating the failure becomes. Helping you get back on your feet again is a very important feature of this chapter.

Gathering the information you'll need

The student guides you receive while taking the Microsoft courses listed in Table 1-1 are your most important asset in taking an exam, especially if you take good notes during class. There are two operative phrases here. First, you must take the Microsoft courses to obtain the Microsoft view of networking, operating systems, or application product use. Second, you must take good notes in class. Unless you perform both of these steps, there is a good chance that you will fail at least once for each exam. The reason for this failure is simple. While you may have a great understanding of networks or the application you use in general, you need to know the Microsoft way of doing things to pass the exam.

The importance of the Microsoft courses

Your instructor is specially trained to help you understand networking from a Microsoft perspective. A Microsoft certification is

a credential that tells the world you know what you're talking about when it comes to Microsoft networks. This implies that you know the Microsoft way of doing things. While you could argue that there are probably many other ways of performing a specific task, the certification implies that Microsoft has provided you with training in the Microsoft way of doing it.

It may seem that prescribing one way of doing things when there are many other equally correct ways of doing them is unnecessarily restrictive and oppressive. However, Microsoft cannot test everyone's methods of doing a task, yet they must ensure that the methods used by the people they certify are correct. Any other course would make people ask, "Why should I trust anyone you certify to maintain my network or train my employees?" As you can see, what may seem restrictive at first is simply a way of making sure that everyone can perform networking or training tasks in a way that works every time. It also ensures that someone certified by Microsoft fully tests those techniques in a real world environment. When people hire you based on your certification, what they are really hiring is someone who knows the Microsoft way of performing a task, an extension of Microsoft if you will.

So how does this relate to test taking? Since Microsoft must test your ability to maintain a network or use an application and we have seen there is a logical reason for everyone performing those tasks in the same way, it follows that Microsoft will test that one way of doing things. If you walk into the examination room without a knowledge of Microsoft's way of performing the task, then there is no way for you to answer the questions correctly. (The passing requirements are high enough to void just about any possibility of someone guessing their way through the exam.) This is the first point you must remember then. When you take a certification exam, you are getting tested on your knowledge of Microsoft's way of performing a task, not your networking or application knowledge. This is a very important concept to grasp. Failure to grasp it could cost you the exam.

By now you're saying, "But Jane over there never went through the courses and she passed the exams without any problem." There is a simple answer to this question as well. You can only perform some tasks one way. When you come across questions that ask about that one way, you will find that you can answer them even if you haven't gone through

the Microsoft courses. This is how some people get by without taking the Microsoft courses. They learn enough about the Microsoft methods to pass the exam based on their own knowledge. Of course, these are the same people who usually have several years worth of networking or application experience, and a few degrees as well. Unfortunately, unless you are very skilled in networking, the cost of approaching the exams from this angle can be high. Failure to prepare yourself costs you both time and money paid for failed exams.

⇨ Taking good notes

Another piece of information you need to collect before you can study for an exam is a set of good notes. What makes the difference between a good note and a bad one? Actually there are no bad notes (with the exception of wrong information). There are good notes that help you study, and ones that won't. While both convey information, one doesn't provide the correct type of input.

Notes are somewhat difficult to quantify until you actually need to use them. You may think something the instructor said is of the greatest importance during class, only to find that you never use the information afterward. Watching what information you use and what information you don't is one way to improve your note-taking skills. Everyone differs in their ability to retain information. One person may need to write just about everything down on paper or he will not remember later, while another person will fail to hear an important fact if they are too busy taking notes.

Part of the problem is levels of concentration. How well do you concentrate? Can you work on complex problems for hours without getting mentally tired? Do you remember what you read in trade journals long after the information is no longer useful? You may find that taking a minimum of notes and really concentrating on what the instructor has to say is your best method of retaining information. In fact, some people don't take any notes at all during class. They save that activity for after class as a technique for going back over the information the instructor presented.

If you find that you can't remember anything without writing it down first, you may want to consider two other methods of taking notes.

Some people use the outline approach. They write quick notes about what the instructor said as an outline on a separate sheet of paper. This allows the note taker to concentrate on what the instructor has to say. After class these people fill in the outline. This helps reinforce what the instructor said during class.

Another group can actually concentrate on two things at once. They can write complete notes and still pay attention to what the instructor is saying. This is the same group of people that you find talking on the telephone while working away on their computer. This is a talent that some people possess, and you can use it to good effect in class. Make sure you use every resource to ensure you get a good set of notes to use for study later.

A final group of people need to resort to high technology to make sure they get all the facts. Simply take a tape recorder with you to class, record what the instructor has to say, and transcribe it later. This tends to reinforce the lessons you learn in class and still allows you to get complete notes. (Make sure you ask the instructor's permission before you start recording the session; some people may object to the use of recording equipment in class.)

As you can see, there is a variety of ways to take notes. This is the first thing that you must learn to do. Get the information down on paper so you can use it later to study. If you find that at the end of the day you cannot remember what the instructor said, then you may be using the wrong note-taking technique. You should rely on your notes as an aid to memory, not as a replacement for your memory. Force your brain to do a little of the work required to remember what the instructor said during the day. Work with a variety of methods until you find the one that works best for you.

The second part of this note-taking procedure is to take notes that you will actually use. This differentiates a good note from one that you took and don't need. Taking good notes always helps you in the long run; the other kind of note is a waste of time. Unfortunately, this is something that you learn from experience. A valuable note for one person may not provide any information for someone else. Here are some rules of thumb that you can follow to maximize the possibility that the notes you take are as useful as possible:

➤ Take complete notes. Never write down just a few words without filling the note out later. This is especially important if you use the outline approach to note taking. Some people take good notes during class, but fail to fill them out immediately afterward. When they try to use the note to study for an exam, or for part of their work later, they find the note is incomplete or indecipherable.

➤ Take specific notes. Don't talk about generalities in your notes. Always make them as specific as possible. If the instructor provides an example in class, adding this example to the notes can help you get the most out of the notes later. Making the note specific also helps trigger the memory process later. We tend to remember specifics, not general information.

➤ Don't take notes out of context. Always provide enough surrounding information so you can get the full flavor of the note. Never jot down a quick idea that you could misinterpret later. Always provide yourself with all the details. Have you ever heard of the guy who took notes about preparing a chicken for dinner? One of the notes said "Cut off head." So he cut off his own head instead of the chicken's head. Don't let this happen to you. Take complete notes that give you the whole story.

As you can see, note taking is an important part of the learning process. Always increase your chances of passing an exam by taking good notes in class. Take the time to check the usefulness of your notes after you write them. If you find that you don't use the contents of a note later, then don't waste the time required to take that type of note again. In addition, if you find that you can almost, but not quite, remember something the instructor said, it is a sure sign that you needed to take a note. Make sure you remember to record this type of information during courses you take in the future.

The test taker's study guide

You're sitting at a table or desk, with your student manuals on one side and a stack of notes on the other. What do you do now? What is the best way to study for your certification exam? This question plagues just about anyone who takes an exam. If you leave your study

area and go to the exam with this feeling, you may actually psyche yourself into failing it.

No matter how you slice it, passing an exam means that you must perform some type of study before you take it. Whether you use the formal approach of classes or something a little less conventional, like tapes or self-study guides, you need to prepare yourself to take the exam before you enter the test area. This section helps you develop the good study habits that you need to get the most out of your study time.

A good study regimen does not mean spending a long time in study; it means studying efficiently. There are four major areas of concern: quality, environment, goals, and techniques. Each area will help you improve your study habits to obtain the best overall efficiency without reducing the effect of your study. If anything, these techniques will help you study faster and better.

The first part of this section helps you set time aside to study. Let's face facts. Everyone has a very busy schedule, and it's not always easy to get a quiet place to study. In fact, home and job probably consume more time and energy than you really want to admit. However, here is another fact to consider. If you are so busy taking care of other things that you cannot concentrate on what you want to study, then your retention rate will fall to near zero and there is no reason you should even make the effort. This may seem a bit harsh, until you really think about it. Why waste your time? Part of studying smart is to set aside a special time and place to study. Don't let anyone or anything interfere with it. You will find that you can study for a lot less time and actually get more out of it. This will help you free more of your time for those home and work duties, in the long run.

The next area I look at is creating a good study environment. Some people try to study in the living room with both the TV and the radio blaring in their ears. Of course, this type of setup is hardly conducive to effective studying. There are seemingly innocuous things that affect the study environment as well. You may not notice how much direct light tires you out, but your retention rate will certainly reflect this factor. The right kind of comfort is essential to a good study environment. This part of the section looks at the total study environment. We will look at things like getting the correct materials

together and making sure that you have enough of the right kind of light. This section also looks at the physical requirements for study. For example, the type of chair you choose can greatly affect comfort, which in turn affects how much you get out of a study session.

The third part looks at setting goals for a study session. You need to know what you plan to accomplish during any given session. Few people realize just how much their mind can wander during a study session. Do you find yourself thinking about the work you need to get done tomorrow while reading that test question? Setting goals keeps your mind focused. A failure to set goals may lead to random study that does not accomplish the goal of passing the test. Consider how well you would do on the job if you didn't set and meet goals. You may not always meet those goals within the time frame you set, but you *must* meet them to maintain your productivity. Studying is no different from any other human activity in this regard.

Finally, I look at study techniques. The technique that works best for you is a very personal thing. Not every test taker can use the same technique. The same individuality that lends interest to life in general makes it difficult, if not impossible, to create a sure-fire study technique that will work for everyone. As a result, I will not even try to propose one standard way to study for your certification test. This part of the section looks at a variety of study techniques that you can choose from to create your own strategy. At least one of the methods will meet the needs of every reader who looks at this section. Hopefully you will use a variety of study methods to make your study time interesting.

Setting aside adequate study time

Time is a quantity that seems in shorter supply today than ever. Its use is closely guarded by all of us in our everyday dealings. In fact, many of us are even more careful with our time than we are with our money. Time is a quantity that you can never have enough of. This time shortage invariably extends into your studies as well.

Unfortunately, some people will try to cram everything in their Microsoft manuals, third party books, and self-study guides into just one or two day's worth of study. They will further cheat themselves by using only one of the teaching aids that Microsoft provides. While this may work for some of the simpler exams, it probably won't do much good for the majority of them. The average human being needs a lot more in the way of study to really pass the certification exams. You will want to set aside at least a full week of study for each exam. Most people will require two weeks of study to really understand what the exam requires.

Fortunately, there is an answer to this problem of time and how it impacts your certification. There are two things you need to do to ensure you get the maximum benefit from your study time: control the starting time and control the length of study. Controlling the starting time is important because that influences how you approach your study time. Controlling the length of study ensures you maximize the effect of your study time. The following rules of thumb should help you in both regards.

➢ Always study when you feel well-rested; never study when you feel tired. Not only are you apt to get facts that you study confused when you feel tired, but you will remember them for a shorter length of time. Studying with a clear mind helps you retain the facts you learn for a longer period of time. Studying when you feel well-rested also improves your attitude.

➢ Try to study at the same time each day. This helps you develop a study habit, rather than forcing you to go through the inconvenience of study. It also improves your ability to study. You will find that your body actually anticipates the demands of studying and prepares for them. Make your study time a treat instead of a dreaded job each day.

➢ Choose a time of day when you are relaxed and there are few interruptions. Trying to study right before or right after meal times probably isn't a good idea in most cases (most people are a little too relaxed right after a meal). You will want to pick a time when your surroundings are quiet and you can spend some time hitting the books. This means that you won't want to study during your lunch hour at work. Use your lunch hour as a time to rest in preparation for your study time that night. Trying to take care of the kids while you're trying to study probably won't work well either.

➤ Never study more than two hours. Most researchers indicate that one hour of study is about what most people can tolerate. Have you ever gone to a seminar where they try to cram as much as possible into the two or three hours allotted? It seems that, with all the excitement, everyone should be ready to go for at least that long. But what happens after about an hour? People start leaving for places unknown, or fidget in their seats; they simply cannot absorb more than an hour or two of lecture. Likewise, as a person spends more time in study, their attention slowly drifts to other topics, and away from the area they want to study. If you really want to study more than two hours, make sure you take plenty of breaks. One way to extend your study time is to study for an hour, take a fifteen-minute break to relieve the stress, then study for another hour.

➤ Use an alarm or other timing device to keep yourself on track. This will help reduce the chance that you'll spend more time watching the clock than you do studying. Decide how long you need to study for a particular session, set the timer, then forget about clocks until you hear the alarm. Of course, using this technique will also keep you from studying too long and losing the good effect of your study time.

➤ Try varying your study technique. You might try having someone quiz you one night and do some memorization another night. Another way to vary your schedule is to spend the first half an hour studying and the second half an hour having someone quiz you. Make sure you use more than one of the methods of study presented in this section to help obtain this goal. Varying your study technique can reduce the boredom that naturally occurs as study progresses.

As you can see, planning for your study time is fairly important. It really helps if you can study without fear of interruption or of going to sleep. It also helps if you can maintain the most positive attitude possible; you want to study without getting bored.

One technique that helps prevent boredom is to read or study with a big bowl of popcorn. As you study, munch on the popcorn. The action of moving your hand from the bowl to your mouth will stimulate your other muscles just enough to keep you alert. (Make

sure you don't douse your popcorn with too much butter; you don't want to complete your certification weighing in at 400 pounds.)

Variety is essential to meeting your nightly study goals. After all, this is your future livelihood. Why should you work at something that bores you? Give yourself every advantage. Pick the times when you are best able to study. Make sure you study long enough, but not too long.

 # Creating the right study environment

Creating a productive study environment can prove daunting in the average home. No one wants to maintain a quiet environment after spending the day locked in a classroom or office. In addition, few homes contain a dedicated study area. More likely than not, you will find your study area located in the kitchen or a bedroom. Other possible areas you may want to use for study include the library, park bench, beach, or your own backyard. Problems aside, you need to find a place that satisfies at least the majority of the hints provided in this section, even if it means studying outside your home. With a little work you can probably satisfy most of them. Figure 4-1 shows some typical study area needs.

Notice that the requirements for a good study area are fairly simple. You can group them into three areas as shown in the picture: optimum study environment, personal study needs, and a lack of distractions. Actually attaining these goals is a whole different matter. Let's look at the requirements in a little more detail.

You have the greatest control over the study environment. It doesn't get tired or have a bad day. In addition, it usually stays in place once you set it up. As a result, this is the area you should concentrate on first. Make sure you take some time to get this part of the study environment up to par, because the other areas are subject to change. For example, a few dollars spent for a better computer chair today can continue to net results for many tomorrows. Normally you will spend a lot of time in front of your computer studying for the certification exams, so it really pays to invest in this area. Don't

Figure 4-1

Make sure you observe all the required precautions for using your computer. This includes sitting at least 30 inches from the screen and using a wrist pad to prevent carpal tunnel syndrome. Keep your display and other parts clean, too.

Go ahead and get relaxed, but not too relaxed. Remember, the whole idea is to study for your certification exam. Maintaining the correct posture and body position can help you focus on the job ahead.

Avoid study area distractions. A lack of light or the wrong kind of light can reduce your ability to see. Try to use indirect light. TV and radio can interfere with studies as well. Never try to study while doing chores.

Sources of distraction.

overlook things like an antiglare screen if you need it. Many newer displays provide an antiglare surface, but you may require more.

One of the most important (yet often overlooked) requirements is the screen distance. If you can't see the screen at 30 inches without squinting, then there is something wrong. Take the time to check for glare conditions or dirt. You may want to change the size of the font to make it easier to see from a distance. Getting glasses specifically designed for computer work can help a great deal as well.

A comfortable office chair that is adjusted to fit your body is also a must. Take the time to adjust it to meet your needs. Your calf and thigh should form a 90-degree angle and your thighs should be parallel to the floor when you adjust the chair properly. Check out your arms. Do you have to reach up to touch the keyboard? Your upper arms should rest against your body and your upper arm should form a 90-degree angle with your lower arm. Make sure you provide plenty of support for your wrists.

You can usually control the second area pretty well. A look at your personal study needs is always a good idea. Maintaining a positive mental attitude will help you get the most from your study. Trying to study while tired does not accomplish much. If you feel bad, take the night off. Get relaxed, but not too relaxed. If you are too tense, then you will tire easily. You need to relax to go the distance during your study time. Of course, getting too relaxed will allow your mind to wander. A wandering mind does not remember much; not even what you were thinking about instead of your studies.

Distractions, the third area of concern, are the hardest part of the equation to get under control. Don't try to study while performing chores around the house. One of two things always results. Either you will perform the chore with your usual flair and forget everything you studied, or you will end up frustrated because you cannot perform both tasks at the same time. Don't fall into the trap of having someone quiz you while you perform chores either. This is still a form of study; give it the respect it deserves.

Avoid too much noise as well. A television or radio is a good companion when you work around the house, but they produce

devastating results when you study. Do you ever find yourself singing a song on the radio instead of paying close attention to your studies? This is the natural result of noise in the study area. Of course, the same thing holds true for people who insist on talking to you while you study. Take the time to look away from your work, listen to what they say, take care of anything they need, politely ask them to leave you alone, and get back to work. Any other course will surely frustrate both of you.

Subliminal distractions are the worst of the group. Ever have a dripping faucet ruin a good night's sleep? The same thing happens when you get distractions that are just beyond the range of your senses during your study time. The amazing part of this is the variety of forms that subliminal distraction can take. For example, you might need to remove the clock from your study area because it makes too much noise. Even a source of light can provide a subliminal distraction. Try using indirect light instead of a lamp while you study. You will probably feel more relaxed because you don't have light glaring in your eyes. Using indirect lighting also means that you can use the proper light level. Some people get rid of the glare by getting rid of the light. Taking time to figure out those subliminal distractions may not rapidly improve your test scores, but they will make your study time a lot more comfortable.

Setting up the right study environment is just as important as any other factor in studying effectively. Make sure you don't ignore it. A good study environment can help you optimize your study time and reduce the fatigue most people associate with it.

⇨ Goal-setting strategies

Setting goals for each study session is extremely important. You need to decide where you are now, and where you want to get by the end of the study session. Using this technique will help you keep your mind focused on what you want to do. Maintaining your focus is one of the most important parts of any study regimen. If you don't keep your mind on what you are doing, it will drift to other, "more interesting" topics and you may as well not spend any time studying

at all. Any effort from the time you stop thinking about the exam and start thinking about that next vacation in Tahiti is totally wasted.

Of course, it's equally devastating to rush through a study session simply to meet your goals. Think of your goals as the target that you want to attain. Get as close as possible to that target, but don't shoot yourself in the foot in the process. Rushing is one of the worst things you can do if you want to retain what you learn. Make sure you take the time to fully study each topic.

Getting somewhere between these two extremes is the best way of setting goals for your learning time. Make sure you set a reasonable goal. After all, whom are you trying to impress? Only you will know what takes place during your study sessions, so make your goals difficult to reach, but not impossible. The following tips will help you set reasonable, yet worthwhile goals.

➤ Check your actual progress from session to session. Use this as a gauge for setting your goal for each session. Set a goal a little higher than what you achieve during an average study session. This will challenge you, but keep the goal within the realm of the achievable.

➤ Use the sample questions in this book (appendix D) and the Microsoft Certification Professional Assessment Exams to measure your retention. Make the first goal of each new session to test the amount of information you retained from the previous session. Your score will tell you whether you are rushing or not. The combination of materials provided in your courses, plus the Microsoft manuals and any third-party books, should allow you to retain a minimum of 70% of what you learn. If you do not retain information at this rate, consider slowing down a little and spending a little more time on each topic. If you still can't achieve a high enough retention level and you haven't taken any courses, then consider taking classes at your local Microsoft SP ATC.

➤ Maintain a point system based on the goals you achieve each session. This makes the study session more of a game, and ensures that your interest level remains high. Compete against yourself. That is what you really do anyway, so make a game of

it. You could use the following scoring system. Assign each goal a point level: Hard (3), Medium (2), or Easy (1). Add up the goal points for each goal that you accomplish during a session. Now, multiply this number by the test score you obtain during the following session to obtain your final score. For example, you studied 2 hard, 1 medium, and 1 easy goal during an evening. You obtain a score of 80% on the test during the following session. Your score for the evening is: ((2*3) + (1*2) + (1*1) * 0.8 or 7.2. See how easy it is to use this system? Now you have an easy way to track your progress from day-to-day. Make sure you reward yourself for above-average performance. This is one sure way to ensure continued success.

➤ Set goals based on your ability, not someone else's desires. It is too easy to destroy a study session if you are trying to live up to a boss's expectations or what a coworker achieved. On the other hand, it is equally devastating to hold back your progress because you think you need to spend a specific amount of time on each topic. Each person is an individual and requires his or her own special goal-setting strategy. Use the other tips in this section to stay on track.

➤ Use a weekly test to check your overall retention level. If you plan to spend a few weeks studying for each exam, then keep an overall look at your progress. Don't fall into the trap of thinking that you are doing fine, only to find that you don't remember the things you studied during the early part of your study sessions.

➤ Set your goals based on your current work load. If you have an easy week, then set higher goals. A stress-filled week probably calls for a lower goal level. Don't add to a burden by thinking that you need to maintain the same level of achievement every day.

As you can see, what looked like a difficult task at first may prove easier than you think. Setting goals is easy. Checking to see that those goals are reasonable takes a little more time, but is definitely worth the effort. Make sure you optimize your study time by optimizing your study goals.

→ Using the right study technique

Developing good study habits is important if you want to pass an exam; using the appropriate study technique is an important part of developing good habits. You always want to maximize the impact of each study session by varying your technique over the time allotted. Study techniques are a personal part of the picture. Each person has different needs in this area.

Developing good study habits means a lot more than just getting into the right frame of mind, or using good study practices. Using the right study technique can mean the difference between a boring study session and one that fully meets your objectives. If you enjoy spending a lot of time with other people, a good study technique could include taking the time to converse with your peers about the topics that will appear on the test. You may even want to exchange telephone numbers and addresses with your classmates and set up a study session at one of their houses. Make it a study party and you could be miles ahead in your study goals. Talking with friends is just one more technique you can add to your bag of study techniques. Of course, you will surely fail if this is the only technique you use. You need to combine this technique with some individual study time or other study methods.

There are many ways to help improve your study time. Some methods work for some people, some for others. Everyone is different. You need to develop a set of study habits that works for you. The best rule of thumb is to always analyze both your successes and failures to determine what works and what doesn't. I cannot possibly list all the potential study methods in this book. However, I can look at a few that you can use to develop your own techniques.

> ➤ Try having someone quiz you. Make sure they concentrate on one test at a time, but that they vary the questions from one session to the next. Ask them to ask the same question in several different ways. This will help you develop a thought pattern centered around question content, rather than the question itself.

➤ Discuss the test and other study materials with your peers. You can ask them about problem areas they have and express your own problem areas. Having a group help you with your problem areas not only increases your chances of getting a great answer, it forces you to consider areas that you may not think about normally.

➤ Make a game out of the test. Try making your own flash card system or other game type techniques. You might even want to create a Trivial Pursuit or Jeopardy type game for yourself. Creating these games puts the test in a different light—making it more a challenge than a chore. Try modifying existing games to meet your needs, or use other traditional game methods. For example, you might want to combine correct answers with the ability to move on the game board.

➤ Spend some time in concentrated book study. Look over the Microsoft manuals in depth. Try to find at least one new fact during each study session. Perform the same process with your third-party books and the student manuals. The search will help you focus your thoughts on the test and reduce the chance that your attention will wander.

➤ Some people find that memorization is an easy way to learn. Try to memorize as many of the facts in this book and the Microsoft manuals as possible. Recite them to yourself as you perform other network or application-related tasks. (Always avoid mixing study and chores.)

➤ Consider the hands-on activities in your student manuals and the Microsoft manuals as the basis for your own exercises. Create your own case studies based on your weaknesses and the guidelines presented in this book. Make sure you set a starting point and an ending point. Figuring out how to get from point A to point B is a good way to study. You can even use this in a group setting. Challenge one of your peers to a race. Each of you can set the starting and ending points for the other person. The first person to accomplish their goal wins.

➤ Use association to study. Take the time to associate the items you need to know for the exam with things that you do every day. Some people even create acrostic sayings to learn various

elements of the exams. For example, this works especially well when learning the security portions of an operating system, like the different types of access or the attributes you can assign to a file. Of course, it works equally well when memorizing the various menu functions of an application. You can also use mnemonics for association. To learn the names of the seven OSI model layers in order, try taking the first letter from each word of the saying "All People Seem To Need Data Processing." Each of the letters in this saying are in the same order as the OSI layers Application: Presentation, Session, Transport, Network, Datalink, and Physical.

➤ Take notes as you read the Microsoft manuals, and study the questions in this book. Then, refer to the notes and see if you can remember what you read. See how accurately the notes reflect what the manuals actually say. This can help you find and define problem areas. An alternative to this method is to create an outline of the topics you study, then fill in the blanks later. This forces you to remember what you read, and then reinforces it by having you write the information down.

Of course, this is not the list to end all lists. Do yourself a favor: develop a set of study strategies that work for you. Then, take the extra time to use a variety of techniques to keep your study time from getting boring. The time you spend in this additional effort will pay for itself quickly when it becomes time to get down to work.

Getting the job done right

Learning to study is essential if you want to pass your certification exams. Any other course of action is deadly. This section looks at four major areas in optimizing your study time. More importantly, this section shows you how to retain what you learned. You will never pass the exams if you do not know how to study and, more importantly, retain the information you learn. The following hints will help you develop a study strategy that maximizes the effects of your study time.

➤ Always study your weak areas first, then study the areas you feel more confident about. If you have someone quiz you, make sure they quiz you about the weak areas first and the strong areas afterward. To help determine where your weak areas lie, make sure you look at your notes and sample test results. If you spent the time to take notes about a particular topic, then you are probably weak in that area. If your daily tests show that you miss a lot of questions in a particular area, then spend extra time in that area.

➤ Have someone quiz you on what you learned. (This book provides you with a wealth of sample test questions; form your quiz questions using the same format.) Make a game out of studying. Reward yourself with something special if you get a specific number of points toward your goal. You can use the questions you miss as the basis for the next day's study.

➤ Create a good study environment. Make sure you have a clean desk or table to work at. Reduce any distractions by turning off the radio, closing windows, and asking others in the study area to remain quiet. Adding a good, indirect light source and sitting in a comfortable chair can help as well. Make sure you wear comfortable clothing while you study.

➤ Study the appropriate section in this book for the test you want to take. Some people tend to race ahead or look at previously studied areas when they become bored with the current test material. Doing this can actually confuse you rather than help you study. For example, you may find that you start confusing the feature set for Windows with those found in Windows NT. Each exam only tests one specific set of information. Make sure you study for that particular test. If you find yourself getting bored with the current material, take a short break; get up and move around instead of racing ahead or looking at previously studied material.

➤ Fill out your notes if you use the outline method of taking notes. Even if you don't, you may want to spend part of your study time expanding the notes you took during a previous study session. Make sure you take the question-and-answer portions of this manual into account. This forces you to remember what you read during the previous session, and what

questions you studied. It also increases the usefulness of your notes when you need to use them later.

➤ Spend time discussing the topics you studied with your peers; a particularly good activity if you are part of the network staff for a large company or a local user's group. This allows you to compare notes and ideas about the topics. You may find that someone else has a different viewpoint about how to interpret the Microsoft manuals. (The same thing happens when you ask two people about what happened at an accident site; both will see something different.) Talking with your peers helps you enhance your notes by incorporating their viewpoint as well. It may also help you fill in gaps in your notes. Even the most conscientious person misses things during a study session.

➤ If you are a very motivated person that tends to rush things, never register for the exam until you feel ready to pass it. The only limiting factor on the time you have to study is the schedule for the application or operating system update. Microsoft does not place any other limitations on your time. Make sure you are ready to take the test before you call to register.

➤ If you tend to procrastinate, you may want to register for your exam immediately after the first study session for it. You may even want to register immediately after you complete your courses. Try setting the date for three weeks from the time you begin the topic or two weeks after you complete the course. This will give you a goal to achieve and enhance your study efforts. Don't let your certificate pass you by; register now for the exam.

As you can see, there are a lot of ways to improve your chances of passing an exam. This includes: creating and maintaining a positive study environment, reemphasizing important points through quizzes and discussions with your peers, and taking the exam only when you're ready. Following any or all of these suggestions may just make the difference between passing the exam and failing it. You may want to take some time to add your own ideas to this list. For example, some people may find that studying outside is more beneficial than studying in the house. Each person is different. The study methods used by one person may not help another. Make sure you optimize your study methods to meet your needs.

Registering for the exam

Registering for the exam is one of the easiest parts of the process. All you need to do is have a credit card ready and call the Drake registration number. You can register for any test by calling (800) 755-EXAM. The person on the other end of the line will ask you a few questions for you to answer. That's all there is to registering.

Of course, there are a few pieces of information you need to know before you can call. You will need to know the number of the examination you want to take and the location of your nearest test center. (You can check Table 1-1 for a list of exam numbers.) If you don't know the location of the nearest test center, the person registering you can provide a list of locations in your area. They can usually provide you with directions to the test center as well. You may want to drive to the test center from work at some time before the exam, so you know how long it takes to get there. This also allows you to test the directions you get from the test center, and make any required changes. Make sure you add or subtract some time to compensate for differences in traffic flow at the time you plan to travel to the test center. If you make the trip from work during your test run in light traffic, then try to make it in the same time in heavy traffic, you may end up arriving late.

Make sure you have several exam dates in mind before you call the test center. Otherwise, you may find the test center filled for the date you originally wanted, and you may have to rush to find another one. Once you do get a test date, write it down in several places. Talk to your boss about taking the needed time off well in advance of the test. Make sure you don't schedule other appointments on your test day. Set this day aside for testing and nothing else, if possible. (Of course, most people will have to go back to work after the exam.)

Things to watch for while taking the exams

There are quite a few things people do during the examination; many of them are big time wasters. Some people wander between the

drinking fountain and their desk. Others seem more interested in staring at the dots on the wall instead of answering questions. Make sure you use all the time allotted to take the test; don't waste any of it doing other activities. Try to maintain your concentration during the entire exam. Don't allow interruptions to rob you of the chance to pass. Of course, time isn't the only thing you need to watch during the exam. The following hints should help you take the test faster and improve your chances of passing.

➢ Look at the time indicator on your screen from time to time, but don't waste time staring at it. Make sure you pace yourself; allot enough time for each question you need to answer. You may want to take a quick glance at the time indicator after each question, and ignore it the rest of the time.

➢ Read the entire question. Don't skip over small words like "and" or "not" when reading the question. Small words make a real difference; skipping them could cost you the question. People often miss questions not because they didn't know the answer, but because they failed to read the question fully. Make sure you understand the question before you read the answers. In fact, it is always a good idea to read the question twice before you answer.

➢ Read all the answers provided. Sometimes there is more than one correct answer on the screen. You need to pick the most correct answer that you find.

➢ Remember to put on your Microsoft hat before you enter the testing area. Microsoft uses the student manuals and product manuals as the basis for all the answers in the exam. Even if there is more than one correct way to perform a task, only the Microsoft way is the correct answer on the exam. In some cases you may see more than one correct Microsoft answer to a question. Always pick the most complete answer.

➢ Go with your first instincts. Some people get so psyched out before an exam that they actually overthink the answers to questions. Going with the first answer that comes to mind is correct more often than not, especially if you took the time and effort to study. Don't kill your chances to pass the exam by overthinking the answers.

➤ Maintain your level of concentration. Even though the exam center administrator tries to provide the very best testing environment possible, there are always distractions that try to reduce your concentration level. Concentrate on the test; ignore any outside influences that tend to reduce your level of concentration. You can't perform well on a test that you aren't concentrating on.

➤ Make sure you take care of your comfort needs before the exam. For example, even though you don't normally need to eat breakfast, you may want to do so on the day of the exam to boost your energy levels. You will also want to wear comfortable clothing. Wear your glasses or contacts so you can see the screen without squinting.

As you can see, the things you notice during the exam are really a matter of how well you prepare before you go into the test center. For example, your body's energy level always affects your concentration level. It's also affected by all the environmental factors under your control, like the ability to see the screen and wearing comfortable clothing.

Realizing the effects of environmental factors on your mind during an exam is very important. For example, some people go so far as to make out a schedule for the day of the exam. This can help you get from place to place without rushing. Make sure you allow plenty of time to get from place to place. Taking an exam while you feel relaxed is a lot easier than taking one after you rushed all day. Figure 4-2 shows a typical schedule. Of course, you will need to tailor your schedule for your test needs.

Notice that my schedule contains little housekeeping notes, like the reminders to call work and place the test results in a folder where you can find them later. These may seem like things you shouldn't have to write down, but writing them down does provide a certain peace of mind while you're taking the exam. You don't need to worry whether you took care of a specific item since you have all of the things you need to take care of on paper.

Figure 4-2

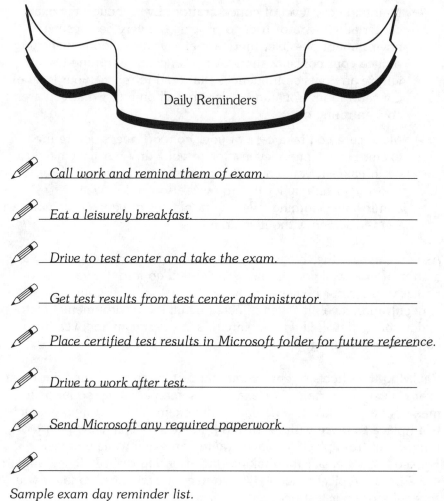

Daily Reminders

Call work and remind them of exam.

Eat a leisurely breakfast.

Drive to test center and take the exam.

Get test results from test center administrator.

Place certified test results in Microsoft folder for future reference.

Drive to work after test.

Send Microsoft any required paperwork.

Sample exam day reminder list.

➡ What do you do if you fail?

Even if you do fully prepare for an exam, there is still a chance that you will fail it. There is no way for you to take every variable into account to guarantee that you will pass the exam. You may not realize that you have a weak area that the test asks you about. A cold or flu may strike on the day of the exam. An accident may delay part of

your schedule, forcing you to rush to the exam. Any or all of these reasons may prevent you from performing your best on the exam.

How you recover from a failure partially determines how you will react during the next attempt. It may even determine whether you make another attempt to pass the exam. Many people try the exams once, fail, then give up on their certification because the failure was so demoralizing. Remember, certification requires a lot of dedication and hard work. If certification were easy, the benefits of certification would be a lot less. Don't give up after one attempt to pass an exam.

Understanding the mechanics of failure

Of course, nothing is more demoralizing than failing the same test twice. There are several things you should do after failing an exam to make sure it won't happen again. For example, you can plan to study the areas that gave you the most trouble in the first exam. The following tips will help you pass the exam the second time around. Unlike the other tips in this chapter, these tips usually work for everyone. Make sure you try them all.

> ➤ Write down the areas where you did well and the areas where you did not. (The test center administrator will provide you with a blank sheet of paper and a pencil you can use for this purpose.) This will tell you where you need to concentrate your study before you take the next exam.

> ➤ Maintain a positive attitude. If you convince yourself that you're going to fail, you surely will. Virtually thousands of other people have gotten their certification; there is no reason that you can't get it with the proper training and study. You need to keep this fact in mind while you study for the retake.

> ➤ Don't overcompensate by studying too much. Many people make the mistake of punishing themselves for failing by spending hour after hour in front of their desk studying for the next exam. This is probably the worst mistake you can make. While it is important to study for the next exam and try to find the weak areas that

caused you to fail the first time, studying too much can confuse you and cause you to fail again. Make sure you don't study more than two hours per day. (You may want to review the study tips in the previous section of this chapter.)

➤ Try to remember specific questions that you may have had trouble with. In fact, you should try to write these down while they're fresh in your memory. Even though it's unlikely that you will see these questions on the next test, they may help you find weak areas in your study strategy. In some cases you may even see the same question worded in a different way. This is where reading the question and understanding what it says really helps.

➤ Always study for a general exam—not the specific exam you took the first time. Trying to study for a specific exam is pointless because each exam contains different questions. Microsoft writes a new exam from questions in a database for each person that takes an exam. That's why it is so unlikely that you will see the same question again.

⇨ Understanding the emotions of failure

Besides the mechanical methods for getting to the next exam, you must deal with the emotional issues as well. Failing an exam always lowers your self-esteem and causes you to doubt your abilities. You need to find outlets for dealing with this problem. Some people perform some physical activity like bowling or tennis after a failure. The activity helps them release the frustration they feel over failing the exam. Other people work on crafts. A creative endeavor allows them to take their mind off the failure and put it to useful work. Whatever method you use to release the tension of failure, make sure you do it as soon as possible afterward. Don't give yourself time to think about the failure too long.

You also need to convince yourself that you can pass the exam. Many of the people who start the certification process never complete it

because they don't think they can pass the exam. Remember, anyone with reasonable computer skills can pass the exams with the proper training and the right amount of study. A positive attitude is one of your best weapons in passing the exam the next time around. Make sure you maintain a positive atmosphere as you study and when you take the exam. Keep telling yourself that you can pass the exam.

CHAPTER 5

Getting the paperwork finished

THE job's never finished until the paperwork's done. This is just as true for Microsoft certification as anything else. Even if you finish all the required tests and training, you can still fumble around for several weeks just getting all the paperwork finished. Failure to take care of the paperwork properly won't cost you your certification, but it will cost you time, and as we all know, time is money.

There are two forms of paperwork required for most certification efforts. The first is Microsoft-related paperwork; you will have very little to do here. The second type is personal; you always have to get this paperwork finished. This chapter describes both types of paperwork and what you need to do to get them completed.

Normally Microsoft downloads your test scores from the testing center automatically. The automated nature of this method is the reason there is little paperwork for your Microsoft certification. When you complete all the requirements for your certification, Microsoft automatically sends you the required paperwork. All you need to do is check the paperwork to make sure everything is correct, then sign the Microsoft Certified Professional Program and Logo Agreement. Sending the signed agreement to Microsoft is the only Microsoft-specific paperwork requirement you have.

NOTE **The MCT program requires additional paperwork that we will discuss in the MCT specific section. The additional paperwork is minimal, but you do need to track it carefully.**

Unfortunately, everything doesn't always go as planned. Test results can get lost or hardware failures could trash the test center files. If any of the test results do get lost, you must provide Microsoft with all

the documentation required to prove that you passed the required exams and took the required courses. Much of the paperwork you will need to fill out comes from a loss of a course certificate or passing exam paper. If you ever need to verify your test status or paperwork requirements, call Microsoft at (800) 636-7544.

Even though there is very little physical paper changing hands, you should still maintain your own logs and other means of verification. The paperwork does not end when you complete your certification; that's where it begins. It also includes follow-up calls to make sure that Microsoft has everything it needs to issue your certificate. You also need to call Microsoft to make sure that nothing gets lost or overlooked. The bottom line is that you need to maintain a line of communication between yourself and Microsoft to make sure the certification gets issued promptly.

Your personal paperwork is essential as well. This second form of paperwork may seem like an unnecessary effort, but you must take care of it or suffer the consequences. If nothing else, you need to at least reflect on a few issues regarding your certification. For example, what did you learn from your certification experience? Where do you plan to go from here? If you fail to learn from past experience and plan for the future, then your career will most certainly suffer. It is no longer enough simply to shuffle to your job each day; it is the thinking person who gets ahead in the Information Age.

This chapter deals with the problem of paperwork by providing you with step-by-step instructions on filling out the paperwork and getting all the required documentation together. It also provides you with the names of the departments you need to talk with, and where you need to send the paperwork to. It tells you what kind of paperwork you should get back from Microsoft, and how long it usually takes to receive it. Finally, I look at your personal paperwork requirements. What should you look at once you complete your certification?

Getting the paperwork started

It is very important that you begin the paperwork process by getting organized. Make sure you can find the items you need for your

conversation with Microsoft by putting them in one easy-to-find place. Putting all your paperwork in one or two folders is a good idea as well. You may even want to create one folder for each course you attend. This way you can keep notes, certificates, and test results for that course in one place. Whatever techniques you use, make sure you keep good records of all the certification items that Microsoft requires. You want to make it as easy as possible to find this information when you need it during a conversation with a Microsoft representative.

You will also want to make a list of the paperwork required for your certification. The figures in chapter 1 help you to do this. Make sure you keep this information in your folders as well. If there was a mistake in what you thought you required for certification, then you will want some basis to discuss the mistake with Microsoft. This may help them improve the level and quality of information that they provide to other candidates in the future. It may also grant you some leeway on getting the required exams taken or other certification requirements finished.

⇨ How long is too long?

The problem you face now is figuring out when to panic if you don't receive word from Microsoft regarding your certification. It is always a good idea to take a proactive approach to your certification. Microsoft downloads the data from the test center every evening. They compare the information they receive to their current database. If someone passes a test, they add it to their existing record. If Microsoft can't find your name on its lists, then it adds you to the database as a new applicant. People who complete all their requirements are issued a certificate. A computer performs all these database functions automatically, making the process nearly foolproof. There is little chance that your examination scores will get lost.

Based on this information, you will want to call Microsoft if you do not receive your certification transcript within about 10 working days after you take your exam. Calling Microsoft ensures that you will receive your certificate on time, and that both of your records are in synchronization. It also reduces the last-minute rush you'll experience

if you wait until you complete all the requirements to call Microsoft. You can take care of each mishap as it happens.

Once you complete all your requirements, take time to call Microsoft again. Make sure you wait the requisite 10 working days after you complete your last requirement. Make sure they received everything. This is the time to ask the Microsoft representative how long it will take to receive your certification. Asking this question will help you know when you've waited too long for your certificate to arrive. Always allow a few days after the deadline before you call Microsoft again. This compensates for slow postal deliveries, especially during the holiday season.

⇨ Maintaining a log of the paperwork

Keeping records is an important part of the certification process. It helps you keep track of where you need to go and what you need to do. Of course, records fulfill an even more important need. Maintaining these paperwork logs may seem like a lot of fuss for nothing, until something gets lost. Chances are good that you won't have any problems, but if you do, the time spent creating these logs will help to resolve any problems or misunderstandings. Make sure you cover all the contingencies by keeping a record of what you do, when you do it, and how you do it. That way you won't have to rely on your memory later when it comes time to figure out what happened. You also want to make sure you maintain good contact with Microsoft without making a nuisance of yourself. Maintaining these logs will help you maintain constant contact without calling too often. Remember, you are the one interested in certification. The Microsoft representative is only there to help you achieve your goal.

⇨ Using the paperwork log

The time may arrive when you need to provide Microsoft with proof that you passed your certification exams. Since proof of requirement

completion is your responsibility, it really helps to keep a complete log of every certification requirement you complete. Remember, normally you do not have to worry about any paperwork with your Microsoft certification; you only need to maintain this log to keep things on track. Drake normally sends the required information directly to Microsoft.

Unfortunately, you may have to prove that you did fulfill the requirements when something goes wrong. Make sure you write down the date that you sent this proof to Microsoft. You will also want to make notes on what method you used to send the certification material. For example, did you fax the material, or send it overnight mail? (If you completed the requirement and simply relied on Microsoft to download the information from the test center, make sure you record this information as well, on the appropriate chapter 1 form.) The forms in this chapter are for emergency use only. Figure 5-1 provides an emergency log you could use for the MCPS certification. Figures 5-2 and 5-3 provide the same logs for the MCSE and MCT certifications. Use these logs to record any paper correspondence with Microsoft. For example, if Microsoft loses your paperwork, you would want to use these forms to record the time, date, and method you used to send them paper copies.

Figure 5-1

MCPS Paperwork Log

Name: _____

Date Started: _____ Date Completed: _____

Date Microsoft Certified Professional and Logo Agreement Signed: _____

Requirement	Course Number	Date Sent	Method Of Mailing	Register Number	Date Received
Submit Operating System Test Results	_____	_____	_____	_____	_____
Submit Application Program Test Results	_____	_____	_____	_____	_____

MCSE Paperwork Log

Figure 5-2

Name: _____

Date Started: _____ Date Completed: _____

Date Microsoft Certified Professional and Logo Agreement Signed: _____

Requirement	Course Number	Date Sent	Method Of Mailing	Register Number	Date Received
Microsoft Windows	_____	_____	_____	_____	_____
Microsoft Windows NT	_____	_____	_____	_____	_____
Microsoft Windows NT Advanced Server	_____	_____	_____	_____	_____
Windows or Windows NT Networking Exam	_____	_____	_____	_____	_____
Elective Credit 1	_____	_____	_____	_____	_____
Elective Credit 2	_____	_____	_____	_____	_____

MCT Paperwork Log

Figure 5-3

Name: _____

Microsoft SP ATC Name: _____

Date Started: _____ Date Completed: _____

Training Skills Requirements Met: _____ Courses Completed: _____

Instructional Skills Self-Assessment Tool Completed: _____

Getting the paperwork finished

Figure 5-3   *Continued.*

Letters of Recommendation and Student Telephone Numbers Collected:

_____

Date Microsoft Certified Trainer Application Signed: _____

Date Microsoft Certified Professional and Logo Agreement Signed: _____

Date Microsoft Trainer-Preparation Course Completed: _____

Requirement	Course Number	Date Sent	Method Of Mailing	Register Number	Date Received
Course Name:					
_____	_____	_____	_____	_____	_____
Course Name:					
_____	_____	_____	_____	_____	_____
Course Name:					
_____	_____	_____	_____	_____	_____
Course Name:					
_____	_____	_____	_____	_____	_____
Course Name:					
_____	_____	_____	_____	_____	_____
Course Name:					
_____	_____	_____	_____	_____	_____
Course Name:					
_____	_____	_____	_____	_____	_____

As you can see, each of the forms addresses the needs of one of the certifications. Using this type of form allows you to make sure you not only sent everything that Microsoft needed, but that you can keep track of when and how you sent it as well. The first few fields of the form contain personal information like your name, the date you started the certification process, and the date you finish it. The table contains a list of the requirements you must pass to get the certification. Some of the information needed to fill in the blanks will come from the worksheets that you completed in the previous

chapters. Notice that the course information is blank. This allows you to tailor the form to your specific needs. The course numbers you place in these blanks reflect your operating system specialty. The other fields in this form contain the date on which you sent proof of passing the requirement to Microsoft, the method used to mail the package, registered mail number (you never want to send this information regular mail), and the date Microsoft received it. You may even want to include the name of the person who verified that Microsoft did receive the package. (This information also appears in the telephone log described later in the chapter.)

One good alternative to using the mail service is faxing your information to Microsoft. You may want to consider this alternative whenever possible. It is much faster than using the mail, and you can call Microsoft immediately after you send it to make sure they received it. Make sure you call and verify that you have the correct fax number, and alert them that you plan to send the information immediately. Once you send the information to Microsoft, verify that someone at the other end of the fax line received the material in good condition. If they did not receive the information in good condition, resend it right away.

⇨ Using the phone log

There is at least one other log you should consider maintaining. This is a record of the telephone conversations with people at Microsoft. Make sure you record the time that you call, whom you talked to, pertinent facts about the conversation, and a few notes about what transpired. Figure 5-4 provides a sample telephone log.

This log file contains enough space for two entries per page. You may want to make a few copies of this sheet to keep on hand for easy reference. Maintaining the log on your computer will allow you to scan the records quickly during a telephone conversation. It also helps you ensure that no information gets overlooked while you talk with the Microsoft representative. This also makes it a lot faster and easier to maintain your logs, and to make sure you haven't forgotten to take care of anything you talked about on the phone or through the mail.

Figure 5-4

Certification Telephone Log

Date: _____ Time: _____ Contact Person: _____

Phone Number: _____ Ext: _____

Topic: _____

Notes: _____
_____
_____

Problem: _____
_____

Resolution: _____
_____
_____

Date: _____ Time: _____ Contact Person: _____

Phone Number: _____ Ext: _____

Topic: _____

Notes: _____
_____
_____

Problem: _____
_____

Resolution: _____
_____

Some database managers, like AskSam, will allow you to enter this type of freeform information quickly. When you need to search for a particular topic, these database managers will look for phrases or whatever else you can remember about the conversation.

Notice that the telephone log contains space for the date, time, and contact person's name. These items are pretty self-explanatory. You will want to include the person's telephone number and extension in the Phone Number and Ext fields of the form.

The Notes field allows you to maintain a record of what each party said during the conversation. Reserve this section for conversation of a general nature. Be specific when taking notes. The more information that you can include, the better your chances of resolving any difficulties. Make sure that you record times, dates, phone numbers, and any names mentioned. If there were any commitments made by either party, be sure to make a note of them as well. After you finish your conversation with the other person, summarize the conversation from your notes before hanging up. This will help to prevent any miscommunications.

If you called about a problem, make sure you record it in the Problem field of the form. Use descriptive terms for this field. Don't write something like "Lost package in the mail." Provide yourself with exact details by writing "Lost copy of the Windows NT 3.1 exam results in the mail." At least this tells you what test the postal service lost for you. In addition to this information, you may want to record the registration and other important facts. If the field does not provide enough room to record all the pertinent information, at least make a note about where you can find the information.

Record the resolution that you and the Microsoft representative talk about in the Resolution field. Again, document as much of the conversation as possible immediately after the conversation. If you wait very long before documenting your conversation, you may forget something. You can use the contents of the Resolution field to help make a to-do list later. Creating a to-do list ensures that you won't forget to follow through on your certification requirements. It also helps you remember when you need to call Microsoft to recheck the results of a problem resolution.

⇨ Filling out the paperwork

There are two sets of paperwork requirements. The standard set applies to anyone who wants to obtain any of the certificates. The

MCT set applies only to people who want to become MCTs. The following paragraphs explain these requirements in detail.

Standard paperwork requirements

The paperwork required for certification by Microsoft is very minimal. Besides the test scores, the paperwork consists of the Microsoft Certified Professional Program and Logo Agreement. (Remember, you are responsible for maintaining a copy of your test scores.) As you complete and pass each test, Drake testing sends an electronic copy of your test scores to Microsoft. This information gets added to the certified professional database automatically. If you are just starting the certification process, Microsoft adds your name and records to the database. As you take each test, Microsoft will add that information to your record. Once you complete all the exams, Microsoft will automatically register your certification. This applies to all the certification goals: MCT, MCPS, and MCSE.

MCT paperwork requirements

The MCT program requires one extra piece of paperwork. You need to apply to become a Microsoft Certified Trainer. The form asks about you, your employer, your instructional skills, and the courses and exams that you've passed. You need to sign the form and send it in to Microsoft. There is a checklist on the last page of the form that you can use to make certain you have met all the requirements.

Verifying that Microsoft receives and processes the paperwork

Even though Microsoft will automatically register your certification, it is your responsibility to follow up. You can never take too many precautions when it comes to your certification. After all, you spent many hours and dollars to get this far. The last thing you want now is to have some lost or misplaced paperwork to hold up your certification or, worse yet, cause you to retake a test. After completing your last test,

give Microsoft about seven to ten working days to process the paperwork. After that time, call Microsoft to check the status of your certification. The people there are very courteous and helpful when you call. Chances are very good that Microsoft already processed your certification and it may be on its way to you. If Microsoft has not processed the paperwork yet, then you will be able to inform them of your standing, and they can start the process.

Make sure you're armed with all the information you need to talk intelligently with the Microsoft representative before you call. This includes your logs and the actual documentation. The more information that you can give the Microsoft representative, the faster and more accurately Microsoft can take care of your paperwork.

When you call in to Microsoft, make sure you have a list of important telephone numbers as well. For example, if you work for a company, make sure you have a fax number that Microsoft can use to send you any required information if necessary.

Victory—getting your certificate

The day of victory is the day your certificate finally arrives in the mail. Your certificate will arrive in your membership kit from Microsoft. There is nothing like the sense of accomplishment you will feel when you finally get to see the certificate you worked so long to get. This is a time when you need to spend a little time with your new credentials. Make sure that Microsoft filled in your name and other important information areas on your certificate correctly. You may want to write down some of the vital information like your Certified Professional number as well. You can provide this number to your clients or potential employer for verification purposes.

The second CP package contains many other items besides the certification certificate. You also receive a Certified Professional logo sheet, a membership card, and a lapel pin. Chapter 6 tells you how to use your new membership card and lapel pin when you want to work for someone else. Chapter 8 will cover the use and purpose of the membership card and lapel pin when you use them as a consultant.

You will also want to take time to get your certification logo put on any business cards, brochures, or sales literature. If you aren't a consultant or in the retail business, you may want to put your logo somewhere on your resume. This may attract the attention of a future employer. You may also want to make some photocopies of the certificate and include it at the end of your resume. Whatever situation you find yourself in, make sure you let everyone know that you finally achieved your goal of getting your certification. After all, you shared your dreams of certification with them. They supported you throughout the courses, long hours of studying, and the testing process. This includes not only telling your friends, family, and co-workers, but also framing your certificate and displaying it. Many companies and resellers will use your certification to add credibility to their organization. This is an important part of making your certification work for you.

 # A look at your personal paperwork requirements

Now is the time to look at your personal paperwork requirements. There are several different things that you should look at. However, the two most important factors are what you gained and what you plan to do now. Other considerations may include looking at the financial impact of gaining your new status, and how well you met the goals you set before you started the whole process. There are a variety of things that you can do to put the finishing touches on your certification process. Many of these items are a personal requirement; other items could pertain to the requirements of the company that you work for. For example, your employer may decide that you need to fill out a report to tell the company how it spent its money. Many companies now require this type of input so they can perform some type of analysis on how money is spent, and what return the expenditure provided.

There is one thing that you should decide not to do. Don't sit back and decide to do nothing. Why would you even want to consider this course of action? Consider all the work it took to get you here. Do you really want to let it go at a simple "I finally finished," instead of

taking advantage of your work? If the certification process taught you anything, it should have taught you to look at where you are now and where you want to go. Setting goals is a very good lifelong activity.

The following paragraphs describe the first two of your paperwork items. The first section talks about what you gained during the certification process. It provides tips on analyzing what you received for the investment you made in yourself. The second section talks about where you plan to go in the future. I will examine this topic in much greater detail in chapters 6 and 8, but you may have personal goals that these chapters don't look at. For example, you may decide that you want to use this experience as a stepping stone for a college degree.

Examining your gains during certification

Some people are probably thinking that there is nothing more to say about the certification process at this point. After all, you came, you saw, you grabbed. What more is there to say about the certification you received? In actuality, there is a lot to say about it. You gained a lot more than a simple piece of paper saying that you are now qualified to work on a network or train people to use an application. If this is all that certification offered, it would still prove worth the price, but it does provide more for those who really look.

Figure 5-5 provides a sample form that you can use if you require some form of written analysis. Many people think better when they write their thoughts down. In addition, the form will provide you with some ideas of what to look for from this accomplishment. However, make sure you tailor the form to your personal needs. Don't take the form as the end all of your certification analysis; use it as the starting point instead.

There are six questions on the form; the "other" entry provides a space for your personal questions. One area that you really need to consider is your outlook on life. The first question addresses this issue. Every time you achieve something new, it does affect how you look at things. It is very important to look at this change when it happens.

Figure 5-5

Post-Certification Analysis

Name: _____

Date Started: _____ Date Completed: _____

Course Completed: _____

What did you accomplish personally? _____
_____
_____

Did this experience provide any new skills besides your certification?
_____
_____

How does your current level of knowledge compare to what you expected to achieve when you started? _____
_____
_____

Would you change any part of the certification process if you went through it again? _____
_____

Did you provide any feedback to Microsoft? _____
_____
_____

What additional education do you feel you need? _____
_____
_____

Other: _____
_____
_____

The second question asks you to examine what new skills you gained from the certification experience (in addition to the certification). For example, the certification process may force you to formulate new ideas about how to organize things. It may have shown you how to juggle a job and educational needs at the same time. There are many new skills that you can learn from the certification process. If nothing else, it should at least show you that you can learn something new and accomplish some worthy goal.

Everyone starts the certification process with some preconceived ideas. One of these ideas is what you expect to learn during the certification process. The third question asks you to take a second look at these preconceptions. How well did you do during the process? Did you get everything you thought you would from the courses? How about the manuals; did they show you everything you thought they should?

The fourth question is not asking you to examine any regrets you may have. What it is asking you to do is look at what you have achieved, and what you would do differently the next time. You can use this as a stepping stone for further education possibilities. Even if you never go back to class, you might want to use this entry as a basis for personal study. Everyone needs to grow in their personal knowledge to remain competitive in today's world.

Providing feedback may be the worst or best part of the course, depending on your personality and other factors. Helping Microsoft develop a better program is not optional. You owe it to the other people going through the courses and certification process to provide Microsoft with some kind of feedback about the process. If you don't like that reason, consider it from a selfish standpoint; providing feedback may make it easier for you to meet your continuing education requirements. Feedback does not have to consist of negative comments. Feel free to tell the people at Microsoft that they did a great job. Whatever your feedback, it will help you as you delve into other certification possibilities and maintain your current certification.

Finally, the sixth question asks you to look at this experience and decide what you might like to do in the future. You should always have some type of educational plans at least on the back burner.

Keeping yourself up-to-date is like an insurance policy. It helps you maintain your job skills at their peak and may provide opportunities for you to advance in the future.

Where do you go from here?

Once you figure out where you are now, it is a good idea to see where you plan to go. This section will help you make some plans for the future. Of course, just like the future everywhere, the help in this section is even less certain than the last section to fully meet your needs. The best idea is to use this section as a springboard for your own ideas.

Figure 5-6 provides a sample form that you could use to help create some goals for the future. Of course, this may or may not reflect what you want to do, so the form also provides plenty of space for your own ideas. Make sure you take plenty of time to fill out the form now, and re-examine it on a regular basis. As you gain further experience, your needs and educational requirements will change. Make sure you change your goal sheet to match.

Figure 5-6

Goals Worksheet

Name: _____

Job Goals: _____

_____

_____

_____

Personal Goals: _____

_____

_____

_____

New Educational Requirement: _____

Date Started: _____   Date Completed: _____

 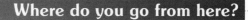

What do you expect to achieve? _____

_____

_____

_____

Other Goals: _____

_____

_____

_____

There are four main sections on this form. The last one, Other Goals, is pretty self-explanatory. Use it to create your own list of goals.

The first part of the Goals Worksheet asks you to examine your future job options based on your current certification. We examine this particular goal in great detail in chapters 6 and 8. However, you may want to take some time to think about this goal before reading those chapters. You may decide to open your own business, or take a different job at your current company. Other plans might include going to another company or starting a partnership with another consultant. The number of possibilities are endless.

You get a chance to look at some personal goals in the next section. For example, what tasks did you have to put off over the last few weeks or months to get your certification? Now might be a good time for that vacation you keep putting off. After all, getting your certification is exhausting work. Of course, this is also the space you could use for other personal items, like getting your degree or building a network at home.

Of course, no future goals worksheet would be complete without a section for future education. The information age requires that you constantly maintain your education and keep up to date on current developments. This section helps you put some of these goals into writing. Of course, this could include everything from reading the trade papers more often to getting your doctorate in some specialty. The choice is up to you.

CHAPTER 6

Using your certification to your advantage

HAVE you ever seen someone who had all the advantages lose out to someone else because they didn't know how to use what they had? It happens all the time in the movies. We find ourselves cheering for the underdog as he or she overcomes the resources of some villain to win in the end. Of course, the movies don't truly reflect real life. In real life, the consequences of not using an advantage you may earn are not nearly so entertaining; in fact, they are downright devastating. Imagine losing a job you really wanted to someone less qualified than you are simply because you didn't market your skills properly. Gaining access to a skill is only the first step in using it as a career enhancing tool. You must learn to use this skill to your advantage in the marketplace.

As you can see, the trick to gaining the full benefit of your certification comes from marketing those skills to a potential employer. Now, this book won't tell you how to write a resume or prepare a cover letter; you can get that information from the wealth of business correspondence books on the market. This chapter does help you understand what you need to do to use the certification you acquire to your benefit. You possess a special skill that these other books just won't help you to market properly. It is essential that you market your skill to its fullest or you won't get that job. This particular chapter focuses on the individual working for someone else. I cover a number of topics from advancing in your current company to getting a new (and hopefully better) job based on that training. (See chapter 8 for information on how consultants can use their Microsoft certification to good advantage in the marketplace.)

In this chapter I cover two main methods of enhancing your career. Either method will help you gain the full benefit of attaining your certification, but use entirely different approaches. Section one covers the possibility of advancing within your own company. This is the route that will appeal to people who are happy with their current company. Many people are very happy with their job. If you fall into this category, there is absolutely no reason to move to a new company.

There is another group of people who only take a job for the short term until they can get something better. (Some employers hire people knowing that they don't intend to stay.) Moving from one company to another can help you gain the recognition you need in addition to improved company benefits. If you want to make a change from your current company, then it pays to follow the two-step plan outlined in section two.

Advancing within your current company

There are a lot of ways to advance within your current company. Your boss may get promoted or leave for another company. If you demonstrate the abilities required to take over that position, then your company may choose to promote you. Another method of advancing is to create your own position. Your company may want to get rid of an old method of doing something and replace it with a newer, more efficient method. If you provide your company with enough reason to make the change, you may find yourself in charge of the group responsible for implementing the change. After the change is finished, you may find yourself in an entirely new position as head of the group. Some companies will simply change your job title to match the work that you're doing. In some cases this includes additional pay or other benefits. Whatever method you choose to follow, you need to create an advancement plan. Don't wait for opportunity to knock, because it seldom does. Create your own opportunities within the workplace.

The fact that your company chose to pay for your certification shows that there is an advancement opportunity waiting for you when you return. Even if your company already has a network in place and you trained to become an MCSE, there is some reason for them to train

you. The same holds true for the MCPS certification. Your company may have some training or user-support position in mind for you. Your first goal in getting a promotion or new position is to find out why you are getting the training. Use this reason as the basis for your advancement plan. Of course this is only the beginning. You may find that you have to do a lot of detective work before you work out an advancement plan. Management often treats new network installations, the departure of a manager, or the need for additional employee training as a closely guarded secret. Finding out what plans your company has may help you prepare for the future. The following tips should help you start to formulate some advancement goals and strategies.

MCSE only If your company already has a network, try to find out if anyone from that section is leaving the company. You may find that you will eventually fill their position if you demonstrate the proper skills to the company. Make sure you concentrate on ways of enhancing these skills. If your company doesn't have a network in place, you can be sure they will. The company would not train you for a position that will not exist. Try to become part of the planning process for the new network. Not only will the information you gain help you prepare for the new position, it will show the company you have the dedication required for the position.

MCPS only If your company already has a training program in place, try to find out if they are expanding that training, or if someone plans to leave the department. Make sure your training will sufficiently prepare you to take over the departing person's position. This includes training on all the applications they currently support. If your company does not currently have a program in place, you may become the founding member of such a group. It always pays to find out what the company plans before you get too far into the certification process. Your attitude has a lot to do with the way the company views your skills. This includes your attitude before, during, and after training. Remember an MCPS is, by necessity, a people-oriented person.

Find out if your company is creating a new workgroup. Some companies create splinter organizations when they want to introduce a new product, or when the current group becomes too large. These splinter organizations always require their own training personnel and network administrators. You may become the network administrator,

trainer, lead person, or even the manager for the new workgroup. Alternatively, the old trainer or network administrator may move to the new group. You may find yourself in charge of the old group when he or she leaves. Make sure you fully understand the current status of this group before you take over.

See if your company recently won a large contract. A company may create a small workgroup to deal with a specific contract. If so, your new position may only last the term of the contract. Figuring out ways to make this new position permanent is a very important consideration. You need to consider the longevity of any advancement or title change you get.

Of course, some employers won't recognize your new status unless you bring it to their attention. There are many problem situations where you may find that your certification is more of a handicap than an asset. Take whatever steps you need to take to prevent this situation from happening. In most cases, your employer will not want to lose the investment in time and money that the company made to get you certified. You can use this as leverage when you try to correct these problem situations. The following paragraphs list some of the problems you may experience.

In some cases a company will help you get your certification and promise you the sun, the moon, and stars until you achieve your goal. As soon as you get back to work, you find that instead of a promotion you got more work instead. Your company may feel perfectly justified in forcing you to perform all your previous tasks in addition to the new network administration tasks. Application program specialists may find themselves training people after hours while maintaining their current work level during the day. Don't let this happen. If your company promises you anything to get your new certification, make sure you get the promises in writing. Verbal promises last only as long as you can hear the words.

A company may ask you to sign a contract promising to work for them for a specific amount of time after you receive your certification. They may also ask you to sign a document promising to pay back the cost of certification if you fail to attain it. Make sure you get some concessions from the company in exchange for these

guarantees. Never give your company something for nothing. In many states it is illegal to hold you to such a contract or make you pay the employer back for education. Make sure you know your legal rights before you sign. Contact your local labor relations board for more information. The Better Business Bureau and your labor relations board can also tell you if your company has any complaints for unfair treatment against it. Make sure you take these complaints into consideration before you sign any kind of agreement.

MCSE only You may find that the level of cooperation drops drastically once you complete a network installation. Without the proper tools and support, you will never maintain the network in peak operating condition. Technology changes every day, but many corporations only update their tools in a crisis. You need to use current technology to help network users get the most out of the network. Make sure you talk to the company about these problems in advance. Don't make your new certification a source of problems.

MCPS only Application program specialists may find themselves in a critical situation once an expansion crisis is over. The company may view you as an expendable resource once you train the staff to use a new version of a word processor or spreadsheet. They may even try to demote or fire you to save some money. You will probably find that the company no longer provides the time and facilities required to enhance the overall education level of the employees you train. Try to find other tasks you can perform in your current position if this happens. For example, you can offer to create macros that will automate many employee tasks. Make sure you keep the company's turnover rate in mind as well. Point out that your job is not finished yet if the turnover rate is high enough. If enough new employees arrive each month, you may find that training becomes a full-time job.

Now that you have some ideas about the positive and negative aspects of getting a certification, you can formulate an advancement plan. As the previous paragraphs showed, there are at least three different ways of getting a promotion within a company. The following paragraphs examine these three methods of advancing within your company. Of course, there are probably many other ways that you could pursue advancement. These methods simply provide ideas that you can use to create your own advancement plan.

 # Advancement through promotion

Many people start at a particular company and stay there for their entire working career. They wait for the person ahead of them to either get a promotion or leave the company. As new positions open, these people try to fill them before someone else does. This is a perfectly good way to advance your career. There are several different ways that you can enhance you chances of getting that new position based on your new certification and the longevity of your relationship with the company.

You can demonstrate an extensive knowledge of the company's ways of doing things. This translates into a network administrator, trainer, or low-level manager who is familiar with company policies. It means that you can do the job faster and more efficiently than someone hired from outside the company.

Longevity also translates into a knowledge of the people working at the company. You probably have a better idea of who is working at the company, how long they have worked there, what their job responsibilities are, and what you can do to help them. All of this knowledge means that you will spend less time getting the network set up and maintaining it. In the case of an application specialist, it means that you can create an environment that enhances overall productivity within the company. In either case, it also means that you will probably make fewer mistakes.

The fact that you have held several positions in the same company means that you can better identify with problem areas within the company. You have a greater understanding of why certain policies are in place and what each person needs to do their work since you have done their job in the past.

The Microsoft certification you receive opens new doors of responsibility. Your past job performance will help you get an advancement based on positive proof that you can handle the added responsibility. Everyone in the company knows that you are capable of doing the job. They don't have to rely on the secondhand information provided by someone you worked for in the past.

As you can see, the means of getting the promotion once a door of opportunity opens is there. Of course, simply because the door opens does not mean that management will put you in the new position. You must earn the new position. As a result, there are other things you need to do as well. For one thing, you can't advance if you don't know where all the windows of opportunity exist. Figure 6-1 shows a typical company organizational chart.

Figure 6-1

Manufacturing Division Organizational a Chart

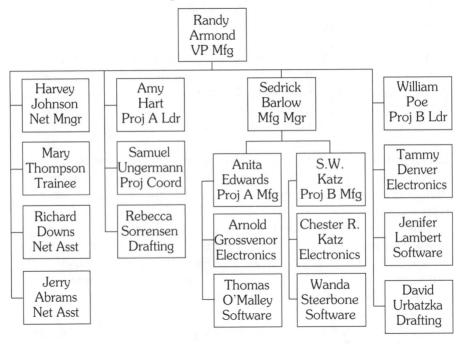

Typical organization chart.

If you are Mary on the chart, the first thing you may think is that your next promotion opportunity is limited to Harvey's job. But there are many other windows of opportunity just waiting for you. For example, as you help administer the network, you will find out about the tasks performed by Amy Hart or William Poe. You may even set your sights higher by trying for the position held by Sedrick Barlow. Of course, your ultimate goal might be the vice president's job. The important thing to remember is the organization of your company;

look for opportunities to advance yourself. You may even want to take this time to get a copy of your company's organizational chart (or make one of your own).

So how does this relate to your certification? Remember, there are many ways to use your certification as a key to future promotions. Don't limit your thinking to a single area or one possible means of using it. You can use the information you obtain from administering the network to prove your worth in other areas of the company as well. Companies look for people who are willing to take charge—people who show a real involvement in their work. They won't promote someone who simply does their work.

Now it's time to combine everything you learned from the preceding paragraphs into a plan of attack. Learning the various pieces of information we discussed should provide you with all you need to know to fill out the advancement form in Fig. 6-2. Notice that this form is specially designed for someone who wants to use the advancement route to improve his or her position at the company.

Advancement Through Promotion Worksheet

Figure 6-2

Date: _____ Current Job Title: _____

Current Pay Rate: _____ Target Pay Rate: _____

1st Advancement Goal: _____

Date of Anticipated Advance: _____

How will your networking experience help you attain your goal? _____
_____
_____

Experience needed to attain goal: _____
_____

Education needed to attain goal: _____
_____

Figure 6-2   *Continued.*

2nd Advancement Goal: _____

Date of Anticipated Advance: _____

How will your networking experience help you attain your goal? _____
_____
_____

Experience needed to attain goal: _____
_____

Education needed to attain goal: _____
_____

The form begins with a little self-examination. It asks you to provide your current position and salary. This gives you a starting point; it shows where you are now. You need a starting point to see how far you progress toward your goal. It also provides a reality check as you set your future goals. Trying to reach president of the company in one step is probably not very reasonable. Reaching for a management position from a technician's job is a little more attainable.

The next two sections of the form provide places for two goals. These are the positions you want to target as potential places for advancement. Make sure you pick realistic goals, or you will find disappointment rather than advancement. Picking two goals is an essential part of the planning process. You must maximize your chances of advancing in the company. As a result, you must always look at more than one place for an advancement opportunity. Of course, you don't want to spread yourself too thin either. Shooting for more than two different positions might make it impossible for you to achieve any of them. Sometimes it's a little better to bypass one potential opportunity to enhance your chances of achieving another. Trying for two different goals offers maximum flexibility with the least amount of risk.

There are four sections in each goals section. The first section asks you to define the goal itself. Make sure you include the title, pay, and

any responsibility you would like to take as part of the advancement. You may even want to include the name of the person (if any) who currently holds that position.

The next thing you need to do is relate your networking or application program experience to the position you want to attain. This serves as a reality check. It asks you to determine how you can use the experience you gain now to help in later promotions. This may seem a little unreasonable for some positions until you consider that your boss may have been in your position at one time. Business is always willing to pay for experience.

The third area asks you to decide what other experience you need to gain to get to the next position. Obviously you don't have enough experience right now to take the position you want, or there is a good chance that you would have it. This is an important consideration because it will allow you to grab opportunities to gain the needed experience. For example, when the boss asks for volunteers for a project, it is really an opportunity to grab some experience.

Finally, the fourth section asks you to determine what educational requirements the new position will require. Management is interested in both knowledge and experience. Don't let someone fresh from college take your position from you. Make sure you prepare for both areas.

One final piece of advice for the person who wants to advance in his or her current company: You need to grab opportunities, because they seldom knock very loud and they never knock very long. Look for opportunities to gain experience and show management that you are ready for a promotion. Always think about the possibilities; don't stoop to reactive attempts at advancement. The proactive approach always yields some result; the reactive approach always yields stagnation. Of course, you need to think about the consequences of your plan before you present it. A proactive approach can have negative as well as positive results. For example, telling your boss that you want their position may get you fired. Make sure you find the opportunities that yield positive results.

 # Advancement by creating a new position

Some people still possess the frontier spirit. They go where no one else will go, and do the things that no one ever thought about doing. Inventors and scientists commonly fall into this category. However, this same set of skills can work to your benefit in the corporate environment as well. Many people have made fortunes by inventing their own position, and then showing management that the company can't survive without it. This is where the network administrator, applications expert, and corporate trainer are today. You have an opportunity to break new ground, to create your own position. These people are truly at the forefront of technology.

Of course, the network administrator, applications expert, and corporate trainer don't always start with many benefits or even any recognition. Sometimes they start as a grunt laborer under someone who doesn't appear to understand what the company needs, and has no desire to learn. For example, you may start out as a computer repair person or someone who gives presentations, instead of the job that you really want to do.

Fortunately, there is another way to approach this problem! Instead of forcing yourself to endure untold hardship under someone who cares little about what you do, turn the situation around. Look at this situation as an opportunity to create a new position. If you can show management that you can produce better results without your current boss standing over your head, you may find that you can create your own position. Of course, the payment for failure to convince management of the benefits of the new position is dismissal in many cases. (Your old boss will likely never trust you again, at the very least.)

As you can see, this method of advancement is not without risks. But the risks are worth it to someone who is prepared to take advantage of the results. Creating your own position means that you control how your job takes shape. It also means that your chances of getting promoted to upper management are much better. If you prove that

you are an idea person, someone capable of thinking on his or her own, management may sit up and take notice.

So how do you start planning for a new position? Everything requires planning. You must take time to create a proposal that demonstrates the company needs the new position you want to create. More than that, you must demonstrate that you are the best candidate for the position. Just because you prove the company needs a new position doesn't mean that you'll get it. You must prove that you are the only person for the job, both through qualifications and in repayment to the company. Figure 6-3 shows a sample of what you can do to start the planning process.

New Position Worksheet

Figure 6-3

Current Date: _____   Planned Presentation Date: _____

New Position Title: _____

Reason the New Position is Important: _____
_____
_____
_____
_____

Cost of Creating the Position: _____

Potential Cost Benefit: _____   Payback Time: _____

Intangible Benefits: _____
_____
_____

Reasons You Should Take the New Position: _____
_____
_____
_____

❏ Cost Analysis   ❏ Full Presentation
❏ Time Analysis   ❏ Handouts
❏ Benefits Analysis   ❏ Graphs and Charts
❏ Requirements for the Position   ❏ Presentation Scheduled

A sample plan for creating your own position.

There are several interesting features of this form. The first section states a starting and ending date to accomplish your goal. Make sure you enter both dates to give yourself a target to reach. Procrastination is the worst thing you can do to your plans for creating a new position. On the other hand, don't be afraid to change the ending date if necessary; you'll want to prepare the best presentation possible. The important thing to remember is that you need to maintain a sense of balance. Get the proposal finished as quickly and as well as possible.

The next section talks about the position itself. It is very important to define a potential title name, indicate why the position is important, conceptualize any potential costs and problems associated with creating the position, and provide management with a projected payback period for their investment. Make sure you list both tangible and intangible benefits. In most cases you will want to create a position that provides a payback to the company in both areas. This does not mean that management never considers a new position that only provides intangible benefits; however, you will likely find your job on the chopping block at the first sign of economic troubles if you take this approach. It is always better to show the company that you can make some money for them.

The third section states why you are the person to fill this position. You must write these reasons down and back them up with good arguments. Make sure you demonstrate beyond a shadow of a doubt that you are the person to fill the position. Of course, it helps that you are the person defining the new position. You can modify the job definition as required to make yourself the only person who can fill the position. This process of give and take provides another reality check. Once you do get to the point where you completely define the job and your reason for filling it, make sure the job still makes sense. Otherwise you may find that management won't even talk to you about it. Don't try to create a position whose sole advantage is a promotion for you.

The final area is a checklist of items you need to complete before you make your presentation. This worksheet is for your benefit; the other items provide the information to management in an easy to understand manner. If you can't express your idea to management, there is no reason to believe they will create the new position for you.

Now it's time to look at some of those additional pieces of information presented on the form. The first item is a cost analysis. You will want to create a full cost analysis showing exactly what it will cost the company to create the new position that you propose. At the very least, it will cost the company a pay raise. (Hopefully you are not going through all this work for the sheer gratification of doing the work.) Make sure you look for hidden costs as well. Consider items like additional staff and equipment. Make sure you show how the company can amortize this investment over a period of time. Any friends you gain in accounting can probably help you in this area.

The next thing you will want to do is create a time analysis. As a minimum, you need to create a milestone chart with goals that you expect to meet by specific dates. Some of the more advanced project management programs could help you in this regard. You might find a computer with one of these programs in the engineering or manufacturing area of your company. Ask the supervisor if you can use the program. (You may need to come in after working hours to perform this work.) Of course, you could even use a standard drawing program to create the charts you need, but the project management software will help you look for potential scheduling conflicts. The project management software will also make it easy to incorporate changes to your plan.

The benefits analysis is one of the most important parts of your presentation. Management tends to focus on the negative element of any form of change—the cost of making it. You need to focus their attention on the positive elements of what they will obtain from the change. Make sure you look at the company's interests when you write the list of benefits, not the elements that are attractive to you. For example, while you may find the increased responsibility interesting, management won't. However, they will find increased revenues or other company-related benefits interesting. One common way for training and network personnel to make their case is to show that the new position will make the company more efficient. A more efficient operation usually spells lower operating costs and higher income.

Provide management with a complete listing of all the requirements for the position. This accomplishes two purposes. First, it defines the position and shows management that you took the time to think this

idea through. It also helps you define your position later. One of the reasons that some new position ideas fail is that they are ill-defined at the very start. Some people actually make their jobs more difficult by not defining what they mean at the start of a project. This leaves the door open for interpretation. Second, you can use the requirements as part of your arguments later. For example, you can use the requirements to show management that you are the only person who can perform the job adequately. Make all the pieces of your presentation fit together into a well-coordinated plan.

Create a full presentation for management. Include slides, graphs, charts, handouts, and anything else you can think of to make the presentation interesting. Remember, you are trying to sell an idea that many people in management will want to resist. This is not a situation where you are starting with an open-minded audience; you have to open their minds to the potential benefits of the new position.

Handouts really help keep people interested if you use them correctly. There are several rules you need to observe during the presentation. For example, have someone help you with this element of your presentation. Don't make the mistake of providing management with all your handouts at once. Give them out as management needs to look at them. Otherwise, you may find that you will lose your audience to the handouts that were supposed to keep them interested in your presentation. The people that you gave the handouts to will skim through them trying to find the bottom line and not get the full picture that you are presenting them. You should also refer to your handouts frequently during the presentation. Otherwise, management will wonder why you took the time to prepare them.

Graphs and charts are an extremely important part of your presentation. Studies show that people can absorb information in graphic form much better and faster than they can in printed form. The printed material is abstract; the graphic form is a lot more concrete. Rather than burden management with a lot of tabular data, present it in graphic form and offer to allow them to see the tables later. Make sure you make the actual data available, but keep your presentation interesting by using graphics.

You will need to schedule your presentation. Make sure you get a specific date from management. A common problem that people face is that management will use the excuse that they want to see your presentation "sometime soon." They keep putting the presentation off until (hopefully) you forget about showing it to them. To get their approval you may need to tell them about some aspects of your idea. Get management as excited as you are about this new position. Make sure you don't tell them everything; keep some surprises for the meeting itself. Schedule a conference room for the meeting. Avoid presenting your idea in someone's office. Reduce the chances of political posturing by holding the meeting in a neutral setting. This helps alleviate the problem of trying to answer questions from someone who only asks them to increase his or her political stature in the company. In addition, holding the meeting in a conference room reduces the risk of interruptions such as phone calls and other people walking in. Get everything ready for the meeting well in advance. Don't wait until the last minute.

As you can see, creating a successful presentation is a challenge in many ways. You need to do a lot of preparation before you will be able to present your idea to management. Take the time to research your company thoroughly. Check your company's history to see what type of ideas management normally approves. Make sure you can tell management everything they will need to know about your idea. Show them that you did your homework, and that you're interested enough in the company to devote the time required to find out about it. You may want to spend some time viewing presentations made by other people in your company as well. Notice the ideas and presentation methods that seem to attract the attention of key management personnel. These are the methods that usually guarantee some measure of success when you make your presentation. Make sure you write these ideas down to use in your presentation as well.

Of course, there are several ways you can use your certification to attain these goals. For one thing, as network administrator, company trainer, or management assistant, you will meet many of the people you need to influence. This personal contact can make the difference between getting the new position approved and looking for a new

job. Make sure you take the personalities of the individual members of management into account as you prepare your presentation.

You can also use your position to obtain information about the company and its operations. As network administrator you will gain access to many areas of the company that many other people may not see. A trainer or management assistant usually has some access to this information as well. You will see the broad view of all the jobs that people in the company perform. Your position will expose you to all the products that the company makes and gives you inside information about how these products could improve. The possibilities for gaining knowledge are almost unlimited.

Finally, your position as network administrator, company trainer, or management assistant will give you a unique view of both management and the employees. You can use this view to provide unique insights as you present your idea to management. Present some of the employee needs from a management viewpoint during your presentation.

Recognition through title change

There is a group of people in any company that don't really want to advance into management. They are happy working at their current position and don't really want the added responsibility that a promotion brings. This is not necessarily bad. Someone has to fill these positions, and if you're happy working there, then a management post may not provide the type of work environment that you want.

Of course, you still want some form of recognition for your achievement. After all, you did go through all the effort required to get your certification and you want management to recognize that achievement. One of the best ways to get the recognition is to provide management with a reason to change your title. You'll work for the same boss at the same pay doing about the same work, but the title change will show that you have made some type of change in your qualifications. So what good is a title change? It will make a big

difference if you ever leave your current company. The title change shows a potential employer that you made some type of effort to get a promotion, even if it didn't result in a pay raise. Of course, a title change in your current company could lead to some additional pay as well. You may not receive it right away; it may come during your annual review instead.

So what do you do to get this title change? First, you could simply schedule a meeting with your boss and ask for the change. You might be surprised to find that your boss will help you get the title change with no additional effort on your part. (You may have to shuffle some paperwork, but this is really a very minor consideration.) A title change on your part reflects favorably on your boss. It shows that he or she is doing their job by helping each employee under their control provide a greater contribution to the company as a whole. You may even want to remind your boss of this fact. It never hurts to show the boss that you have his or her welfare in mind too.

If this first approach doesn't work, put your request in writing. Make sure you state some reasons why the title change is so important. This will give your boss an incentive to tell you why he or she won't consider a title change. It will also provide your boss with something to pass up to his or her superior. The reason that your boss didn't provide the title change could involve a lack of authority to do so. The following paragraphs provide some ideas on arguments you can use to get a title change.

Since your job tasks have changed since you got your Microsoft certification, why not a title change to go along with it? Changes in job tasks should show up in your job title as well. You could even argue that the job title change will help show that the company got value for the money it invested in your training.

A new job title will help distinguish between the tasks you perform and those performed by other employees with the same title. This is especially important for government contractors since the government usually looks to see that they have enough personnel to do the job in a given category before granting the contract. Of course, this reflects well on other companies as well, especially when it comes time to impress visiting dignitaries.

The new job title is a lot less expensive than a raise. (Of course, you can always argue later that your new title entitles you to a pay raise.)

The new job title could potentially add to the company's prestige by showing they have an up-to-date networking system or training specialist. You would need to add some arguments that would show whom this would affect. It may help to show how this new job title could help the company gain new contracts.

Providing you with a new job title could enhance the way management views your boss's position. It would show that he or she had a wider area of responsibility than before. Of course, this appeals to the boss's vanity, but it pays to use whatever will work.

Of course, these are just a few of the arguments you could use to convince your boss to grant you a new job title. The important factor is that you deserve the new title. If your current title is administrative assistant, it hardly reflects your new position as a network administrator, company trainer, management assistant, or product specialist. Even if you perform this job on a part-time basis, your job title should reflect your change in status.

There are several ways that a job title change can help you in the future, even if it doesn't appear to help you today. First, if you do decide to go to another company, the title change will appear as a promotion. There is no way that your future employer will know that you didn't receive any additional benefits for the change in title unless you tell them. Second, it could help you get better raises in your current company. If you demonstrate an increased level of knowledge, then many companies are willing to pay for that increased knowledge. The only problem is that upper management will never know that your status has changed unless you get it down on paper somewhere. The change in title is one of the most efficient and most noticeable methods of doing so.

Getting a title change may not seem very exciting. In fact, it may seem as if you accomplished nothing at all. Of course, nothing is further from the truth. A title change may not dramatically affect your career today, but it could help a great deal in the future. Even if you don't want to get into management in your current company, it is very important that you gain the recognition you deserve for getting your Microsoft certification.

 Getting paid for what you do

The matter of how much of an increase in pay you can expect from a promotion or new position is always a touchy subject. There are no hard and fast rules; the policy in your company and the effects of the local economy make things even harder. Someone who gets a 15% raise in pay in Wisconsin may get only a 3% increase in Texas. There are some general things you can do to get an idea of what kind of an increase you should expect. The following tips provide guidelines, but you will need to tailor them to your specific situation.

Check around the company for clues. Some people will tell you what type of raise they got when going to a new position. However, some companies will fire someone for even talking about their salary, so this may not be an option. Don't expect to go to the personnel department and ask about salary ranges in the company; they won't provide you with the information.

Talk to someone at your local Chamber of Commerce. They track all kinds of business statistics, including pay raise rates. You may even find that they can provide you with an approximate range of pay for your type of position. If you can't get this information at the Chamber of Commerce in your town, then go to the nearest large city and try to find the information there.

Just about every large community has a local business magazine. You won't see it on your newsstand, but you may see it in the lobby or other public areas. Take time to look through the magazine. Many of them provide current trends in business for your area.

Read the business section of your local newspaper. This will give you some economic information for your area. It may also contain news about your company or other information you can use.

Listen to the radio. I was surprised when a local radio station revealed that the average pay raise in my area was running at 3%.

Few radio stations will provide you with everything you need to know, but many will provide you with some clues.

Talk to people in your local user's group. If you don't belong to a user's group, then join one. The people in your user's group work in the same area as you do. Just find someone who performs the same work as you do, and talk to them. What could be easier? Make sure you ask them how long they have worked in their area of expertise, and take this into consideration when you look for a promotion.

There are a few absolutes that you should expect when it comes to pay. You will always receive a salary instead of an hourly rate when working as a network administrator. The same thing holds true for most trainers, unless you work for a company that provides services for others. The reason you get a salary is simple; no company in its right mind will pay you for the extra hours required when working these types of jobs.

You absolutely will not get the same amount of pay as a consultant doing the same work. There are a few reasons for this. First, your company provides benefits that a consultant does not receive. Second, the consultant pays business taxes and other expenses out of the money he or she earns that you do not need to consider. However, you can use the local consultant's fee as a point of reference for your pay. In most cases an employee will earn 25% to 33% of the fee charged by a consultant in the same area. Call at least three consultants in your area, average their hourly rates, multiply by 25%, then multiply by 40 hours to get your new weekly pay. The differential between this weekly pay rate and your current pay rate probably reflects the pay raise you should expect. Remember, this is only an estimate, not a hard and fast reality.

Moving to a different company

Some people work at a company to gain experience and a specific level of education, then move to another company. The reason for this strategy is quite simple; you can advance a lot faster using this technique than you can by staying at your current company. Fast

advances mean faster and higher pay raises. Of course, you give up quite a bit to use this strategy. For example, many companies will not provide you with any kind of retirement unless you stay there for a specific number of years (anywhere from 10 to 20 years). You need to provide your own retirement plan through an IRA or other means. There are other benefits that companies offer as well. For example, in some companies you share in the stock program after you work there for five years. If you move from company to company in pursuit of a better position, you may never meet this requirement. See the section below on getting paid what you're worth to figure out how this reduction in benefits should affect the pay rate you receive.

Once you weigh the consequences of moving around and decide that you want to improve your position more than you want to gain these other benefits, you need to consider how to present yourself to a potential employer. This includes both a written and a verbal presentation. Of course, the written presentation is commonly called a resume, while the verbal presentation is called an interview. The following paragraphs show you how to leverage your Microsoft certification as part of both processes.

⇨ Getting your resume together

Any good book on business writing or communication will show you how to write a stock resume and cover letter. That isn't the purpose of this section. What you need to know is how to modify these stock presentations to emphasize your qualifications. The following tips point out several ideas you need to present in these written forms of communication.

If you are currently a network administrator or training expert, place your experience first on the resume. Make sure you provide detailed information on your network-related jobs. Provide one- or two-sentence summaries of other jobs.

If you recently passed your MCPS or MCSE certification tests, place your education first. Emphasize the fact that you passed your certification test. Don't be afraid to use bold type for this credential

to make it stand out from any others you may have. Add a date of certification to show that you are current.

Always add your logo to both the cover letter and the resume. This will make them stick out from other stock input. Use a logo size of ½ inch square. Figure 6-4 illustrates how the logo can be used on a sample cover letter. Figures 6-5 and 6-6 show two possibilities for resume layouts using the logo.

Place a reference to your certification in the first sentence of the cover letter. Many managers don't read past this point before letter and resume both end up in the circular file.

As you can see, preparing a resume is the same task no matter what job you want to apply for. It is the content of that resume that makes the difference. You get two pages, one for the resume and another for the cover letter, to convince someone to hire you. It's your job to use those pages to good effect.

Emphasizing your qualifications

Everyone knows the basics of going in for an interview. You're supposed to get dressed up and present a clean appearance. Of course, breath mints and a good attitude are important too. All these things are just a part of any interview. However, there are several things you can do to use your Microsoft certification to enhance your interview. The following paragraphs provide you with some ideas on how to do this.

Many Microsoft certificate holders receive lapel pins. Make sure you wear this pin on your lapel during the interview. It serves to reinforce your qualifications every time your potential employer looks at you and sees it.

Take your wallet card along with you. Your employer may ask you to present proof of your certification.

Figure 6-4

John Mueller
2020 Twin Palms Street
River City, CA 92104-3703
(619) 881-7732 Business
(619) 881-7733 Fax
6 March, 1994}

Mary Jones
Engineering Manager
The Industrial Place
3288 The Place Street
Somewhere, CA 92112

Dear Ms. Jones

I recently saw your advertisement for a Microsoft Certified Systems Engineer in the California Job Times. According to the ad, you need someone with a minimum of two years experience and proof of certification. As you can see from the attached resume, I can meet both qualifications. I worked two years at Jobber Industrial and three years at Technical Stuff, Inc. I can provide my certification papers to you on request. (There is a copy of the certification attached to the back of the resume.)

The important consideration for you is that both of my former employers produced about the same products as your company does. In addition, according to your annual report, the corporate structure of all three companies is similar. These similarities mean that you will spend less time training me to fill the position at your company. Hopefully, these qualifications will allow you to consider my application in preference to others who applied.

Sincerely,

John Paul Mueller

Example cover letter.

Figure 6-5

John Mueller
2020 Twin Palms Street
River City, CA 92104
Home Phone: (619) 775-2123

EXPERIENCE:

**Network Administrator, Technical Stuff, Inc.
(July 1990 - August 1993)**

In charge of two assistants at Technical Stuff, Inc. The combination ethernet and token ring LAN supports 150 users and 4 file servers. There are eight print servers attached to the network as well. Most of the print servers had two printers attached, one HP Laserjet III and a high speed dot matrix. All maintenance scheduling went through my office. In addition, I supervised the installation of a new DBMS (database management system) on one of the file servers.

**Assistant Network Administrator, Jobber Industrial
(January 1988 - July 1990)**

Assist the LAN Administrator in maintaining the company LAN (local area network). The LAN supports 40 users and 3 file servers. There are four print servers attached to the network as well. Part of my LAN responsibilities include installing and maintaining Windows. I also performed much of the hardware maintenance.

**Sonar Technician, US Navy
(July 1976 - September 1987)**

Maintained computer controlled sonar and fire control equipment. This equipment ranged from tube-based technology, to solid-state discrete circuitry, to modern CMOS circuitry. Learned to operate and maintain every type of data storage device available today. Most equipment was hybrid digital and analog circuitry.

Designed and was paid for a design change to audio recording equipment. Change decreased recording reproduction time by a factor of four, reducing the per recording cost to the government for a training tape.

Operated sonar equipment which included acoustic signal analysis equipment. Supervised work center personnel. Wrote six part training course using tapes and training books.

Example experience-based resume.

EDUCATION:

Technical Diploma in Electrical Trade, Milwaukee Technical High School, June 1976

Various Military Electronic Equipment Maintenance Courses:

- Basic Electronics and Electricity
- Sonar Specific Advanced Electronics
- Acoustic Analysis Schooling
- Fire Control System Maintenance/Operation Schooling
- Computer Controlled Sonar Maintenance/Operation Schooling
- Other Peripheral Equipment Maintenance Schooling

Bachelors in Computer Science, National University, June 1986

Artificial Intelligence Programming Course, Cubic Corporation, October 1986

Certified Netware Engineer Courses, VITEK Corporation, April 1991

Microsoft Certified Systems Engineer, Chaporal, March 1994

COMPUTER LANGUAGES:

- Pascal - IBM PC knowledge only
- BASIC - IBM PC and Perkin-Elmer mainframe experience (Includes various Windows 3.1 dialects like Access BASIC and Visual BASIC)
- Assembler - IBM PC (DOS, OS/2, and Windows NT environments), Macintosh, and various military computers
- dBase III (Clipper, Force, and FoxPro) - IBM PC
- Prolog - Learning stages, IBM PC knowledge only
- Machine Code (Hex) - IBM PC, Macintosh, and various military computers
- C - IBM PC (DOS, OS/2, and Windows NT environments)

Microsoft
logo here

Figure 6-6

John Mueller
2020 Twin Palms Street
River City, CA 92104
Home Phone: (619) 775-2123

CERTIFICATIONS:

1994 Microsoft Certified Systems Engineer
1991 Certified Netware Engineer

EDUCATION:

1986 Artificial Intelligence Programming Course, Cubic Corporation
Bachelor's in Computer Science, National University

1977 - 1985 Various Military Electronic Equipment Maintenance Courses:
Basic Electronics and Electricity
Sonar Specific Advanced Electronics
Acoustic Analysis Schooling
Fire Control System Maintenance/Operation Schooling
Computer Controlled Sonar Maintenance/Operation
   Schooling
Other Peripheral Equipment Maintenance Schooling

1976 Technical Diploma in Electrical Trade, Milwaukee Technical
High School

EXPERIENCE:

Network Administrator, Technical Stuff, Inc.
(July 1990 - August 1993)

In charge of two assistants at Technical Stuff, Inc. The combination ethernet
and token ring LAN supports 150 users and 4 file servers. There are eight
print servers attached to the network as well. Most of the print servers had two
printers attached, one HP Laserjet III and a high speed dot matrix. All
maintenance scheduling went through my office. In addition, I supervised the
installation of a new DBMS (database management system) on one of the file
servers.

Assistant Network Administrator, Jobber Industrial
(January 1988 - July 1990)

Assist the LAN Administrator in maintaining the company LAN (local area
network). The LAN supports 40 users and 3 file servers. There are four print

Example education-based resume.

servers attached to the network as well. Part of my LAN responsibilities include installing and maintaining Windows. I also performed much of the hardware maintenance.

Sonar Technician, US Navy (July 1976 - September 1987)

Maintained computer controlled sonar and fire control equipment. This equipment ranged from tube-based technology, to solid-state discrete circuitry, to modern CMOS circuitry. Learned to operate and maintain every type of data storage device available today. Most equipment was hybrid digital and analog circuitry.

Designed and was paid for a design change to audio recording equipment. Change decreased recording reproduction time by a factor of four, reducing the per-recording cost to the government for a training tape.

Operated sonar equipment which included acoustic signal analysis equipment. Supervised work center personnel. Wrote six part training course using tapes and training books.

COMPUTER LANGUAGES:

Pascal - IBM PC knowledge only
BASIC - IBM PC and Perkin-Elmer mainframe experience (Includes various
    Windows 3.1 dialects like Access BASIC and Visual BASIC)
Assembler - IBM PC (DOS, OS/2, and Windows NT environments),
    Macintosh, and various military computers
dBase III (Clipper, Force, and FoxPro) - IBM PC
Prolog - Learning stages, IBM PC knowledge only
Machine Code (Hex) - IBM PC, Macintosh, and various military computers
    C - IBM PC (DOS, OS/2, and Windows NT environments)

Microsoft
logo here

Prepare a listing of the hardware you've worked on in the past if you are an MCSE. An MCPS should prepare a list of applications he or she has worked with in the past. Preparing a list of training and presentation duties may help as well. You can use this information during the interview.

Create a list of questions you want to ask the employer. During a successful interview, every employer asks if you have questions. Make sure your questions are based on your knowledge of the company and what it does. This is your opportunity to impress the employer with your knowledge of their company.

The interview is a two-way street; they are not only interviewing you, but you are interviewing the company as well. You need to make sure that this is the company that you want to invest your time and effort into. Just because you conducted some preliminary research on the company doesn't mean they are a good company to work for. The only time you find this information out is during your conversation with your prospective boss. The company must also pass your interview of them. This includes taking a good look at working conditions and other factors as you walk around the company.

During the interview make sure that you maintain eye contact with the person giving the interview, speak clearly, and portray confidence in yourself. If asked a question that you do not know the answer to, do not make one up. It's better to say that you don't know the answer than to lie to them; it shows honesty. You can usually avoid looking like a dunce when this happens by showing interest in the topic. Use the occasion to feed your potential boss's ego. Phrases like, "I didn't know that, please explain it further" go a long way toward making the interview a success. Make sure you show an interest in what the boss knows and what the company needs, rather than showing irritation at not knowing the answer to a question.

Talking about a rate of pay

How much should you get paid for your qualifications? That's a tough question for a lot of reasons. Your past work greatly affects how people

view your certification. Someone who has managerial experience in addition to his or her certification should expect to receive a better job than someone who only has the certification. Likewise, someone with a computer-related degree will receive more than someone who does not possess this credential. The following tips should help you determine what type of pay increase you should expect.

Always use a point of reference based on fact to compute your new rate of pay. You need to know that a change of company is worth the effort. One point of reference that you can use is any proposed pay increase your current company offers. You can also talk to people at a local user's group to find out what other companies pay for similar work. Finally, you can check statistical information contained in business magazines or other sources.

Try to get a pay increase equal to at least twice the current average pay raise rate in your area, if your new job title is about the same or only one level higher than your old one. For example, suppose the newspaper in your area states that the average pay raise in your area is 5% and you currently make $24,000 a year. Simply multiply the rate by 2, then add that percentage to your current pay. In this case you should expect a pay increase of at least $2,400 a year, or a salary of $26,400.

Make sure your new company recognizes any supplemental capabilities you can provide. For example, if you have a degree in computer science, then there is a good chance you can perform some programming tasks in addition to your network responsibilities. A trainer who also has marketing experience can provide a lot more than simple user assistance. Your new company will try to make use of these capabilities, so you should get paid for them.

Be sure you take any benefits your new company offers that your old company doesn't. For example, your new company may offer a dental plan when your old company didn't. This is a benefit you can use even as a short-term employee. On the other hand, a stock option benefit may not be worth much if you don't plan to stay with the company. You also need to ensure that the new benefit is tangible. Use the value of these new benefits to you as part of the basis for the level of pay increase that you're willing to accept.

Of course, these tips merely help you get an idea of a reasonable rate of pay. Here are some absolutes you need to consider. First, you always have to get more for a transfer to a new job than a promotion at your current company. There are a few simple reasons for this, but most of them have to do with a loss of benefits. Companies do not provide very many benefits to short-term employees. If your current company offers you a promotion, double the amount of pay increase (not the pay itself) and add it to your current salary. This is what you need to receive from your new company to make the move worthwhile.

The second absolute is that no one ever got a pay increase for doing the same job at a new company. If you are a trainer with the current title "administrative assistant," then you should look for some type of training-related title in the new company. Your old title does not match your new job, and you will not get the pay raise you deserve using that old title. The same holds true for a network specialist. If you previously had the title "maintenance technician," look for a new title, like "network administrator" or "assistant network administrator."

CHAPTER 7

Planning for continuing education requirements

YOU finally made it! The certification that you so diligently worked for is finally yours! Take some time to feel good about yourself and your accomplishments. After all, you worked hard for it and deserve to take a little bit of a break.

Once you have had time to reflect on your accomplishments, you must begin to think about and plan for what it will take to maintain your precious certification. The certification that you obtained, while yours at the moment, is revocable by Microsoft if you do not meet the continuing education requirements. Remember, your certification says that Microsoft tested your knowledge and found that you meet their stringent requirements; it is an affirmation that you know what you are doing.

Don't let the continuing education requirements scare you. They are not difficult. Nor are they an every-other-month demand designed to squeeze more money out of you. Microsoft only asks you to recertify if there is a major change in the technology associated with your certification. These requirements are necessary to keep your knowledge of Microsoft products and technology current. You are Microsoft's best representative and salesperson, because you are the one that is on the front line with the customer. If your knowledge of the product is not current or not accurate, Microsoft's credibility as

well as yours may be in question. The last thing that they want is to have a customer think that either Microsoft or your skills are not what they expected. If customers are not comfortable with Microsoft's reputation or yours, they will most likely take their business elsewhere. What this means to you is that you will miss out on a potential sale of your services. The result is a loss of income for both you and for Microsoft.

Of course, the process of planning for continuing education does not stop at what Microsoft requires of you. This only skims the surface of what you need to know in the real world to conduct business. You must constantly enhance your knowledge to keep an edge in this industry; limiting your horizons is the surest way to short-circuit your business. Keep your eyes open for other opportunities to learn more about your trade. This includes reading books and trade magazines. It also involves a certain amount of research and perseverance. You need to take an interest in yourself to maintain your educational advantage over the competition.

In this chapter, I discuss your continuing education responsibilities to maintain your Microsoft certification. Because the education process does not stop with the Microsoft training, I will also cover topics that help you to remain current in the market of your choice. These additional topics include tips on where to find this information; after all, the search is at least half the effort in any endeavor of this sort. The ideas in this chapter are only a beginning. As you gain experience and accumulate time plying your trade, you will find your own additional sources of continuing education that meet your particular needs.

Looking for more information

The real expert in this business, be it the system administrator, management assistant, trainer, consultant, analyst, or instructor, is the one who takes the time to learn. For the expert it's like an obsession. The more information and knowledge that you have, the more you want. This is an industry where the more you learn about a topic, the more you find out how little you really know about it. Our industry

develops new technologies every day. It expands every moment, and no one can hope to know everything there is to know. Ours is also the only industry where technology changes and advances so fast that the trade journals have a hard time keeping up (about the only other group of professionals with the same problem is the medical community). Every week you'll read about a new technology, only to find that it's already old news. To keep up with this industry means a dedicated and concerted effort to remain current and on the leading edge of technology.

These facts should tell you two things. First, what you learned today is probably old news tomorrow. By the third day, you had better put anything you know today aside and make room for new information. What you learn today is not useless; it builds the base of knowledge you need to take the next technological step. However, it is still out-of-date. Second, these facts show that you need to select the information that you want to learn. You can't play the role of a sponge and expect to gain any useful information. The computer industry requires more; it requires that you create a plan of attack to maintain your educational edge.

Filtering your input

The first problem is easy to solve, so let's look at the second. The key to staying current is finding the information that pertains to your situation. We are living in an age of information. The problem that most of us face is information overload. The faster that you read about new technology, the faster that word on still newer technology seems to arrive. Every vendor wants you to know about their great new product or strategy. Every magazine says that they are the key resource you need to improve your business. The first step you need to take to control information overload is to know where your interests lie and what types of information you need. The worst thing you can do is use the shotgun approach to learning; it only frustrates you and makes it even more difficult to concentrate on your real goals. Likewise, attempting to learn advanced techniques while you are still at the novice level is an exercise in frustration. You will never achieve anything by trying to learn something you cannot comprehend.

So how do you put this concept into practice? It takes a conscious effort at first. Limiting your information exposure is not easy because everything looks pretty interesting at first. Let's look at an example. Suppose that you are a system administrator for a small firm with 10 to 12 users. You are using Microsoft Windows for Workgroups with no access or connections to a mainframe computer. Your network deals with word processing and spreadsheets. In all aspects, this is a fairly simple installation. *Heavy Metal Computers*, a magazine that deals with mainframes, sends you a free issue. Unless you are personally interested in mainframe computers and may someday need this information, allocate your time gathering information to products and techniques related to Local Area Networks (LANs). In other words, you'll probably want to toss that copy of the magazine and look at something else.

This is not to say that all sources of other information sent your way are not important or worthwhile. There are many situations where even an offbeat magazine can provide invaluable information that you need occasionally. For example, a magazine that contains an article on troubleshooting Ethernet connections might prove useful someday, but not today. What you need to remember is where your priorities are and what your main interests are. Make a mental note of where you stored this (or any other information, for that matter) for future reference. When you need this information to troubleshoot your network, you will know where to start looking for it.

Now it's time for you to take charge of your own information needs. Figure 7-1 helps you get a handle on what information you need to read. It contains a survey of the things you need to read about to maintain your certification and personal learning goals. This is your personal road map to learning. You could also look at it as an information filter. Every time you get a new magazine, compare its contents with this survey. See how much value you will get for your learning investment. Once you get used to thinking before you read, you will find that you read less, yet learn more. That's the trick to keeping on top of the educational pile; learn only what you really need to know and file the rest away for future reference.

Reading Interest Survey

Figure 7-1

Name: _____ Date: _____

Position: _____

Hardware Needs:

❑ PC   ❑ Mainframe
❑ Macintosh   ❑ Minicomputer

Software Needs:

Word Processing: _____ Database: _____

Spreadsheet: _____ Accounting: _____

Communications: _____ Other: _____

_____ _____

Peripheral Devices:

❑ Tape Drive   ❑ CD-ROM/WORM Drive
❑ Sound Board   ❑ Mouse
❑ MODEM
❑ Printers: _____ _____

❑ Other: _____ _____

Network Specific:

Network Type: _____ Bridges/Routers: _____

Operating System Version: _____ Print Servers: _____

Other: _____ _____

Personal Needs:

_____
_____
_____

Sample reading interest survey.

The survey provides you with some ideas of what you need to read to maintain your level of knowledge. It may seem a bit overwhelming if you are a product specialist; you can ignore the sections that don't pertain to you. To use the form, simply fill it out and then look for those areas in the magazines and trade papers that you read. You may even want to use a highlighter at first. Go through the magazine or trade paper and look at the article titles. Highlight those that appear to answer your reading needs. Ignore the other articles when you go back through to read the articles you highlighted. It takes a little practice, but you will find it a very practical alternative to reading the entire magazine.

There is another way that you can use this survey. Some people get so much mail and so many magazines to read, that even a focused approach to reading will not help them get through everything they need to look at. They usually resort to using a clipping service—a company that sends you clippings from magazines and trade papers in your areas of interest. A more cost-effective method of doing the same thing is to have a secretary or other assistant use the survey as the means for going through the magazines and trade papers for you. They simply clip out the articles that you are interested in. This alleviates the need to go through all the magazines and trade papers yourself. It also helps you maintain your concentration level by removing sources of other nonessential information.

⇨ Sources of information

The basic information needed to maintain your certification will come from Microsoft in some fashion. This may include instructor-led courses, videotapes, manuals, bulletins, or seminars. There are also special training groups, product demonstrations, and satellite conferences available from time to time. This information is very Microsoft-specific. It will only help you with the Microsoft products and your certification. Because most people have an interest in the complete scope of networking, product support, or training, using Microsoft as your only source of information will not get you very far. In the real world, people use a variety of solutions; you must make sure you are ready to handle them. For this reason you need to use

other sources of information including magazines, trade papers, books, on-line services, and electronic media. Figure 7-2 shows these typical sources of information, and provides a little guidance on how to allocate your time.

As you can see from Fig. 7-2, you need to spend the majority of your time with non-Microsoft sources of information. These other sources of information will help you to not only maintain your Microsoft certification, but obtain other certifications or a better position. Balance is the name of the game here; study what you need to study at the proper level and in the right amounts. Do not fall into the trap many people fall into, of thinking "now that I have my certification, I can stop studying." Nothing is further from the truth. Now that you have your certification, you must work just as hard to maintain it.

Organizing your information

Organization is a major key to retaining a vast amount of knowledge without juggling it in your head all the time. Trying to keep all your knowledge balls in the air at the same time is just plain silly. Put the balls down so you can get some real work done. The important idea here is to group the information into easily digested chunks, then find a way to access those chunks quickly. Of course, the exact method of organization you use varies by the type of information you want to store. The most flexible media are trade magazines and books. Notes and brochures from seminars are also fairly easy to store. You will find it a lot more difficult to store information from satellite conferences and special training sessions. Information collected at user's group meetings may prove to be the most difficult source of all to organize.

One way to organize this information is to photocopy the table of contents. Put the photocopied table of contents in a notebook. Divide the notebook into sections; you could have sections for magazines, trade papers, books, electronic sources, and others. You can also divide it by magazine/trade paper title. Ordering your magazine and trade paper articles in this manner allows you to quickly locate what you need. Of course, part of this maintenance is removing old

Figure 7-2

Microsoft-
Specific Sources

Instructor-Led Courses,
Seminars, Product
Demonstrations, and
Special Training Groups

Manuals and Bulletins

Video Tapes

Satellite Conferences

Other
Sources

Magazines, Trade Papers
and Third-Party Books

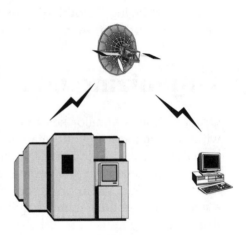

On-Line Services and
Electronic Media

Follow the 70/30 rule when updating your knowledge base.
30% Microsoft and 70% Other

Sources of continuing education information.

information from the folder as well. For example, you wouldn't want
to keep articles that told you about the latest version of the PC—the
8088. Keeping your information up-to-date is part of the work
required to reduce information overload.

Another way to reference information is to use a free-form text database such as AskSam. The benefit of using AskSam is that you are not restricted by the usual limitations of a standard database. This product is designed to provide storage for data that may or may not fall within a predictable pattern. In fact, it is the perfect database for storing notes and other hard-to-organize information. With this program you can quickly and easily create an infobase with all the above mentioned information. You can also add a paraphrased summary of the articles, books, or other information to help narrow your search of a particular topic. You could scan entire articles into the database using a scanner. While this organization technique requires a little more time to create and maintain the infobases, it does allow you to find the information that you are looking for faster.

Other methods of recalling this information may include creating a database using your word processor or spreadsheet. While these applications do not provide the same flexibility as a product like AskSam, you probably have them right now and know how to use them. There are probably a lot of other ways of converting the data into an electronic format that's retrievable at a later time using a computer. This section shows you just a few of the more common methods. Whatever method you use to keep track of the important information you find, the key is to record and document your findings. Do not entrust this information only to memory.

Ziff Publishing provides a unique method for accessing their articles and reviews. You can order Computer Library Plus for a nominal fee. Every month you receive a new CD-ROM disc containing the latest articles and reviews about any topic you can think of. The CD contains the complete text (excluding graphics and advertisements) of over 170 publications. It also includes 13,000 company profiles and a complete computer glossary. The search engine included as part of the library system allows you to conduct key word searches throughout the entire database. You can order Computer Library Plus by calling (800) 827-7889. The cost is about $1,000 per subscription. Microsoft provides the same type of library through the Microsoft Developer Network. It contains the latest issues of *Microsoft Systems Journal* and many of the Cobb Group newsletters. You can order the Microsoft Developer Network by calling (800) 227-4679. The cost is about $195 per subscription.

⇨ Magazines

Magazines are an excellent source of information. By subscribing to a few good magazines, you can remain current on most aspects of your area of expertise. Many publishers produce their magazines on a biweekly or a monthly basis. There are two types of magazines that you can subscribe to: mandatory and interest. Mandatory magazines contain information crucial to your certification or your job. These are the magazines that help butter your bread; you must read them to remain current. Interest magazines fulfill the need to expand your horizons. They help you see the world view of the computer world.

Mandatory magazines tend to come out on a monthly basis. They do not contain information that you will read today and toss tomorrow. Read the mandatory magazines when you have a large chunk of time to devote. Because you have a couple of weeks to read the magazine, you can study when you have the time. Taking your time allows you to absorb and retain what you read. Make sure you add the table of contents of this magazine to your database.

Interest magazines usually come out on a weekly basis (although some will certainly come out on a monthly basis, depending on your certification and job requirements). These magazines tend to contain news items and short interest articles. You can use this type of magazine as a time filler. Ever find that you have five or ten minutes during the day where you need to simply wait? You can't start a new project, but you can't get the pending project done either. This is the time to check out the interest magazines. Make sure you add only the valuable articles to your information database. Don't bother to log the articles that don't meet a specific need or interest.

Finding one or more great magazines doesn't present a problem either. There are many excellent magazines on the shelves at your favorite bookstore (you may need to check a local technical bookstore). You will also find that there are as many magazines that never make it to the bookstores or magazine racks. It's not that these magazines are of any less quality; they may just have a different market targeted. They usually get mailed directly to your home or business. You can usually find business reply mail cards for these

magazines in the card stacks that you get in the mail, as part of software packages, or within other magazines. For example, most of the Cobb Group newsletters are sold as part of the software package you purchase. They also perform direct mail based on the registration cards you send back to the vendor.

Deciding which ones you will buy is a very difficult decision and one you should not rush. Spend the time to research each one of them, looking for the ones that center on the topics that concern you. You can't buy and read every one of them. Even if you had the money to do so, it would require many hours or days to read them all. You must again narrow your search to the few good magazines that address your areas of interest. By reading the magazines written with a focus on your area of interest, you won't have to wade through a group of articles that you have no interest in.

Many magazines on the newsstands contain too many advertisements, and in some cases the ads get priority over the articles. This becomes very annoying when some of the articles seem too short and the editor leaves out important information because the ads needed more room. Sometimes you can't get around these types of magazines. Even though they have a lot of ads, they may still contain some good information. As you spend time looking at the magazines month after month, you will begin to notice which ones are ad magazines and which ones have the substance of good articles. (Many good magazines try to achieve a 60% ad to 40% article ratio; some of the bigger magazines achieve an even higher ratio of articles.)

You will also begin to see patterns with the type of articles written for the different magazines. Some magazines are into home computing, some the latest gadgets, others focus on networking, and still others cover every other aspect of computers or electronics. Find the ones that deal with your needs; these magazines will become part of your required reading list. Make sure that you read them each month first; they are your windows into the industry. Always read the articles that are of importance to you first. Then spend some time skimming the other ones to get an overview of what they are trying to convey. If you find something interesting, then read it. After you have read the required magazines, then read the others if you have time or want to. If you try to read everything, you are just wasting your time.

The MCPS should look at one or more product-specific magazines. The Cobb group provides a very good set of newsletters that contain not one ad. They pack these newsletters with a plethora of tips and techniques that can and will make your job a lot easier. You will probably want to look at one of these newsletters as a major source of information. The Cobb group mails out subscription information to people who purchase a product they support. They usually get your name from the registration card you send back to Microsoft. This is just one reason to make absolutely certain that you send in a registration card. Make sure you look at a major magazine as well. Magazines tend to provide a better world view of the product than a newsletter will.

For the MCSE there is at least one magazine that you should not miss. McGraw-Hill publishes *LAN Times*, a newspaper-type magazine that contains all the news you'll ever need about the networking industry. This biweekly publication covers everything from routers to the latest cabling technology. It is also one of the most objective magazines available. It doesn't matter who is doing good or bad; *LAN Times* will write about it. The magazine includes articles on the latest technologies, internetworking, applications, and network management to name a few. There is also an article in every issue that covers a "hands-on" topic. This article covers some networking-specific topic that provides you with the theory, use, and procedures.

LAN Computing is another good newspaper-type magazine for the MCSE. Cardinal Business Media, Inc. publishes it on a monthly basis. A typical issue contains news, analysis, viewpoints (opinion pieces), columns, features, and at least one lab article. This magazine tends to provide a very detailed look at the networking industry. The articles are at a higher level than those provided in *LAN Times*, and each issue is smaller.

There are many other magazines that also deal with PC networks. You need to research each of them to find the ones appropriate for you and your needs. Some of the magazines are free to consultants, administrators, and businesses. When you find the magazines that you like, call or write to the circulation manager and ask about a complimentary subscription. Often you will find that complimentary subscriptions are available for the asking. Sometimes they are on a trial basis of one to three issues. If you cannot get them for free, then

spend the money for them; you need some access to the technology. In most cases, the magazine subscriptions are tax-deductible as a business or education expense.

Once you finish reading the magazines, remember to document the contents and then store the publication in a safe place. You will only remember a small fraction of the information contained within the articles, but by using some form of documentation you will be able to access more information when you need it in the future.

As your experience and knowledge change, so should the magazines, trade papers, and books that you buy. If you find that a particular publication is no longer teaching or informing you, then it may be time to drop the subscription. If you keep reading the same material that you already know, then you are just wasting your time.

⇨ Trade papers

The weekly trade papers (or trade journals) that you receive are packed with the latest information about the computer industry. Subscriptions to a few of the more popular trade journals will keep you up to date on what the hardware and software vendors are doing. You should always subscribe to at least one of these publications. However, always remember that the information the trade papers contain is very transitory. Never forego your meat-and-potatoes articles in a magazine to read a trade paper.

Trade papers have several distinctive characteristics. They always have articles about new gadgets, state-of-the-art technology, and trends. Also included are columns about what certain industry people are doing and what company they are working for this week. This is very important information. A tip you receive from one of the trade journals can help you prepare for a future change in your company. For example, you may see an article that tells about a new release of your favorite application or networking product. A new gadget may perform a task that the boss has asked about for many months; knowing about it could save you a little time in answering questions or stalling until you find a solution.

As with magazines, you must find the trade papers that meet your needs and make them your top reading priority. There are just too many on the market to read every one of them. Some of the trade journals you will find are very pro-IBM, or pro-UNIX, while others only concern themselves with what Microsoft is doing. It is very important to remember this bias as you read the articles. Whenever you see articles of this type within a magazine or trade paper, remember that they only express the opinion of the author. These articles do not necessarily represent the right or wrong view of the industry, but only one person's view. Of course, these people maintain their positions because they are either controversial or correct more often than not. Make sure that the trade journals you decide to get objectively cover the topics that interest you.

The trade papers, when read in addition to the regular subscriptions of books and magazines, will keep you informed about the industry. Trade papers usually have a lot of articles that are unrelated to what you are doing, and they contain a ton of ads. Like magazines, the publisher sends trade papers directly to your home or place of business on a weekly or biweekly basis free of charge.

Always organize the information you find in the trade papers. Keep in mind that you can use some of the same ideas that you used for magazines to document the useful information. Find the articles of interest, make photocopies of them, then place the articles into a binder. Record the entries in a table of contents for future reference. You might try scanning the articles into a free-form text database if you want to use an electronic storage method. After you save the articles that interest you, discard the original trade paper, or preferably recycle it. If you try to save every back issue of the paper, you will soon find that you need a large garage to keep them all.

A few of the trade papers that you may want to invest in are *Network World*, *Computer Technology Review*, *Computer Reseller News*, and *PC Week*. Getting subscriptions to some or all of these provides you with complete coverage of the industry. Appendix B contains a complete list of addresses and telephone numbers for all these trade papers.

⇨ Books

Books provide another excellent source of information. You can find a book on just about any topic that comes to mind. There are so many good books on the market that you will probably run out of room to store them before you run out of books to buy. Of course, the first step in buying your library is finding a place to store it. Buy one or more heavy-duty bookcases; the light-duty bookcases in many of the variety stores won't do the job. Put the bookcases in a convenient place. You want to find your books with the least effort possible. Make sure you don't stack your books in double rows; make the bindings easy to read.

Most of the books written about a software product contain the same information as is supplied by the vendor manuals. The difference between third-party books and the vendor manuals is that the information written in the third-party books is usually more concise and to the point than the manuals. They often have real-world examples, and the author writes them in terms that most readers can easily understand. While these books contain a large amount of information, they are not for everyone. This is the type of book that the novice reader will want to get.

The expert reader needs to exercise a little more discretion when buying a book. Make sure you get books that address a specific need. A "how-to" book that addresses the needs of the novice probably won't do much for the expert user. There are exceptions to the rule that every third-party book repeats the information in the vendor manuals, and it's the exceptions that you want to look for. For example, you may find a book on creating Microsoft Word macros. This book probably contains information that the Microsoft documentation does not provide. Even if it doesn't, it will probably contain some sample macros you can use for your next macro programming job. Either way you win, because you are getting an expert-level book.

Microsoft Press has an excellent reputation for producing high-quality, expert-level books. You may want to make this source of information a first stop if you are an MCPS. Of course, there are

many other publishers on the market as well. Some of them may not appear in your local bookstore; you may have to check a technical bookstore to find them. You'll want to check the card decks that arrive in the mail as well. Some publishers use the mail as their exclusive advertising media. These card decks seldom advertise novice-level books. The reason that the books are in there is that they address the needs of the expert. The publisher usually feels that they can reach the expert reader better by using the card decks.

The MCSE may find it even more difficult than the MCPS to find high-quality books. The market is flooded with network-related books, but many of them address concerns that the MCSE may never encounter. Even worse are the books that contain nothing more than the vendor-supplied information. You need to check the book thoroughly before you buy it because the title seldom conveys the full intent of the book. The MCSE will also want to check out *The Hands-On Guide to Networking* by John Mueller and Robert Williams (ISBN 0-8306-4439-3), published by Windcrest/McGraw-Hill. This book provides you with a lot of tips and techniques for getting your network running smoothly and keeping it that way.

⇨ On-line services

Microsoft offers a wide range of services to all their product users and support technicians. Besides the standard magazines and books, Microsoft offers electronic on-line services as well. There are two basic services: Microsoft Online and Microsoft's forums on CompuServe. With these services you can use your computer to stay in touch with Microsoft. The Microsoft Online service is by subscription only, so I won't cover it here. This section does cover Microsoft's CompuServe forums, a vast array of places you can use to get answers for every question conceivable. These forums also offer download services that provide you free updates for your Microsoft products (of course, you'll only see this service when the update is free of charge). Figure 7-3 provides an overview of Microsoft's CompuServe forums.

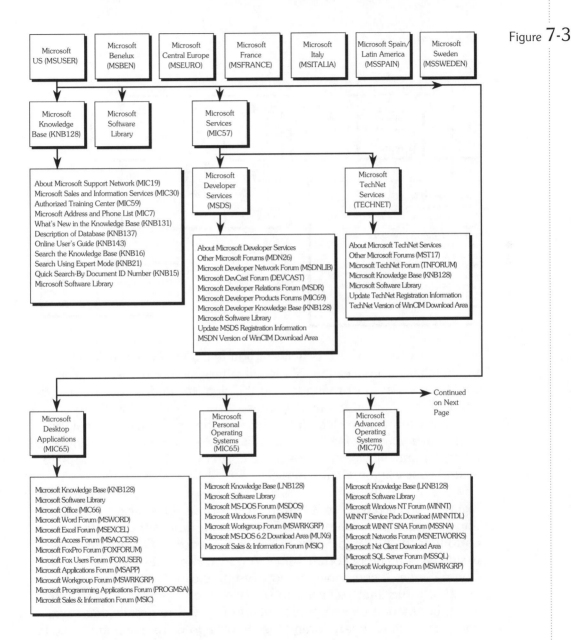

Figure 7-3

Microsoft CompuServe forum structure.

Continued on Next Page

Figure 7-3   *Continued.*

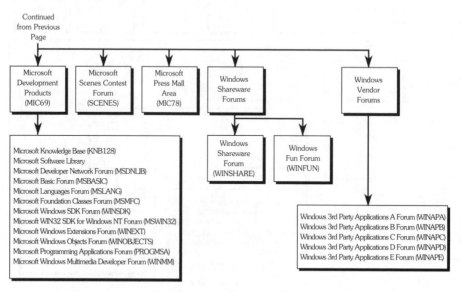

As you can see, Fig. 7-3 is huge. If you feel a little overwhelmed by the number of services that Microsoft offers, you're not alone. You could spend days just trying to find the right forum for your particular needs. For that matter, unless you use a product like WinCIM to maneuver through the labyrinth of CompuServe menus, you may not even reach your destination. Using Fig. 7-3 should make your job a lot easier and allow you to use more cost-conscious tools like TapCIS to find your way on CompuServe.

Figure 7-3 is arranged in a hierarchical format. This means that the upper level menus appear first. The actual forums appear at the bottom of the hierarchical tree. Notice the word "GO" in parentheses beside each menu or forum name. A go word provides a shortcut on CompuServe. If you know the go word, you can go directly to the menu or forum that you want to see. Not every menu entry has a go word, but there are enough provided in Fig. 7-3 to greatly decrease your search time. Every forum does have a go word, making it easy to get to any forum you want to visit.

Notice that the upper-level menu doesn't list product areas or forums. What this level does provide is access to Microsoft forums in various

languages. This allows you to communicate with Microsoft using a language you understand, rather than try to get through using English. Unfortunately, not every language provides all the services that the Microsoft U.S. section does, so you may need to use this section in some cases.

There is one special go word that the figure does not contain. You can use GO MSP to get to the Microsoft Press section of the mall. A previous section mentioned the books you can get from Microsoft Press; you can use this forum in the CompuServe mall to order books or a catalog. Using it will save you a trip to the bookstore, and it provides you with a complete list of the books you can order. Even the best-stocked bookstore in the world may miss a selection or two out of Microsoft Press's vast selection. The following paragraphs describe the sections that you'll find in the Microsoft U.S. section.

Information on Microsoft

This section offers four services. The "About Microsoft Support Network" service tells you all about Microsoft's service support offerings. It specifically looks at the Microsoft Support Network and what it offers. Use the "Microsoft Sales and Information Services" selection to obtain sales and service information. The "Authorized Training Center" service provides information about Microsoft's authorized training center program. It also provides a phone number you can use to obtain further information. Finally, the "Microsoft Address and Phone List" service provides a complete list of telephone numbers and addresses. This includes individual product service numbers as well as numbers for various Microsoft subsidiaries.

You can download any of these four services for future reference. Each one tells you about a different component of Microsoft. Unfortunately, this section does not provide any interactive capability. Microsoft provides these services through the plethora of forums described in the following section. Overall, this section provides you with quick references. Essentially it contains the telephone numbers you need to obtain further information.

 # Microsoft Knowledge Base

The Microsoft Knowledge Base contains a vast wealth of information in an article format. These articles talk about everything from methods for accomplishing specific tasks to bug fixes for Microsoft products. In many cases, a forum sysop will ask you to search one of these articles instead of providing a direct answer to your question. This is the place to go when you need to know more than the manuals provide. The seven menu entries provide everything from instructions on how to use the knowledge base to access to the search engine itself.

The first three entries tell you about the knowledge base and how to use it. The "What's New" section tells experienced users about new items in the knowledge base. Microsoft constantly updates this source of information, so you'll want to check this entry out on a regular basis. Every first-time user should read the "Description of Database" materials. This tells you what you can expect to find in the knowledge base. Finally, you will want to download the user's guide. This tells you how to get the most out of the knowledge base in the least amount of time.

There are three search engines for the Microsoft knowledge base. Each engine has its own entry and serves a different need. Novice users will want to use the "Search the Knowledge Base" entry. This section provides a menu-driven front end to the knowledge base. You can use these menu entries to narrow your search criteria and finally look at the articles that the knowledge base finds. Once you get the hang of using the knowledge base, you might want to switch to the "Search Using Expert Mode" entry. There is no menu-driven front end when using this selection, but it is faster and more flexible. Finally, you will probably want to use the "Quick Search by Document ID Number" entry when a forum sysop tells you to look for a specific article. Every article has its own number, and using this search engine entry will help you find what you need to know in one try.

The final entry in this section is the Microsoft Software Library. I describe this entry in further detail in the next section.

Microsoft Software Library

The Microsoft Software Library provides access to a wide assortment of Microsoft-tested and approved software. This is differentiated from the software that you normally download from forums, which Microsoft may or may not test. The software library uses a search engine similar to that used by the knowledge base. Of course, there are a few differences due to the differences in the tasks performed by these two services.

Once you find the software that you need, the software library provides you with the opportunity to download it. There is no real difference between the download procedure for the software library and any other service on CompuServe. All you need to do is provide a filename for your computer and specify the download protocol. In most cases your communication software will take care of the rest.

 # Microsoft Services

The Microsoft Services menu entry contains two submenus: Microsoft Developer Services and Microsoft Technet Services. The Microsoft Developer Services entry provides access to all the developer-related services like the Microsoft Developer Network forum. A developer is someone who writes applications using any number of tools including compilers and debuggers. This particular forum is heavily tied to the Microsoft Developer Library (formally Microsoft Developer Network) subscription service. This is a CD-ROM packed with information, knowledge base articles, books, and even some software. You can even download a special version of WinCIM (a Windows-based communication program specifically designed for use with CompuServe) in this area. This version provides special menu entries that relate to the Microsoft developer services.

Like the developer services area, the Microsoft TechNet Services area revolves around a CD-ROM subscription service. In this case, the subscription is called the Microsoft TechNet CD-ROM-based information service. This service is designed for people who require in-depth information on Microsoft products and how to support those

products. This differs from the programming language and operating system support provided by the developer's network. The TechNet forum allows users to exchange ideas and provide feedback to Microsoft. It also provides access to TechEd information. As with the developer services area, you can download a special version of WinCIM for this area. This version provides special menu entries that relate to the Microsoft TechNet services.

Microsoft Desktop Applications

This area of Microsoft CompuServe support provides access to all the user-oriented tools. This includes products like Word, Excel, Access, and FoxPro. In fact, these four products have their own special forums. FoxPro rates two forums: one for developers and the other for users. You can usually obtain information about the other Microsoft applications by going to the Microsoft Applications forum.

Four special menu entries allow you to access the knowledge base, software library, sales, and the Programming Applications forum. All four entries work just like their counterparts in other areas.

Microsoft Personal Operating Systems

Microsoft differentiates between single user and multiuser operating systems. This area deals with the single user (or personal) operating systems. There are three operating systems in this category: MS-DOS, Windows, and Windows for Workgroups. The menu entries for each area are pretty obvious in this case.

Notice the special entry for the Microsoft MS-DOS 6.2 Download Area. Going to this entry allows you to download the MS-DOS 6.2 step-up software free of charge (except for connect time). As with other areas described in this section, Microsoft provides access to its knowledge base and software library in this area as well.

Microsoft Development Products

There is a special area besides the Developer Network section for application developers. The development products area is a lot more general in nature. It provides access to all the language products that Microsoft provides. Notice the special forums for BASIC users and multimedia developers.

If you are a developer, then you will probably find a need to visit more than one of these forums. For example, if you develop Windows applications, then you will probably need to visit the Languages forum and the Windows SDK forum. There are even situations where you may want to visit three or four forums. Talk about information overload! If you don't monitor your time carefully, you could easily spend all your time gathering information instead of performing useful work. Fortunately, you'll probably find that you won't need to read all the messages on the forum, just the few related to your specific areas of interest.

Microsoft Advanced Systems

Microsoft set aside a special area for users of advanced operating systems. Currently there is only one operating system, Windows NT, that falls into this category. However, you can see from the figure that there is a lot going on with this one product. Notice the special areas for SNA and SQL Server. As with the other areas described in this section, this one also contains access to the knowledge base and the software library.

If you are a developer, then you will probably find a need to visit more than one of these forums. For example, if you develop Windows NT applications, then you will probably need to visit the Windows NT and Networks forums. Some developers visit three, four, or even more forums daily. Visiting that many forums could easily lead to information overload! If you don't monitor your time carefully, you could easily spend all your time gathering information instead of performing useful work. Fortunately, you'll probably find

that you won't need to read all the messages on the forum, just the few related to your specific areas of interest.

An application user can probably get by with just one forum. In most cases, a visit to the Windows NT forum is all it takes to get all the information you need. Unlike the developer, you work with the operating system to a greater extent in getting applications to work together properly. As a result, you will probably want to download all the messages in this one forum. Check the section titles carefully; you might find that you can eliminate one or two of them from your list. Remember, you will probably want to visit this forum in addition to any application-specific forums that you visit.

Microsoft Scenes Contest Forum

This is a temporary forum (just how temporary remains to be seen) that allows you to submit your photographs to the Microsoft Scenes contest. There are a few limitations and some rules that you must follow to enter.

Microsoft Press Mall Area

This is a special area for the computer press. You will not need to go here in most cases, unless you are interested in the press releases and so forth.

Windows Shareware Forums

Many people discount the value of shareware, but Microsoft obviously doesn't. Shareware can provide the same or better quality than an off-the-shelf commercial product and at a greatly reduced price. It always pays to check this area for special needs. You never know when you'll find something that a client has asked for in the past but you couldn't find.

The Windows Shareware Forums area is split into two forums: Windows Shareware Forum and Windows Fun Forum. As the name suggests, both forums are designed to provide a venue for you to talk

with shareware authors who create Windows products. The main difference between the two forums is that one is for application products you can use for serious work, and the other provides items like screen savers that you can use for fun.

Windows Vendor Forums

This group of five forums is a place for smaller commercial product vendors to provide their services. Each vendor occupies one section of the forum (there are 18 sections in each forum, but at least one section is private in most cases). This includes one message and one library area. They all share the conference rooms. You may want to check each area to see if a vendor of a product you use is present.

Electronic media

Microsoft offers two main CD-ROM subscription services. (There are a variety of other electronic media services, but we won't look at them here.) The first service is the Microsoft Development Library. This product answers the needs of most application product developers. It is especially suited to the Windows developer, but the wide range of information will appeal to developers on other platforms. For example, the CD-ROM contains the complete text of Ray Duncan's "Advanced MS-DOS Programming" book. Product specialists may find this product handy as well, because it contains tips and hints for many application products. The CD-ROM contains the complete text of the Microsoft Word for Windows 6.0 resource kit.

The second service is Microsoft TechNet. This product is designed to help people who need up-to-the-minute information on what products Microsoft offers. This is an especially important service for MCPSs who want to provide training or other consulting services to corporations. The following paragraphs describe both services in detail.

Microsoft Development Library

This is the service to get if you develop any kind of application program using a Microsoft operating system or development tool. It

covers quite a range of topics and needs. In essence, if you are a developer, you need this product.

The CD-ROMs for the Microsoft Development Library come out on a quarterly basis and offer a wide variety of information services. The annual fee for Microsoft Development Library level 1 support is $195 U.S. ($275 Canadian) for a single-user license or $595 (U.S.) for a 5-user license. Level 2 support costs $495 U.S. ($695 Canadian). A level 1 developer can update to level 2 support for $395 U.S. ($555 Canadian). To enroll in the Developer Network program in the U.S. and Canada, call (800) 759-5474 anytime. In Europe, call +31 10 258 88 64. All other countries, call (402) 691-0173 in the U.S. for local contact information. Pricing and availability may vary outside the U.S. and Canada. Post questions in the Gen/Admin section of the Microsoft Development Library forum (GO MSDNLIB) or email the Developer Network at >INTERNET:devnetwk@microsoft.com.

The main audience for this product is the software developer, but other people may find it useful as well. For example, the product support specialist will find the application sections of the CD-ROM especially interesting. Anyone who deals with any of Microsoft's networking products will like the technical articles section. This section isn't limited to programming selections; it contains a lot of application and server information as well. The following paragraphs provide a brief summary of some of the items you'll find on this CD-ROM.

➤ Complete text of Charles Petzold's *Programming Windows 3.1*.

➤ Complete issues of the *Microsoft Systems Journal*, including sample code.

➤ Microsoft Visual Basic programming system articles from the Cobb Group and *BasicPro Magazine*.

➤ Complete Microsoft Developer Knowledge Base, a database created and maintained by Microsoft's product support engineers. It contains more than 8,000 short articles, including problem reports and workarounds, on all of Microsoft's development products (Microsoft's C/C++, Visual Basic, Microsoft Access database management system, Microsoft FoxPro database, LAN Manager, and SQL Server).

➤ Complete documentation for Visual C++.

➤ Dozens of new technical articles written by the Developer Network.

➤ New content covering Visual Basic and Microsoft Access.

➤ Complete Object Linking and Embedding (OLE) 2.0 Beta Software Development Kit, which includes documentation, libraries, and sample code.

➤ Latest specifications and white papers from Microsoft, covering critical new technologies and APIs.

➤ Complete sets of developer product documentation on the Windows 3.1 SDK and DDK, the Win32 SDK for the Windows NT operating system, C/C++ 7.0, the Visual C++ development system version 1.0, Visual Basic 2.0, Microsoft Excel 4.0 SDK, and the Word for Windows Macro Development Kit.

As you can see, this service packs quite a bit of information into one disk. While this small sampling of items is only enough to give you the slightest hint of what this CD-ROM contains, it's enough to show you just how valuable this product is. Whether you are a product support specialist, a full-fledged developer, or a network administrator, the Microsoft Developer Library can provide the information you need.

There are two levels of service offered for this product. The previous paragraphs tell you about the level 1 support. This level is sufficient for most consultants and nonprogramming professionals. The programmer may want to consider getting level 2 support. This level includes everything in level 1 plus a copy of the operating systems and SDKs for all Microsoft-supported platforms. This means that the developer with level 2 support will always have access to the latest technology, the most current information, and the best tools available to get the job done. As you can see, getting level 2 support is probably overkill for most people, but there is no doubt that the programmer really needs this kind of information.

Microsoft TechNet

Anyone who spends time helping companies create solutions to their application or networking problems can really benefit from the

Microsoft TechNet service. This service is an annual program designed for those who require timely, in-depth information on Microsoft products and on supporting Microsoft-based solutions. While this may not answer every question you ever had about every solution available for a given situation, it will provide you with the Microsoft solution.

The annual fee for Microsoft TechNet, which includes monthly Microsoft TechNet CDs and quarterly Microsoft TechNet Supplemental CDs, Drivers, & Patches (among other benefits), is $295 (U.S.) for a single-user license or $695 (U.S.) for a single server/unlimited users license. To enroll in the TechNet program in the U.S. and Canada, call (800) 344-2121 ext. 124 anytime. In Europe, call +31 10 258 88 64. All other countries, call (402) 691-0173 in the U.S. for local contact information. Pricing and availability may vary outside the U.S. and Canada. For more information, download the TechNet datasheet in the Gen/Admin library of the TechNet forum (GO TNFORUM). Post questions in the Gen/Admin section of the TechNet forum (GO TNFORUM) or email TechNet at >INTERNET:technet@microsoft.com.

The main audience for this product is the solution provider. A consultant or a trainer would probably benefit most from the information provided by this package. Consider the TechNet service as an enhanced catalog of services available from Microsoft; it is the handbook you need to provide your customers with the best possible information. The following paragraphs provide a brief summary of some of the items you can expect on the TechNet discs.

> ➤ The *Microsoft Services Directory* provides detailed information on Microsoft services, including a telephone directory. It also lists over 3,500 Microsoft Solution Providers and nearly 60 Microsoft Case Studies.

> ➤ Complete Microsoft Knowledge Base, a database created and maintained by Microsoft's product support engineers that contains more than 8,000 short articles, including problem reports and workarounds, on all of Microsoft's application products. This database comes in a variety of languages including English, French, and Korean (Hangeul).

> ➤ Microsoft Access Performance Tuning articles.

➤ Microsoft Access Survey Wizard articles.

➤ Datasheets for FoxPro Developer Tools, Microsoft Mail Post Office, and Windows Sound System 2.0.

➤ Open Database Connectivity (ODBC) Drivers Directory.

➤ MS Development Tools Catalog for Windows NT.

➤ Microsoft DevCast 2 case studies w/supporting files.

➤ Microsoft FoxPro Developer Conference notes.

➤ WinCIM v1.1, a communications program specially designed for CompuServe. This special edition contains everything you need to access the Microsoft TechNet forum with the least amount of effort.

As you can see, this service packs quite a bit of information into one disk. While this small sampling of items is only enough to give you the slightest hint of what this CD-ROM contains, it's enough to show you just how valuable this product is. Whether you are a product support specialist, a trainer, or a consultant, the Microsoft TechNet service can provide the information you need.

MCPS continuing education requirements

You must update your certification from time to time as an MCPS. There are at least two good reasons why Microsoft forces you to do this. First, these continuing education requirements help you maintain a specific level of expertise with the Microsoft products. The better you know the current Microsoft products, the easier it is for you to keep your business running at its peak. This is an especially important consideration for the trainer or product specialist. Unlike a network professional, people who require your services normally use the newest version of a product. Second, recertification also helps Microsoft market their products by showing the customer that they will receive qualified support. This may seem a little self-serving until you think about the ramifications of this viewpoint. The more products that Microsoft sells, the bigger the market for your services.

Microsoft usually introduces a continuing education requirement when they release a new product, and then only if they feel that all MCPSs should know about the updates. Of course, this depends on your specialty. For example, if you are a Word for Windows product specialist, then you will probably have to recertify if Microsoft introduces a new version of Word for Windows. On the other hand, you may not need to recertify if they introduce a minor modification to an operating system. You would only need to recertify if Microsoft changed the way that the operating system reacts from a user standpoint. This means that you can usually expect to recertify every one to two years—not an overwhelming burden by any standard.

You will receive some type of mail notification when Microsoft decides that you need to recertify. After Microsoft notifies you of the update, you have 90 days to fulfill the requirements. In most cases, this means that you must pass a competency exam.

Microsoft will not leave you in the dark about what they expect. They usually provide one or more classes that teach you the new information. Armed with this information, you can usually pass the competency exam the first time around. Remember, even though the product changed, you still have some experience under your belt.

Don't wait too long to take the competency exam, even though Microsoft provides you with 90 days to meet the certification requirements. Try to recertify as soon as possible. Of course, you will want to take the time to fully learn every feature of your product speciality. You will also want to test your new skills. Make sure you study for this exam with the same vigor as your initial exams. Remember that the more pressure you are under, the higher the odds of failing.

MCSE continuing education requirements

You must update your certification from time to time as an MCSE. There are at least two good reasons that Microsoft forces you to do this. First, these continuing education requirements help you maintain a specific level of expertise with the Microsoft products. The better you know the current Microsoft products, the easier it is for you to

keep your business running at its peak. Second, recertification also helps Microsoft market their products by showing the customer that they will receive qualified support. This may seem a little self-serving, until you think about the ramifications of this viewpoint. The more products that Microsoft sells, the bigger the market for your services.

Microsoft usually introduces a continuing education requirement when they release a new product, and then only if they feel that all MCSEs should know about the updates. For example, you will probably have to recertify if Microsoft introduces a new version of Windows NT that drastically changes the way the operating system works. This means that you can usually expect to recertify every one to two years—not an overwhelming burden by any standard.

You will receive some type of mail notification when Microsoft decides that you need to recertify. After Microsoft notifies you of the update, you have 90 days to fulfill the requirements. In most cases this means that you must pass a competency exam.

Microsoft will not leave you in the dark about what they expect. They usually provide one or more classes that teach you the new information. Armed with this information, you can usually pass the competency exam the first time around. Remember, even though the product changed, you still have some experience under your belt.

Don't wait too long to take the competency exam, even though Microsoft provides you with 90 days to meet the certification requirements. Try to recertify as soon as possible. Of course, you will want to take the time to test your new skills on your network. Make sure you study for this exam with the same vigor as your initial exams. Remember, the more pressure you are under, the higher your odds of failing.

MCT continuing education requirements

The Microsoft MCT is a little different from the MCSE and MCPS when it comes to recertification. For one thing, the MCT can expect to recertify a lot more often than the other certified professionals do.

The reason is simple; you will not only need to specialize in more areas as an MCT, but you need to know about *every* nuance of a product as well. For example, if Microsoft introduces even a new minor version of Windows NT, you will probably have to recertify.

There are some similarities in the programs, though. For instance, you will probably attend a class to learn the new material before you take the test. Unlike classes for the other certifications, a Microsoft instructor will usually teach your class, because there will be a lack of certified instructors to perform the task. You will need to take good notes, because Microsoft may not have complete course materials available.

After completing the course and receiving the certificate, the instructor must pass the competency exam just like everyone else. Once you complete this step, Microsoft will recertify you to teach that particular course. As you can see, the procedure is about the same as with the MCPS and MCSE programs, but just a little more stringent and time-critical.

The instructor must stay up-to-date on all continuing education requirements because they are the ones in the front of the classroom trying to teach the material. If the instructor does not fully comprehend the material, there is no way that Microsoft can expect his or her students to understand it. This is why Microsoft requires the MCT to meet such a high standard before they allow her or him to teach the classes.

CHAPTER 8

The consulting approach

MANY consultants make a living installing and maintaining local area networks (LANs) or providing application support for those networks. A LAN needs hardware, software, and user support. Installing and maintaining LANs became a very lucrative business when large corporations decided to downsize their database applications from mainframes and minicomputers to PCs. The LAN environment offers too many advantages for these companies to ignore. In addition, many small businesses are starting to see the benefit of networking their computers to enhance productivity. A sneaker net often wastes more time than it could ever save, and management has started to realize it. Add to this the increasing number of mid-sized businesses, and you have a climate ripe for the entrepreneur.

Of course, once you start adding a new environment with its requisite applications, you need to train company personnel to use them. Power never comes free, and this includes the new power of LAN-based application software. This is where the company trainer comes into play. While there are a variety of training environments available to companies today, training by the company trainer is still the least expensive and most efficient method of getting the job done. In many cases the need for a trainer is short-term; this represents a good opportunity for the consultant. Small and medium-sized businesses usually can't afford a full-time trainer. This is a perfect opportunity for any consultant. As the business market gets more competitive, the consultant should see an increase in business.

Of course, not all consultants will see an increase in their customer base. The difference between a successful consultant and one that simply maintains his or her current installed base is recognition. Unless

you get recognition for your achievements as a businessperson, there is little chance that you will increase your client base.

There are benefits to enhancing your recognition level other than simply working more hours per day as your client base increases in size. For example, with an increase in capability, you can charge higher per-hour fees. It is not unusual for a networking consultant to make $100 or more per hour. A certified trainer can charge $800 per student per class (assuming a three-day class).[1] Compare this with $60 per hour for the average consultant, or $500 per student per class for the average trainer. Of course, what you see in your business depends on a lot of factors that we will discuss later. Because of this increase in pay, you may find that you can afford to hire a helper. This allows you to concentrate on the "fun" jobs and give someone else the headaches. As you can see, the benefits to a Microsoft certification are many. However, to get the benefits, you must first gain recognition.

This chapter specifically targets the networking and training expert. It provides the consultants with ideas on how they can improve their business through proper use of Microsoft-supplied aids. It also examines some of the ways that the consultant can use his or her certification to gain and keep new clients. Finally, this chapter examines some thorny issues like what to charge the client for network and training services, and how to maintain a professional relationship with the client.

Using the Microsoft logo

Once you get your certification, you need to tell someone about it. Clients usually aren't very thrilled with wasting time hearing about your latest achievement, so you need to tell them in an almost subliminal manner. One of the ways you can do this is to add the Microsoft logo to all your business correspondence, price lists, business cards, and other areas of your business. Of course, you need to follow all the rules regarding the use of your logo. You will find these rules in the contract

---

[1]Prices based on a survey of 52 consultants and the average price charged by businesses in Southern California area. Prices vary widely by area of the country. Prices do not include consultants who work in conjunction with another business like a computer store.

you signed at the completion of the certification process. The following paragraphs discuss some of the ways you can use the Microsoft logo to tell your clients about your capabilities.

Advertisements

There are two elements to advertising: design and distribution. The first topic is subject to much debate. The number and variety of advertising brochures that you get in the mail demonstrates this problem. The second topic is a little easier for the consultant to master. As a consultant, there are only a handful of truly effective ways to distribute your advertisement.

Designing your brochure

Let's tackle the first problem: how to design your brochure. Your best source of information on how to solve this problem is the junk mail you receive. Collect the brochures, newsletters, and assorted advertisements for a few weeks. It usually pays to fill a small box up before you begin the next step in this process. Don't bother to save items that have nothing to do with your business (like the sale brochure at the local clothing store); save only the business-related mail.

Now start looking through the pile of mail that you've accumulated. What kinds of mail attract your attention? Go ahead and write down which vendors do a good job of attracting your attention. Give the same junk mail to a few people willing to help you out. Make sure they at least have an interest in computers. You may even want to approach a few of your better clients. Ask them to show you what junk mail attracts their attention. The larger your sample size, the better. Get as many people involved as possible. Collect all the attractive junk mail and throw the rest of it away (unless you really need it). Going through all the mail that attracts your attention will give you ideas of what works and what doesn't. You may want to perform the same kind of analysis on magazine advertisements and store brochures if you intend to pursue those routes. Always look at what the successful competition is doing, then add a few ideas of your own to come up with a truly winning combination.

The junk mail you collect represents an idea base—a source of modules that you can use to create your own brochure. All the mail in this pile contains something that attracted you or your helpers. Go through your idea base and figure out what appeals to you the most. Don't worry if you have too many ideas; you can easily narrow this list down later. Once you do get a few ideas together, you need to create an advertisement.

Creating an advertising brochure is not a scientific process; it lies on the artistic edge of maintaining a business. In fact, it is one of the fun things that you can do. It allows you to exercise your creative talents. Part of the problem is that an effective advertising brochure usually attracts our attention because we can understand what the author is trying to say. As a result, a brochure that works fine in one area of the country may fail in another part because the cultural connection isn't as strong.

How do you find out if your brochure is a success? When people call your business, you may want to take the time to ask them how they found out about your business. Keep track of what types of advertising work and what types don't. If you don't get enough calls in response to a particular brochure or advertisement, then it wasn't a success. The places you choose to advertise make a big difference, too. A good brochure may not do very well if you pick a poor place to put it. Make sure you weight the scores to account for the types of client you like to work with. If your advertisement always attracts the wrong kind of client, it's a sure sign that you need to create a different type of brochure or to pursue a different distribution medium.

There are several common elements that you need to put in a brochure. First, you need to identify yourself. Unless people know whom they're dealing with, you won't get any sales. Second, you need to consider adding a list of services. You can do this in a number of ways. For example, stores usually use graphics to tell people what services they offer. (What else do you call a picture of a computer with a price listed below it?) Some businesses use a simple list that looks much like a price list. Still other businesses use descriptive paragraphs or other methods to tell people what services they offer. The choice is up to you. You may want to include price as part of your brochure, but this usually isn't the best idea for consultants.

Keeping your price as part of a price list that you give the client after you make your sales pitch is usually a better idea.

Every form of advertising you create should mention your Microsoft certification. Have you ever noticed how other vendors use this technique to attract potential clients? You need to avail yourself of this potential sales tool as well. Make sure you look at these other sales brochures for ideas on how to present your certification. Two methods that you should always consider are including the actual logo as part of your advertisement, and then adding some text that says, "Fully Microsoft Certified to work on your network," or "Get your training from someone certified by Microsoft."

Distributing your brochure

The second problem that you need to deal with is distribution. Some businesses resort to mass mailings and all kinds of other methods to attract new clients. While this may work fine for your local food store, it usually doesn't work all that well for a networking professional. Studies show that response from mass mailings is approximately 7% to 10% for an average business. A networking business gets a much lower response, somewhere in the neighborhood of 2% to 3%, because there are fewer people who can use your services. That's two to three people per one hundred mailings. If you close 2% of your sales, you need to mass mail to ten thousand companies to get four to six new clients. So how do you get new clients? An advertising brochure is still a good method of gaining new clients, but the method of distribution can make all the difference in the world.

Word-of-mouth is a very good method for a consultant to gain new clients. Other professionals, like doctors and lawyers, have relied on this method of gaining new clients for years. Have you ever noticed the other method that these professionals use? Referrals are a common method of gaining new clients in both of these fields. A generalist will refer you to a specialist for particular kinds of work. The same holds true for professionals certified by Microsoft. You need to rely both on word of mouth and referrals for new clients. However, the job doesn't end there. The computer business is a lot

more complex than other businesses. Every day there are new developments in industry that other people may not know about. Certainly they won't know everything you do about your business. The reason for advertising becomes very clear when you look at it from this perspective.

You may find that your local newspaper or computer magazine are good places to advertise. This is a means that is secondary to word of mouth and referrals as a way of gaining new clients. Experience shows that about half the people respond to either word of mouth or referral. Only 1% of the people you reach with a magazine advertisement will respond. Of those who respond, only about 1.5% will actually turn into clients.[2] This means that you would have to reach a minimum of 10,000 people with your newspaper or magazine advertisement to get a potential client. The numbers on telephone book advertisements are even smaller, because the audience is less inclined to need computer services. As you can see, the one or two clients you gain using advertisements need to pay off with large work loads and lots of referrals to make the effort worthwhile.

⇨ Brochures, business cards, and price lists

There are three classes of documents that do not fall into the advertisement category, but can act as subtle reminders of the services you offer. They include: brochures, business cards, and price lists. All three of these items end up in the hands of your current clients. If you can get the client to look at these items from time to time, the subtle reminders you leave will help them remember what services you offer. They will also serve as reminders that the client needs to tell others about the services you offer. Remember, referrals are one of the best means at your disposal for gaining new clients.

A standard business card offers very little room for advertising, let alone subtle reminders. By the time you add a name, address,

---

[2]Results obtained from a survey of 50 computer consultants who relied on all three methods of gaining new clients.

telephone number, and fax number, there is little room left for anything else. However, you can usually add a logo or two plus a slug line. You normally add your business logo on the same line as (or directly below) the name of your business. The logo identifies your business to people. They may actually look for the logo instead of your name when they look for your business card. Adding your Microsoft certification logo to the bottom right or left corner of your business card adds a subtle reminder about one of the types of service that you offer. This little graphic says a lot about you and your business. The slug line usually includes one- or two-word reminders of services you offer, or perhaps the guiding ideas of your business. Make sure you add a reference to your Microsoft certification here as well. It doesn't have to contain many words. Simply saying "Microsoft Certified" usually gets your point across to the client.

There is another type of business card that you may or may not want to overlook. Have you ever considered what a calendar or a pen/pencil with your company name on it represents? You have to get past the free gift aspect to realize that these items are simply another form of business card. There are some plusses to using this medium. A calendar certainly offers more room than a standard card for advertising. It also offers the possibility of telling people who visit your client's office about your business. A pen or pencil may receive a lot more use than any other form of business card you may provide the client. This form of business card is almost certain to get passed from person to person during its useful life. Of course, there are some negative aspects as well. A calendar may never see the light of day if your client gets inundated with them from other businesses. Eventually your client will toss both of these other media into the garbage, while a business card could last for years. These other forms of business card are also a lot more expensive than your standard business card. The best way to test this form of business card is to simply hand it out. You may find it useful with some clients and not with others.

Price lists are a very important part of your business. Some clients may actually believe that you go out of your way to overcharge them if you don't provide such a document. In addition, some clients view the lack of a price list as an indication that you are willing to negotiate on your prices. If you are not willing to make this concession, a price list is the best means of telling the client.

Providing them with a document that spells out what you charge and how you apply those charges is very important to maintaining good client relations.

Printing a price list may provide the client with a little peace of mind, but it doesn't do much for your pocketbook. You need to make the price list pay some dividend in increased sales or other tangible benefits. This is where adding your Microsoft certification logo comes into play. Adding something as small and unobtrusive as a logo can provide a big payback. As your clients peruse your price list, they also get a complete reminder of why you charge more than Joe or Sally down the street. Your certification logo reminds them that they are paying for a higher-quality service than they might otherwise obtain. It also reminds them to tell their friends about the quality service they receive from you. Even a price list can serve as an advertisement. Make sure you get the full benefit from the investment you need to make in this document.

The final document is a brochure. This is a relatively undefined piece of information you provide to the client. It includes everything from advertising brochures (covered in the previous section) to documents designed to help the client use your services more efficiently. For example, how often has the client asked you about what your certification really represents? It makes good sense to create a brochure that tells the client about your certification and why it is important. If your business uses more than one level of certification, you can use the brochure to help the client understand what services he or she can expect from each of your employees. Make sure you create valuable tools of this type to reduce the time you spend answering client questions. Of course, adding the logo to brochures of this type only serves to show the client your level of dedication and professionalism. Make sure you add the certification logo whenever possible.

Carrying your ID card

The first thing that comes to many people's minds about a badge is identification. It is true that your Microsoft badge will identify you to your clients. It provides them with a name and a certification number

they can use for reference. This provides the client with a sense of security; they know who you are and what you represent. The badge also tells the client what you are qualified to do; it lists the Microsoft certifications that you possess. Of course, this really doesn't tell you much more than you already knew.

If you spend any time at all going from site to site, you soon realize that clients judge you by your appearance and not your professionalism, at least on the first few visits. This is a sad fact, but true. Your manner in dealing with client questions also makes a big impact. A charming idiot will obtain more clients than a surly genius. (Keeping them is another matter; the surly genius who gets the job done usually wins on this count.)

The most obvious answer to the question of physical appearance versus reality may appear to lie in good communication skills. You may want to tell the client who you are and what you represent. Unfortunately, blurting out all your qualifications may make it appear that you're more a boastful oaf than a professional and thoughtful consultant. So how do you tell the client about all your qualifications without making your sales pitch seem rude? Brochures, price lists, and advertisements all help with the sales pitch. However, there is another method that many consultants fail to consider. We all know the importance of dressing for the job and making sure we present a clean appearance, but this only skims the surface. Use subliminal methods to tell people about you and your business. For example, wearing your Microsoft badge can go a long way toward starting a client-initiated conversation about your qualifications. (They may simply ask why you're wearing the badge.) If you can get the client to ask about your qualifications, they are less apt to think that you're boasting about your qualifications and more likely to think that you provide complete and reasonable answers to their questions.

Your badge says a lot more than what you can do. Wearing your badge helps people see that your qualification means a lot to you. It also shows your professionalism; it demonstrates that you have the knowledge required to keep their network running or to get their employees trained to use the latest applications. People tend to maintain the first impression that they get from you. It is very difficult for a consultant to overcome a negative first impression. Make sure

you make the right first impression by helping people see the professional side of your business.

 # Determining what services to offer

Determining what services you want to offer is a matter of taking inventory of what skills you have to offer and what skills pay the best. You also need to consider what the clients in your area need the most and what they view as the most valuable. This is one of the reasons that you decided to pursue your Microsoft certification. The first part is fairly easy; simply create a list of your skills and then rank them from 1 to 10. Figure 3-1 provided you with an opportunity to survey your networking and training skills before you became certified. Figure 8-1 provides the same opportunity with your skills as a whole. Notice that each section provides additional spaces for you to add specialized skills. Use this figure after you become certified.

Notice that there are five sections to this survey. The first section asks you about your hardware experience. The second section asks about your general software expertise. This looks at your ability to install and maintain the software, rather than use it or teach someone else how to use it. The third section asks about your Microsoft product-specific skills; they should have improved from the levels in Fig. 3-1. The fourth section asks about your other types of training experience. These are the four major areas of participation for a consultant. There are other areas as well. For example, the fifth section contains a listing for the lucrative area of technical writing.

How do each of the areas addressed in Fig. 8-1 relate to your Microsoft certification? As you gain knowledge and experience with networks, your hardware experience will grow. Companies will call on your networking experience when they try to get their software to work. Passing this knowledge onto other people is always a marketable skill. As you gain knowledge and experience in training people, your software and training knowledge will increase. You may find that you gain the knowledge required to make network applications to work together while you exercise your ability to train other people. How many times

Overall Skills Survey   Figure 8-1

Hardware

SKILLS	LEVEL									
	HIGH									LOW
	10	9	8	7	6	5	4	3	2	1
Cable Installation										
Computer System Building										
Computer System Installation										
Computer System Repair/ Maintenance										
Routers/Bridges/Hubs/etc.										
Mini and Mainframe Connections										
Scientific/Specialty Installations										
Others:										

Software

SKILLS	LEVEL									
	HIGH									LOW
	10	9	8	7	6	5	4	3	2	1
Programming										
Installation/Upgrades										
Configuration Management (The software configuration for each machine.)										
License Management										

Network consultant's skills survey.

Figure 8-1   *Continued.*

SKILLS	LEVEL									
	HIGH									LOW
	10	9	8	7	6	5	4	3	2	1
Fault Resolution (Making the hardware and software work together)										
Others:										

Microsoft Specific Networking and Training

SKILLS	LEVEL									
	HIGH									LOW
	10	9	8	7	6	5	4	3	2	1
Microsoft Windows										
Microsoft Windows NT										
Microsoft Windows NT Advanced Server										
Microsoft Word for Windows										
Microsoft Excel										
Microsoft Project										
Microsoft Mail for PC Networks - Desktop										
Microsoft Mail for PC Networks - Enterprise										
Microsoft Windows for Workgroups										
Networking with Microsoft Windows for Workgroups										
Networking with Microsoft Windows										
Microsoft SQL Server Database Administration for OS/2										

SKILLS	LEVEL									
	HIGH									LOW
	10	9	8	7	6	5	4	3	2	1
Microsoft SQL Server Database Implementation										
Microsoft SQL Server Database Administration for Windows NT										
Microsoft TCP/IP for Microsoft Windows NT										
Microsoft LAN Manager Network Administration										
Microsoft LAN Manager Advanced Network Administration										
Others:										

Other Training

SKILLS	LEVEL									
	HIGH									LOW
	10	9	8	7	6	5	4	3	2	1
Database										
Spreadsheet										
Word Processing										
Graphics Software										
Custom Software										
Network Maintenance/ Administration										
Hardware Maintenance/ Repair										
Technical Support Technician										

Figure 8-1   *Continued.*

SKILLS	LEVEL									
	HIGH									LOW
	10	9	8	7	6	5	4	3	2	1
Technical Support Technician										
Peripheral Device Support (Print Server Support)										
Others:										

Other

SKILLS	LEVEL									
	HIGH									LOW
	10	9	8	7	6	5	4	3	2	1
Technical Writing (Network Documentation and User Manuals)										
Others:										

have you walked into a situation where the client had little or no documentation for their network? The need for technical writers becomes obvious when you look at this need. As you can see, you can enhance each of these skills when you get your Microsoft certification. You cannot live in a vacuum; exercising one skill necessarily affects all your other skill levels as well. Marketing these advanced skills is the sign of good business management.

You can answer the second part of the new services equation in two ways. First, you can simply survey or ask your clients what they need in the way of service. You may want to ask them leading questions that produce more than a yes or no answer. Make sure you look at their business for opportunities. You might find that the client hadn't considered this service item in the past. Don't be surprised if the client turns down some of the ideas you have. They may not see a need to pursue them and any arguments on your part may serve to alienate the client. Figure 8-2 provides you with a simple survey you can ask the client to fill out or simply use as a reference document when you ask the questions in person.

Sample Customer Survey   Figure 8-2

1. In what ways do you see your need for customized software support growing in the future? How far into the future?

2. What types of new products are you planning to build in the future? How will this affect your network?

3. When do you plan to downsize your current mainframe database to a PC LAN?

4. How can we improve the reliability of your network? What types of hardware and software purchases are you willing to support to make these changes?

5. Are there tasks that you would like the network to perform but that you can't get it to do?

6. Have you considered any contingency plans if the network fails? If so, have you actually tested them?

7. Which methods do you find most effective for protecting your software investment?

8. Are there any other ways you could see my business help in making yours grow?

9. What level of training do your employees currently have? What level would you like to see them have? Do you have any goals set in this area?

10. Do you see the need to use any new software in the near future? What types and why?

The sample survey shows you how to phrase an open-ended question. Notice that I didn't ask the client if she planned to expand the number of products they produced, but what new products they already have in mind. This open-ended question assumes that the client's business is in good shape and that he or she plans to grow. You really wouldn't want to assume anything else. You also want to explore the outer reaches of networking with your questions. For example, I asked the client about his mainframe database. Many clients do not even think of downsizing their current applications until you ask them about it. Make the client see your visions as their own ideas. Asking questions like the ones shown in Fig. 8-2 will make it appear that the client had the idea, not you. (Putting the client into the driver's seat is the easiest way to ensure he or she will accept any proposals you make as a result of the survey.)

The second way you can determine what services the client needs is to look in your local newspaper and read the case studies in the magazines or trade papers. These sources of information serve as a source of ideas that you can add to your survey. You may even want to simply offer the service and see how many clients respond. Often clients will say they are not interested in a service if you ask them first, but respond favorably if the service is already in place.

Making your clients aware

Your clients may not even know what your certification means. After all, until you read this book you may not have known what certification involved, or what you would get out of it. Your clients are probably less informed than you are about Microsoft certification, yet this is one area that they really do need to know about. It always pays to keep your clients informed. A little information goes a long way when it comes to helping the client see the need for a particular course of action.

As a Microsoft-certified professional, you can usually charge a little more than your noncertified competition for the same service. The reason is simple; you have demonstrated that you possess a set of fully developed skills while the competition hasn't. (Demonstration in

this case means a full examination by a competent authority.) Clients will not see the value of this demonstration until you tell them about it. Until they do understand the significance of certification, their reaction to the higher rates you charge will range from accusations of overcharging to threats of retaining someone else's services. However, many of these objections go away once you make them aware of the advantages of certification.

The approach you take to this education process depends on the techniques you use to run your business. A hard-sell consultant may want to schedule a meeting with the client to talk about this new certification and to make a proposal based on what it represents. A soft-sell consultant may choose to simply print a brochure that fully explains what certification means and provide it to their client during a scheduled visit. Other consultants may use a combination of both approaches, or may even simply mention it during the course of a regular meeting. Your methods of managing your business determine which techniques feel the most comfortable to you. However, the question of informing the client is clear. If you don't tell your clients why your certification is important, then they will never know. An uninformed client is your worst enemy.

There are specific advantages to each technique we describe for keeping your client informed. For example, brochures can double as advertisement. If a client passes your brochure on to a friend, you may find yourself with a new client. On the other hand, the direct special meeting approach may yield a new networking job. The instant cash after you get your certification can improve your self-esteem. A mention during a regular meeting may improve the intimacy between you and your client. She may feel that you're letting her in on something special. This often translates into greater customer loyalty and support.

You also need to consider the temperament of your clients when approaching them with news of your certification. Some clients like to talk with a consultant who lets them think about whatever the consultant has to say. They like to take the time required to fully think about what the new certification does mean to their business. For example, many educational and professional organizations like lawyers

and doctors fall into this category. Other clients may appreciate the hard sell. They take it as a sign that you are an aggressive businessperson when you present your certification quickly and then add a proposal on how they could use the certification within their business. Many retailers fall into this category. Using the mention during a meeting approach with a small business client really works wonders. A small business needs to maintain the feeling of intimacy rather than the cold business approach often used by corporations. Whatever method you use, make sure you take your temperament and that of your client into account before you pursue it.

Determining what to charge

Figuring out what to charge is always a difficult question. Charging too much will yield a dead business when your clients go to your nearest competitor for their networking and training needs. Charging too little may give you more business, but not too much profit. You need to find the middle ground between charging too much and too little. Unfortunately, this is like one of those psychology tests that we all hate. There are no right answers, just right answers for you. No matter how little you charge, someone who really wants a lower price can probably find it. The same holds true for higher prices. Of course, the people who determine this middle ground are your competitors. Your competitors are the ones who will steal your clients and put you out of business if possible. (Of course, you'll do the same to your competitors given the chance.) The bottom line is this: If clients see an opportunity to get the same level of support that you provide from someone else at a lower cost, you can be sure that they will use it.

So how do you determine what the middle ground is? You can start by doing a little research. Simply call the competition to see what they charge for specific services. Some consultants charge by the hour, others by the job. You may need to do some conversion to make a comparison between their rates and yours. There is no reason for them to withhold the information from you if you call as someone looking for information rather than as a competitor. Another place to look is your local computer magazine or newspaper. Vendors often publish their rates for a specific type of installation.

Sometimes the previous methods don't produce any results. When this happens, you can resort to a number of alternative methods to get the information you need. For example, if you have a large enough client base with fairly new LANs, you can always ask them what they paid for the service. Of course, this only helps if you weren't the one installing the LAN. Federal, state, and local governments keep statistics of what businesses charge for certain services. You could find what you need to know from these sources as well.

There are other resources you should consider using. For example, CompuServe and other on-line services host a wide variety of consultant-based forums. You can usually find out the current rate for a given service by polling this group of people. One word of caution here; many of the consultants that frequent these on-line services are at the upper end of the pay scale. You may not get a true reading on what the actual average rate of pay is for a specific service.

The following numbers may help you out as well. A recent survey of 52 MCSEs showed that only 15 of them charged by the job alone, 6 charged by the job or by the hour depending on the client and the task they wanted performed, and 31 charged exclusively by the hour. The average charge for on-site hardware repair was $80 per hour. This went up to an average of $100 for networking services and down to $40 for things like software installation. Most MCSEs that also provide training services charged an average hourly rate of $35. The problem with these general prices is that they aren't tailored for the area you work in. What you need to do is get at least a few comparison prices, then modify these numbers as required. All these numbers provide is a range of prices based on a specific service.

Every MCPS I talked with charged a per-student/per-class fee. That is, every student paid a standard rate based on the class they wanted to attend. In most cases, this price is based on the length and complexity of a class. A poll of 18 MCPSs revealed an average rate of $100 per day for a simple class, $125 per day for an average class, and $200 per day for a complex class. Using these rates, a 4-day class of average complexity would cost each student $500. These rates included all the required student materials, like books, pens, and paper. The instructor was also responsible for supplying all teaching aids and performing all on-site setups. The prices for the

services provided by an MCPS are less likely to change by area of the country, but you still need to check what the competition in your area is charging.

As you can see, the only limits on the sources of information you use are the resources you want to tap. Deciding what you want to charge doesn't stop here. You also need to resolve such issues as what to charge for parts. Some consultants don't charge anything at all. They make up for any parts sales by charging higher hourly rates. Other consultants tack 10% to 15% onto the price of the parts they sell and charge a lower hourly rate. Both approaches are equally useful. You need to decide which approach your clients will appreciate more.

There is also the issue of when to apply different rates. Some consultants offer more than one service. You need to decide if you want to charge the same rate for software installation as you do for network maintenance. You need to decide whether you will even provide any kind of software installation services. The same holds true if your specialty is training. Do you want to charge different rates based on the complexity of the class? What courses do you want to offer? If you do decide to charge one all-inclusive rate, you may find that some customers balk when you present a bill for software setup that costs the same as their network installation. Make sure your client knows that you charge one rate up front.

If you decide to use different pay scales for different services, you need to decide when one pay scale ends and the other begins. This is one area where consultants can run into trouble. Some clients will try to cheat the consultant by saying that the service they performed was for a lower rate than the service the consultant actually performed. For example, what happens if the client constantly interrupts you with questions during a network installation? Do you charge them the network installation rate or the lower training rate? The client may choose the training rate (and in fact an unscrupulous client will do just that). They may not feel you deserve the full networking rate since you spent that time training them. The best course of action is to tell the client what rate you are charging for the work you are performing. Make sure you inform them when the rate changes because the task you perform changes. Another alternative is to schedule separate tasks for separate sessions. In other words, you

would charge one rate per session, but base that rate on the task you were hired to perform.

As you can see, rate setting is not the easiest part of consulting. You need to expend the energy required to provide the client with written rates and methods you use for charging them. You also need to make them aware of when that rate changes and why. If possible, always make sure you write down the rules for rate changes and get the customer's signature. (Many consultants refuse to work without a signed contract; it's very easy to see why.)

Professionalism

Respect—it's not given, it's earned. That is a saying that many of us hear from more than one source as we advance along our career paths. Yet, how many of us really know what the saying means? Professionalism in the way you perform your job is what earns the respect of your clients. Professionalism means that you are proud of your abilities and the work you do. It also means that you set certain standards for yourself and stand by the work you do. Some people call this type of behavior old-fashioned or out-of-date, but most clients appreciate a professional when they see one.

Where do you stand on this issue? How do you know when you achieve professional status? Some people set up a stiff set of rules and call it professionalism. Nothing could be further from true professionalism than a set of stiff rules. Even crooks and thieves set up rules for themselves. They always use the rules as a means to skirt their real responsibility and neglect to fulfill their promises. Professionalism is more a mindset, and less a stiff set of rules, than many people think. A professional needs to bend with the changing circumstances of everyday living. Figure 8-3 provides you with a checklist that you can use to measure your professional standing.

As you can see, there are many situations where you might need to take time to think about the consequences of your actions before you actually do them. For example, when does a client deserve warranty

Figure 8-3

A Guide to Professionalism

❏ Consider using high quality parts whenever possible. High quality does not necessarily mean high cost. Look for product reviews in trade magazines and newspapers. It also helps to look for opinions from other network professionals via CompuServe or other on-line media.

❏ Try to reduce costs whenever it will not affect the quality or usefulness of a product the client needs. If a product breaks the first time you use it or the part does not perform the task the client requires, then buying it at a discount does not solve any problems. In fact, it actually creates more problems. However, buying a high priced product simply to get the name value discredits your ability to help the client make prudent buying decisions.

❏ Always consider the cost of losing a client versus the cost of losing the money from one job. Losing a client always costs you more money than you'll lose from one job. If the client assumes that you mistreated him or her, find out what it will take to restore confidence. Often this means that you'll lose the profit from one job to save the client's trust.

❏ Never break the law to meet the demands of an unyielding client. For example, some clients will insist that you install pirated software on their network even though they know such an act is illegal. It is always better to lose a client than to knowingly break the law. Otherwise, the client will expect you to break the law as often as they see fit. In addition, you will share in the client's guilt if you get caught performing the illegal act.

❏ Try to honor your warranty whenever possible. Many clients will try to convince you to honor unreasonable interpretations of the warranty you offer as part of your services. It often helps to honor the unreasonable request to maintain the client. Of course, this can backfire if the client starts expecting you to perform this service every time there is a dispute. The most reasonable course of action is to make sure the client understands that you are honoring the unreasonable request in the hope of maintaining the good relationship.

❏ Use the clearest wording possible in any written documentation that you provide the client. This includes contracts and warranties. Make sure you go through the contract or warranty with the client and explain anything they don't understand. Using this technique helps reduce confusion later. It may also prevent you from losing a valued client by reducing the chances of misunderstandings.

Professional network consultant's business guide.

❏ Always perform the work to the best of your ability. Even if the client does not possess the level of technical competence that you do, they do know what task the network should perform when you finish. Make sure that both hardware and software are up to par. Alert the user to potential problems with equipment that you did not install. Help the client understand why there are specific limitations to the installation you create for them.

❏ Never be afraid to admit that you can't perform a specific task. The client can respect you if you simply say that you can't perform a specific task that they need help with. Trying to perform the task when you lack the skills will make the customer less likely to hire you again in the future.

❏ Always make sure you train the client fully. This means working with the client until he or she completely understands the application or procedure. Test the client to make sure they fully understand what you taught them. Sometimes this means that you may have to provide a little work for free when time runs out during the training session. Don't make this a continual practice; some clients will start to take advantage of you.

❏ Always test your installation completely. This isn't limited to hardware or software. It includes procedures and other intangibles as well. If you train someone to do something, it means that you test their knowledge of the topic before you leave.

service rather than pay for a new piece of hardware? There are gray areas that make these hard questions to answer. Yet, if you do not answer the question, you may find yourself in a no-win situation. Imagine that a client calls you in for warranty service on a drive that broke during use. If it appears that the client broke the part, you might feel he or she should pay for it. On the other hand, the client may have used the part in the manner prescribed by the vendor. The vendor may make it so poorly that there is no way to use the part without breaking it. What if this is a very expensive part and the vendor has a reputation for not honoring their warranty? (This happens more often than you might think with inexpensive parts.) If you perform the warranty service, you will lose money on the job. On the other hand, if you don't provide warranty service, you will lose a valuable client.

The same problems hold true for a consultant that offers training services. How much additional training time does a client deserve when it becomes obvious he or she didn't learn what you meant to

teach them? While this type of claim by the client doesn't fall in the realm of warranty service, you may still find yourself providing the client with some free training time to maintain a good relationship. You must always honor any guarantee you provide, whether it is a guarantee on a part or for a service. Fortunately, it is a lot easier to maintain control over the training situation than it is for the networking consultant.

Perhaps the most difficult part of being a professional is figuring out when actions on your part could prevent a situation from happening at all. For example, in our previous example you might choose to use a higher-quality part during installation. The higher-quality part might last longer, and you wouldn't need to figure out whether to honor your warranty. Because you used a higher-quality part, both you and the client are happy with the results. Setting a standard for yourself may cause you to lose a few jobs because you can't compete on cost, but it may prevent you from losing money later when the inexpensive parts break down. Every job has potential risks and paybacks. The professional weighs the cost of each action during a job and chooses the course that produces the best long-term results.

Professionalism is important for another reason. When people see you as a technician certified by Microsoft to maintain their network, they expect a higher standard of service than they would get from just anybody. After all, you convinced the client to pay you a higher hourly rate based on the assumption that they would receive better service. You are supposed to represent the best that the client can get in regard to quality workmanship. Your certification proves that you care more about how people perceive your services than the person who does not choose to get certified. When you are on the job you represent not only yourself, but every other certified individual who follows you.

As you can see, professionalism is not a mere word. It represents a way of doing business and a particular mind set. There are many "experts" performing network installations and providing training services today, but few professionals. You need to work to maintain the professional mind set as your career progresses if you expect people to regard you as something more than a hammer mechanic or

a parrot who reads from the manual. Maintaining such a high standard is hard work, but it pays many dividends.

So what will professionalism buy you? It may buy you some peace of mind. Peace of mind may not seem like very much until you face hostile clients a few times. A professional gets a happy greeting from the client every time he or she goes in to do work. The reason is simple; the client knows that the professional will do the best job possible to get the network up and running and get the employees trained to use any new applications. More important than a great customer relationship, professionalism will buy you customer loyalty. Customer loyalty translates into regular paychecks with a lot less effort than finding a new client. Every time you have to find a new client, you need to set up a new contract, get to know the installation, and perform a lot of unpaid work. This really reduces the benefit you see from working for the client. It isn't until you work for the client for a while that the relationship begins to pay off. (This does not mean that one-time jobs are not profitable; it simply means that long-term relationships are even more profitable.)

Even if professionalism is old-fashioned, people still respect it and look for it whenever possible. They want to know someone who takes the time to get the job done right the first time. Any other course of action is a waste of their time, your time, and materials, and reduces the impact of your certification. Remember, you worked hard to become certified by Microsoft to do the work you do. Keep up the good work. Maintain your professionalism.

A

Important phone numbers

CompuServe Registration: See your start-up kit for instructions.

✳ **Drake testing registration**

(800) 755-EXAM

✳ **Microsoft certified professional sales team**

(800) 636-7544

✳ **Microsoft consulting services**

Australia: (2) 870-2200
Brazil: (11) 530-4455
Canada: (416) 568-0434
France: (1) 6986-4480
Germany: (89) 3176-0
Hong Kong: (852) 804-4200
Italy: (2) 210-7361
Mexico: (5) 325-09-10
Singapore: (65) 227-6833
Sweden: (46) (8) 752-5600
United Kingdom: (734) 270-001
United States: (800) 922-9446

✳ **Microsoft developer network**

(800) 759-5474

✳ **Microsoft download service (BBS)**

United States: (206) 936-6735
Canada: (905) 507-3022

✳ **Microsoft education services**

United States: (800) 277-4679
Canada: (800) 563-9048

✳ **Microsoft FastTips service (FAX Back)**

Desktop Applications: (800) 936-4100
Personal Operating Systems: (800) 936-4200
Development: (800) 936-4300
Advanced Systems: (800) 936-4400

✳ **Microsoft general sales**

United States: (800) 426-9400
Canada: (800) 563-9048

✳ **Microsoft sales**

(800) 227-4679

✳ **Microsoft solution providers**

(800) SOL-PROV

✳ **Microsoft subsidiary offices**

Albania: 089/3176-0
All Other Countries: 1-206-936-8661
Argentina: (54) (1) 814-0356
Australia: (612) 870-2200
Austria: (43) (1) 68-76-07
Belgium: (32) (2) 7303911
Bolivia: (54) (1) 814-0356
Brazil: (55) (11) 530-4455
Bulgaria: 089/3176-0
Canada: 1-416-568-0434
Central America: (52) (5) 325-0910/11
Chile: (56) (2) 218-5771
China: (86) (1) 849-2148-50
Colombia: (57) (1) 618-2245
Croatia: 089/3176-0

Czech Republic: (42) (2) 268-320
Denmark: (45) 44-89-01-00
Ecuador: (59) (3) (2) 460-447/451/452/453/454/455
England: (44) (734) 270000
Estonia: (007) (095) 262-1213/1013 (Local Use Only)
Finland: (90) 525-501
France: (33) (1) 69-86-46-46
French Polynesia: (33) (1) 69-86-46-46
Germany: (49) (89) 3176-0
Greece: (30) (1) 6893-631
Hong Kong: (85) (2) 804-4200
Iceland: (45) 44-89-01-00
India: 91-11-644-4457
Indonesia: (65) 227-6833
Israel: (972) (3) 575-7034
Italy: (39) (2) 369121
Japan: (81) (3) 5454-8000
Korea: (82) (2) 552-9505
Latvia: (007) (095) 262-1213/1013 (Local Use Only)
Liechtenstein: (41) (1) 839-61-11
Lithuania: (007) (095) 262-1213/1013 (Local Use Only)
Luxembourg: (32) (2) 7303911
Malaysia: (603) 230-0299
Mexico: (52) (5) 325-0910/11
Middle East: (971) (4) 513-888
The Netherlands: (31) 2503-89189
New Zealand: (64) (9) 358-3724/5
Northern Ireland: (44) (734) 270000
Norway: (47) (22) 02-2500
Papau New Guinea: (612) 870-2200
Paraguay: (54) (1) 814-0356
Peru: (59) (3) (2) 460-447/451/452/453/454/455
Phillipines: (65) 227-6833
Poland: (48) (2) 661-54-33
Portugal: (351) (1) 4412205
Republic of Ireland: (44) (734) 270000
Romania: 089/3176-0
Russia: (007) (095) 262-1213/1013 (Local Use Only)
Scotland: (44) (734) 270000
Serbia: 089/3176-0
Singapore: (65) 227-6833
Slovakia: (42) (2) 268-320
Slovenia: 089/3176-0
South Africa (All Countries): (27) (11) 444-0520
Spain: (34) (1) 804-0000
Sweden: (46) (8) 752-56-00

Switzerland: (41) (1) 839-61-11
Taiwan (ROC): (866) (2) 504-3122
Thailand: (662) 231-3920/1/2/3
Uruguay: (54) (1) 814-0356
Venezuela: (58) (2) 91-64-43/33-42
Wales: (44) (734) 270000

✳ Microsoft technical information network

United States: (800) 344-2121 (Ext 455)
Outside the United States: 1-206-936-8661

B

Sources of additional information

It's essential to know where to get additional information about your trade. This appendix provides a few sources you can tap for information. Of course, this list is far from comprehensive. There are literally thousands of sources you can use to improve your knowledge. The following tips will help you find these additional sources and improve the level of information you get from them.

Always make certain that you keep your specific needs in mind when looking for a new source. This is the information age, and it lives up to its name. You can bury yourself in information, yet not improve your business one iota. The secret to success is to make very narrow searches for the information you need.

The best way to find sources of information that don't appear in this appendix is to ask your friends or members of the local user group. You can also check on-line services like CompuServe. Many of the forums can provide you with a wealth of information and ideas on where to find more.

Once you meet your basic information needs, it's time to look beyond at other sources of information. This keeps you from stagnating and helps you improve the number and types of services you can offer.

Never take someone else's word for it when it comes to the information you need. Read the front matter of a book and look through the table of contents before you buy. Don't settle for a quick sweep of the book. The same holds true for magazines. Look through the magazine to see what topics it covers. Read the editor's column to see what direction the magazine is taking. Always check out at least three editions of the magazine before you order a subscription.

Now that you have some of the basics down, look through the following list. It's organized by type of information to make it easy to find what you need. Remember, if you don't see it here, it probably does exist, but you'll need to look for it yourself.

Books

Books are a difficult thing to generalize. What appeals to one person may not appeal to someone else. It is imperative that you really look at what a book has to offer before you buy. Of course, you don't have to read the book. Just look at the front matter and table of contents to see if the book contains the type of information you need. Check out random sections to see if you like the author's writing style. It also pays to look at the tables and figures to make sure you can understand what they have to offer. Make sure you download a copy of Microsoft's Certification Road Map from CompuServe to obtain a complete list of book offerings from Microsoft Press. Chapter 7 provides complete details on how you can use CompuServe to best advantage.

Hands-On Guide To Network Management
Windcrest/McGraw-Hill
Blue Ridge Summit, PA 17294-0850
Ph. (717) 794-2191
ISBN # 0-8306-4440-7

Magazines

Magazines are a semipermanent form of information. You usually get them on a subscription basis once a month or every other month. They don't have the longevity of books, but they can provide those missing pieces of information that you can't find elsewhere. They also provide a secondary source of news you can use to keep up to date. While the news in a magazine is not as current as the material that you'll find in the trade newspapers, it usually contains a lot more detailed information.

There are quite a few things you need to check when considering a magazine. First, what direction does the editor intend to take? You need to ask this question, because the editor normally decides what material the magazine will present. Second, individual authors decide what bias the articles in the magazine present. In an ideal world, no one would have any bias at all when it came to presenting product information; you would always receive the most objective information possible. In reality, every author has a specific style and bias when writing. You need to decide whether or not this bias coincides with your view of the computing arena. Look at the writing style to make sure you can understand what the author intends to say. Finally, you need to determine how much information you receive for your investment. If you find that each issue provides

only one or two articles of interest, you may want to consider some other form of information input. Strive for a usage level of 25% to 30% when looking for a magazine to read.

Computer Technology Review
924 Westwood Blvd. Suite 650
Los Angeles, CA 90024-2910
Ph. (310) 208-1335

Data Communications
1221 Avenue of the Americas
New York, NY 10020
Ph. (800) 525-5003

Data Based Advisor
Data Based Solutions, Inc.
4010 Morena Boulevard
Suite 200
San Diego, CA 92117
Ph. (619) 483-6400
Fax (619) 483-9851

PC Magazine
Ziff-Davis Publishing Co.
One Park Avenue
New York, NY 10016
Ph. (212) 503-5255

PC Novice
Reed Corporation
120 West Harvest Drive
PO Box 85380
Lincoln, NE 68501
Ph. (800) 544-1264

Systems Integration
Cahners Publishing Associates/
Reed Publishing (USA), Inc.
275 Washington Street
Newton, MA 02158
Ph. (617) 964-3030
Fax (617) 558-4506

Trade papers

If you need up-to-date news about product releases or the latest technology, then you need to look at one of the trade newspapers (or trade paper) on the market. These sources of information come out on a weekly or biweekly basis. In many cases you can get them in one of two ways: by paid subscription, or free. A trade paper will generally offer free subscriptions to qualified people. Everyone else has to purchase them. It is usually best to try for the free subscription first, even if you don't qualify.

Most trade papers offer a wide variety of news. They all have some type of orientation, but you can usually get what you need by reading one or perhaps two of them. For example, *LAN Times* specializes in network news; you probably won't find much application news here. *PC Week* is a lot more generalized. You will find the latest product information in here. This includes general network news, as well as specific application information. Look for a trade paper with the bias that best fits your business needs. In addition, check the quality and quantity of articles that you actually use. While this percentage will be a lot lower than for a magazine, you should still be able to use 10% of the information in a trade paper to make it worthwhile.

LAN Computing
Professional Press, Inc.
101 Witmer Road
Horsham, PA 19044
Ph. (215) 957-4269

LAN Technology
PO Box 52315
Boulder, CO 80321-2315
Ph. (800) 456-1654

LAN Times
Publication Office
1900 O'Farrell St., Suite 200
San Mateo, CA 94403
Ph. (800) 525-5003

Network Computing
CMP Publications
600 Community Dr.
Manhasset, NY 11030
Ph. (516) 562-5071

Network News
CNE Professional Association
Mail Stop E-31-1
122 E. 1700 S.
Provo, UT 84606-6194
Ph. (800) 926-3776

Network World
161 Worcester Road
Framingham, MA 01701-9172
Ph. (508) 820-7444

PC Week
Customer Service Department
PO Box 1770
Riverton, NJ 08077-7370
Ph. (609) 786-8230
Fax (609) 786-2081

CD-ROM references

This is a fairly new category of long-term information storage. Some CD-ROM references are a once-in-a-lifetime purchase, just like a book. In fact, you should use the same criteria for selecting one of these once-in-a-lifetime purchases as you would a book. Normally you find this information on the CD-ROM package rather than paging through the book. Other references are on a subscription basis like a magazine. These subscription services usually provide updates on a quarterly or semiannual basis. You should use the same criteria for selecting a subscription service as you would for a magazine.

Microsoft Developer Network Development Library
Microsoft Developer Network
One Microsoft Way
Redmond, WA 98052-6399
Ph. (800) 759-5474
Fax (206) 936-7329, Attn: Developer Network

C

Course descriptions

Appendix C provides you with a complete list of the Microsoft classes available to you. Some of the classes directly relate to the existing MCSE and MCPS certification programs. Other classes will come into play when Microsoft introduces its MCD program. All of these courses apply to the MCT. These classes always tell you about the related exam number. You can cross-reference this information with the certification requirements listed in Table 1-1. Another group of classes will appear in the developer certification that Microsoft is currently developing. They don't have exam numbers now, but will in a future edition of the book. Finally, there are some classes in this section that you could take for your own personal knowledge or as part of a job requirement. All of the course descriptions include information on the type of instruction you will receive and the concepts you will learn. They also include a list of the topics that each course covers. Unfortunately, each training center sets its own price. Call your local training center to obtain price and availability information.

Introduction to programming in Microsoft C

This course teaches the student how to create applications using Microsoft C. It is designed for programmers, system analysts, developers, and other support professionals. The course concentrates on the programming skills required to create applications using Microsoft C. This course provides a special emphasis on students who already know how to program in COBOL or Computer Associates' Clipper. Upon course completion, the student can develop simple applications using Microsoft C. This includes creating menu-driven front ends and other standard application constructs. The course topics include the following.

> History and anatomy of C programs
> Printing data to the screen
> Operators
> Flow control
> Functions
> Arrays and pointers
> Input and output
> Libraries
> Structures
> Solving common problems

This is an instructor-led course that concentrates on lecture and hands-on exercises. The overall course goal is to build competency in using Microsoft C. Subgoals include the ability to create very simple C applications.

The prerequisites for this course include at least six months programming experience on a minicomputer or mainframe (Xbase language programmers may not meet this requirement). A good knowledge of how to program in a high-level language like COBOL, Natural, dBASE, Clipper, or BASIC is also a requirement. This means that the student should know how to compile and link an application. Finally, a good knowledge of MS-DOS at the user level is also required for this course. The student can meet many of the prerequisites by completing Microsoft MS-DOS 6 Step-by-Step and Microsoft Windows Step-by-Step. You can purchase these self-paced tutorials by calling (800) MSPRESS and getting further details on these products.

Course length: 3 days
Course number: 85
Test number: N/A

New architectures for enterprise computing

This course provides a general survey of the concepts, terminology, and application of new technologies for enterprise computing. The course includes information about client-server systems, graphical user interfaces (GUIs), local area networks (LANs), and new application development environments. The course content is not limited to Microsoft products. Upon completion of this course, the student will understand enterprise computing from a management point of view. In other words, this course does not prepare you to become a networking technician. The course topics include the following.

> Business computer architectures
> Operating systems and environments
> Local and wide area networks
> Client-server systems

This is an instructor-led course consisting of lectures and team-building activities. The goal is to increase the knowledge level of the management of your company. It includes increasing the level and quality of communication between managers and the end-user community.

The prerequisites for this course include a general familiarity with computers and data processing. This means that you will need at least a fundamental understanding of client-server basics to gain the most from this course. A very basic knowledge of networks and operating systems is also helpful.

Course length: 3 days
Course number: 106
Test number: N/A

 # Managing the migration to client-server architectures

This course helps information systems managers, application development managers, project managers, systems analysts, systems architects, and other computing professionals make the transition between traditional and client-server computing. Upon course completion, the student will possess the knowledge required to implement a client-server system in their company. This includes an understanding of client-server development and deployment methodology and requirements. It also means that the student will fully understand the strategies required to manage a dispersed system that client-server computing represents. The course topics include the following.

- ➤ Definition of client-server computing
- ➤ Application architecture
- ➤ Data architecture
- ➤ Technical architecture
- ➤ Selecting candidates for client-server applications
- ➤ Organizational roles and issues
- ➤ Production framework
- ➤ Application framework
- ➤ Client-server system development life cycle

This is an instructor-led course consisting of lectures and case studies designed to help managers change from traditional systems architectures to client-server architectures. It includes case studies that explore the development of an application, data, and technology architecture. The overall goal of the course is to provide managers the information they need to make the transition from mainframe computing to networks.

The prerequisites for this course include a basic understanding of the system development process and the components of client-server technology. This implies that you have a better-than-average understanding of what client-server

computing involves and are fully aware of the terms used within that environment. You should also take the "New architectures for enterprise computing" course (course number 106) or view the *Understanding New Technologies* video series (course number 295).

Course length: 3 days
Course number: 124
Test number: N/A

 # User interface design workshop

This is a one-day course designed to help user and programmer alike know the difference between a useful and an unusable interface. It does not include any programming-specific information; the student will not use any type of language product during the course. Upon course completion, the student will know what constitutes a user-friendly interface. This includes such diverse concepts as color coordination and screen organization. The course also explores subjects like what constitutes the look and feel of an application. The course topics include the following.

> ➢ Designing the interface
> ➢ Graphic design: developing the look and feel of an application
> ➢ Usability testing

This is an instructor-led course consisting of lectures and hands-on sessions. It also explores the book *The Windows Interface: An Application Design Guide* from Microsoft Press. This book provides the reference material required by the student after he/she completes the course. The overall goal of this course is to teach the student the basics of interface design. It does not teach how to actually program an interface.

The prerequisites for this course include knowing how to use some basic Windows applications. It is the insight of application use from the user point of view that makes this course unique. A good understanding of several products from various vendors is very useful, but not required.

Course length: 1 day
Course number: 126
Test number: N/A

 # Inter-networking with Microsoft TCP/IP

This course teaches the student about the inter-networking capabilities of Microsoft TCP/IP protocols and utilities in a Microsoft LAN Manager environment. It is designed for developers, network integrators, systems

engineers, and other support professionals. The course concentrates on the skills required to use Microsoft TCP/IP in local and wide area networks. Upon course completion, the student can install, optimize, customize, and support Microsoft TCP/IP in local and wide area networks. This includes the ability to define a subnet mask and IP address range for multiple TCP/IP networks, install and use Microsoft SNMP service with a third-party SNMP manager to monitor network activity, use Microsoft TCP/IP utilities to connect to and use resources on TCP/IP-based host computers, and diagnose and solve TCP/IP-related problems. The course topics include the following.

- ➤ Introduction to Microsoft TCP/IP
- ➤ IP Addressing concepts and implementations
- ➤ Resolving TCP/IP names and addresses
- ➤ Performance optimization and configuration
- ➤ Connectivity solutions
- ➤ Network management with the SNMP protocol
- ➤ Troubleshooting the Microsoft TCP/IP protocols and utilities

This is an instructor-led course that concentrates on lecture, labs, and hands-on exercises. The overall course goal is to build competency in installing, customizing, and supporting Microsoft TCP/IP. Subgoals include the ability to troubleshoot TCP/IP-related problems.

The prerequisites for this course include completion of the "Advanced network administration for Microsoft LAN Manager" course (number 239) or equivalent knowledge. The student must know how to install, configure, and perform basic maintenance for a LAN Manager network. In addition, the student must understand LAN hardware, including network interface cards, bridges, and routers.

Course length: 2 days
Course number: 146
Test number: N/A

 # Performance-tuning and optimization of Microsoft SQL Server

This course teaches the student how to optimize and tune a SQL Server implementation. It is designed for server database owners, designers, system analysts, developers, and other support professionals. The course concentrates on the skills required to perform this task. Upon course completion, the student can tune SQL Server to achieve the best performance in a multiuser transaction processing and decision support environment. This includes diagnosing and resolving performance problems based on specific performance needs. The course topics include the following.

- ➤ Overview of performance issues
- ➤ Platform optimization

➤ Denormalization for performance
➤ Data storage structures
➤ Selecting indexes for queries
➤ The query optimizer overview
➤ Phases of query optimization
➤ Processing strategies of the query optimizer
➤ Using stored procedures
➤ Database consistency and concurrency
➤ Other performance issues
➤ Problem analysis

This is an instructor-led course that concentrates on lectures, labs, and hands-on exercises. The overall course goal is to build competency in tuning SQL Server. Subgoals include building the knowledge level required to optimize database design, design indexes, write queries, and use various optimization tools.

The prerequisites for this course include a familiarity with the relational database concepts originally presented by E. F. Codd. You must complete the "Microsoft SQL server 4.2 implementation" course or equivalent. The student should also know how to create devices and segments, back up and recover data, and import and export data using the Bulk Copy utility. You must have at least six months worth of Microsoft SQL Server experience, experience in analyzing, designing, configuring, and tuning databases, and experience with SQL or ISQL Administrator, or SAF.

Course length: 5 days
Course number: 153
Test number: N/A

Programming in Microsoft C

This course teaches the student how to create applications using Microsoft C. It is designed for programmers, system analysts, developers, and other support professionals. This course is the follow-up to "Introduction to Microsoft C" (course number 85). The course concentrates on the programming skills required to create applications using Microsoft C. This course provides a special emphasis on ANSI C and the Microsoft add-ons to this language standard. Upon course completion, the student can develop simple to complex applications using Microsoft C. This includes creating menu-driven front ends and other standard application constructs. The student will also gain a familiarity with many of the tools provided with the Microsoft C compiler. The course topics include the following.

➤ Common elements of a program
➤ C data types
➤ Getting and displaying text
➤ Control statements
➤ Functions and prototypes

> Identifier scope and storage class
> Working with macros
> Working with files
> Using standard in and standard out
> Single-dimension arrays
> Pointers
> Using pointers to modify arguments
> Common string functions
> Arrays of pointers
> Pointers and memory models
> Bitwise operators
> Dynamic memory allocation
> Structures and unions
> Linked lists
> Function pointers
> Bitfields
> Advanced uses of the Microsoft compiler and linker
> NMAKE and Make files
> Using the Microsoft Visual Workbench Debugger
> Microsoft LIB utility
> Using the Microsoft EXEHDR utility
> Naming conventions

This is an instructor-led course that concentrates on lecture and hands-on exercises. The overall course goal is to build competency in using Microsoft C. Subgoals include the ability to create simple to complex C applications and an ability to use all the Microsoft-supplied utility programs.

The prerequisites for this course include familiarity with a high-level language like FORTRAN, Pascal, or PL/1. Experience with Macro Assembler will meet this requirement as well. The student should know how to work with binary and hexadecimal numbers. The "Introduction to Microsoft C" course is recommended, but not required.

Course length: 5 days
Course number: 155
Test number: N/A

Microsoft SQL Server 4.2 implementation

This course teaches the student how to implement an SQL Server solution. It is designed for programmers, system analysts, developers, and other support professionals. The course concentrates on the programming skills required to perform this task. Upon course completion, the student can develop complex applications using SQL Server by writing Transact-SQL-code. This includes creating database devices, databases, and tables. The student will also be able to

write Transact-SQL statements to perform all the normal functions required by a database management system including data import and export. The course topics include the following.

- ➤ Data modeling
- ➤ Data definition
- ➤ Data manipulation
- ➤ Indexes
- ➤ Views
- ➤ Defaults and rules
- ➤ Programmability
- ➤ Triggers
- ➤ Server options
- ➤ Performance optimization
- ➤ Application development and open data services

This is an instructor-led course that concentrates on lecture and hands-on exercises. The overall course goal is to build competency in creating applications for SQL Server.

The prerequisites for this course include a familiarity with the relational database concepts originally presented by E. F. Codd. One month's experience with OS/2 and Microsoft LAN Manager is also required. The student should also have some experience with SQL-Administrator or ISQL and the Microsoft Windows operating system.

Course length: 5 days
Course number: 158
Test number: 70-21

 # Microsoft Windows 3.1 for support professionals

This course teaches the student how to set up Microsoft Windows 3.1 and assist users in its use. It is designed for developers and other support professionals. The course concentrates on the training skills required to perform this task. Upon course completion, the student can install, optimize, customize, and support Windows version 3.1. This includes product installation over a network. The course topics include the following.

- ➤ Introduction to Windows 3.1
- ➤ Examining the Windows environment
- ➤ Memory use with Windows
- ➤ Optimizing Windows
- ➤ Customizing Windows initialization (INI) files
- ➤ Running MS-DOS-based applications in Windows
- ➤ Customizing MS-DOS-based application sessions

➢ Sharing data between applications
➢ Registration editor
➢ Fonts used by Windows
➢ Customizing Windows setup
➢ Troubleshooting Windows
➢ Windows operation on a network
➢ Network setup and administration
➢ Specific network topics related to Windows

This is an instructor-led course that concentrates on lecture, labs, and hands-on exercises. The overall course goal is to build competency in installing, customizing, and supporting Windows 3.1. Subgoals include the ability to troubleshoot user-related problems.

The prerequisites for this course include familiarity with installing Windows 3.0 or later. The student must know how to work with PC end-users. In addition, the student must possess an operational understanding of the following topics: BIOS, memory, hard disks, types of CPUs, communication ports, printer ports, display adapters, and network hardware. Finally, the student must have a working knowledge of MS-DOS. The student can meet the MS-DOS knowledge portion of the prerequisites by completing *Microsoft MS-DOS 6 Step-by-Step*, a self-paced tutorial. Call (800) MSPRESS for further details on this product.

Course length: 4 days
Course number: 161
Test number: N/A

Application development using Microsoft Excel

This course teaches the student how to create applications using Microsoft Excel. It is designed for programmers, system analysts, developers, and other support professionals. The course concentrates on the programming skills required to perform this task. Upon course completion, the student can develop complex applications using Microsoft Excel. This includes creating menu-driven front ends, interfacing to other applications, and other standard Windows application constructs. The course topics include the following.

➢ Introduction to using a spreadsheet as a development tool
➢ Getting started with the macro language
➢ Macro language syntax
➢ Looping, control, and user input
➢ Creating dialog boxes
➢ Menus, toolbars, and buttons
➢ Talking to other applications with DDE and OLE automation
➢ Polishing your application

This is an instructor-led course that concentrates on lecture and hands-on exercises. The overall course goal is to build competency in creating applications around the Excel spreadsheet.

The prerequisites for this course include a good familiarity with spreadsheets in general, and Excel specifically. The student must know how to create and maintain spreadsheet databases and other complex structures. A basic computer science background is a plus, but not required. The student can meet many of the prerequisites by completing *Microsoft Excel Step-by-Step*, a self-paced tutorial. Call (800) MSPRESS for further details on this product.

Course length: 4 days
Course number: 164
Test number: N/A

 # Supporting Microsoft Windows for Workgroups

This course teaches the student how to set up Microsoft Windows for Workgroups and assist users in its use. It is designed for developers and other support professionals. The course concentrates on the training skills required to perform this task. Upon course completion, the student can install, optimize, customize, and support Windows for Workgroups. This includes setup, installation, and troubleshooting of the workgroup network, workgroup electronic mail post office, and shared workgroup scheduler. It also includes an understanding of how multiple Windows for Workgroups networks interoperate and how to administer security. The course topics include the following.

- ➢ Introduction to Windows
- ➢ Examining the Windows environment
- ➢ Memory use with Windows
- ➢ Optimizing Windows
- ➢ Customizing Windows initialization (INI) files
- ➢ Running and customizing MS-DOS-based applications in Windows
- ➢ Fonts used by Windows
- ➢ Data sharing and registration editor
- ➢ Customizing Windows setup
- ➢ Troubleshooting Windows
- ➢ Setting up Windows for Workgroups
- ➢ Windows for Workgroups architecture
- ➢ Mail and Schedule+
- ➢ Sharing information between PCs
- ➢ Securing the system
- ➢ Customization and optimization
- ➢ Network interoperability
- ➢ Workgroup design and implementation

This is an instructor-led course that concentrates on lecture, labs, and hands-on exercises. The overall course goal is to build competency in installing, customizing, and supporting Windows for Workgroups. Subgoals include the ability to troubleshoot user-related problems.

The prerequisites for this course include familiarity installing Windows 3.0 or later, or Windows for Workgroups. The student must know how to work with PC end-users. In addition, the student must possess an operational understanding of the following topics: BIOS, memory, hard disks, types of CPUs, communication ports, printer ports, display adapters, and network hardware. Finally, the student must have a working knowledge of MS-DOS. The student can meet the MS-DOS knowledge portion of the prerequisites by completing *Microsoft MS-DOS 6 Step-by-Step*, a self-paced tutorial. Call (800) MSPRESS for further details on this product.

Course length: 5 days
Course number: 178
Test number: 70-45

Programming for Microsoft Win32

This course teaches the student how to create 32-bit applications for Microsoft Windows NT using C. The course also shows how to port existing 16-bit applications to the 32-bit environment. Ported applications will use threads, structured exception handling, and asynchronous I/O. It is designed for experienced Windows programmers, system analysts, developers, and other support professionals. The course concentrates on the programming skills required to perform this task. Upon course completion, the student can develop complex applications using Microsoft C. This includes creating menu-driven front ends, interfacing to other applications, and other standard 32-bit Windows application constructs. The course topics include the following.

➢ Architectural overview topics
➢ Porting
➢ Design goals, objects, and the registry
➢ Structured exception handling
➢ Getting/starting a process
➢ Threads and synchronization
➢ Standard I/O
➢ Memory management
➢ Dynamic-Link Libraries (DLLs)
➢ Performance measurement tools for Win32-based applications
➢ Remote procedure calls (RPCs)
➢ Internationalization and unicode
➢ Win32s

This is an instructor-led course that concentrates on lecture, lab sessions, and hands-on exercises. The overall course goal is to build competency in creating applications for the Win32 environment.

The prerequisites for this course include six months experience writing C applications. The student must successfully complete one of the following courses: "Programming for the Microsoft Windows environment" (course number 303), "Exploring programming for Microsoft Windows 3.1: video training for developers" (course number 297), or six months of 16-bit Windows event-driven application programming experience. Other requirements include experience using the Microsoft Windows interface and an operational understanding of Windows environment programming constructs and theory. This includes the following concepts: messaging, objects, DLLs, switch statements, C pointers, define statements, and debugging.

Course length: 4 days
Course number: 210
Test number: N/A

 # Supporting Microsoft Windows NT

This course teaches the student how to set up, install, implement, and support Windows NT. It is designed for developers and other support professionals. The course concentrates on the skills required to perform this task within the workgroup environment. Upon course completion, the student can install, configure, troubleshoot, and optimize a Windows NT installation on the workstation and within the workgroup. The student will also possess a fundamental understanding of the network connectivity features of Windows NT.

➤ Windows NT architecture overview
➤ Installing Windows NT
➤ Booting Windows NT
➤ Configuring Windows NT
➤ Security architecture overview
➤ Setting up user and group accounts
➤ Managing files
➤ Running applications on Windows NT
➤ Printing from Windows NT
➤ Administering mail and schedule+
➤ Configuring multiple disks
➤ Backing up and restoring files
➤ Performance optimization and tuning
➤ Configuring the Windows NT network components
➤ Network interoperability
➤ Troubleshooting

This is an instructor-led course that concentrates on lectures, labs, and hand-on exercises within a workgroup. The overall course goal is to build competency in

installing, configuring, optimizing, and troubleshooting a Windows NT installation. Subgoals include building a basic knowledge of the network connectivity features of Windows NT.

The prerequisites for this course include familiarity with using or administering a network operating system like Novell Netware, Microsoft LAN Manager, or UNIX. You must have experience installing and using Microsoft Windows version 3.1. The student must also possess an understanding of the following topics: MS-DOS, BIOS, memory, hard disks, types of CPUs, communications ports, printer ports, display adapters, workstations, servers, LANs, shared resources, and user-level connectivity.

Course length: 5 days
Course number: 211
Test number: 70-40

 # System administration for Microsoft SQL Server for Windows NT

This course teaches the student how to implement an SQL Server solution that runs under Microsoft Windows NT. It is designed for programmers, system analysts, developers, and other support professionals. The course concentrates on the programming skills required to perform this task. Upon course completion, the student can install SQL Server for Windows NT. This includes creating database devices, databases, and tables. The student will also be able to manage user accounts and permissions, import and export data using the Bulk Copy utility, manage remote servers and logons, troubleshoot system problems, and set server, database, and configuration options to fine-tune performance. The course topics include the following.

> SQL Server features
> Installing SQL Server
> SQL Server integration with the Windows NT environment
> System administration tools
> Managing storage
> Backup and recovery
> Managing user accounts
> Managing user permissions
> Monitoring SQL Server activity
> Fine-tuning
> Data import and export
> Diagnosing system problems
> Managing remote servers
> Extended stored procedures

This is an instructor-led course that concentrates on lecture, labs, demos, and hands-on exercises. The overall course goal is to build competency in administering SQL Server running under Windows NT.

The prerequisites for this course include a familiarity with the relational database concepts originally presented by E.F. Codd. The student must take the "Supporting Microsoft Windows NT" course (number 211) or have equivalent knowledge. In addition, the student must have experience using the Microsoft Windows operating system, have a knowledge of networking concepts like sharing and accessing network resources, and possess a basic knowledge of SQL syntax. The student can meet the Microsoft Windows prerequisites by completing *Microsoft Windows 3.1 Step-by-Step*, a self-paced tutorial. Call (800) MSPRESS for further details on this product.

Course length: 5 days
Course number: 213
Test number: 70-22 and 70-23

Microsoft SQL Server 4.2 system administration

This course teaches the student how to implement an SQL Server solution that runs under Microsoft LAN Manager. It is designed for programmers, system analysts, developers, and other support professionals. The course concentrates on the programming skills required to perform this task. Upon course completion, the student can install SQL Server for Windows NT. This includes creating database devices, databases, and tables. The student will also be able to manage user accounts and permissions, import and export data using the Bulk Copy utility, manage remote servers and logons, troubleshoot system problems, and set server, database, and configuration options to fine-tune performance. The course topics include the following.

> SQL Server features
> Installing SQL Server
> System administration tools
> Managing storage
> Backup and recovery
> Managing user accounts
> Managing user permissions
> Managing remote servers
> Fine-tuning
> Data import and export
> Diagnosing system problems

This is an instructor-led course that concentrates on lecture, labs, and hands-on exercises. The overall course goal is to build competency in administering SQL Server running under Microsoft LAN Manager.

The prerequisites for this course include a familiarity with the relational database concepts originally presented by E.F. Codd. The student must possess a basic knowledge of OS/2 and MS-DOS operating system commands. In addition, the student must have a knowledge of networking concepts like sharing and accessing network resources, and possess a basic knowledge of SQL syntax. LAN Manager experience is recommended, but not required to start the course.

Course length: 4 days
Course number: 214
Test number: 70-20

 # Advanced programming for developers on Microsoft FoxPro 2.5

This course teaches the student how to create applications using Microsoft FoxPro 2.5. The course concentrates on the programming skills required to perform this task. It starts where "Intermediate training for developers on Microsoft FoxPro 2.5" (course number 231) left off. The course is designed for programmers, system analysts, developers, and other support professionals. Upon course completion, the student can develop complex applications using Microsoft FoxPro 2.5. This includes creating menu-driven front ends, interfacing to other applications, and other standard Windows application constructs. The course concentrates on showing the student how to use DDE and OLE. It also provides instruction on the API and how to incorporate C routines into your application. The course topics include the following.

➢ Event-driven introduction
➢ Event-driven step 1: the event loop
➢ Event-driven step 2: modal sessions
➢ Event-driven step 3: semimodal sessions
➢ Event-driven step 4: leaving Windows on the desktop
➢ Event-driven step 5: returning to the previous session
➢ Event-driven step 6: remembering window locations
➢ Event-driven step 7: remembering variable values
➢ Event-driven step 8: closing leftover sessions
➢ Event-driven step 9: controlling browses
➢ Event-driven miscellaneous considerations
➢ Multiuser constructs, edit, add, delete, terminator, and multitable updates
➢ Transaction tracking
➢ Object Linking and Embedding (OLE)
➢ Dynamic Data Exchange (DDE)
➢ Incorporating C-language routines
➢ Advanced SQL-Select
➢ Advanced browse
➢ Data dictionaries
➢ Low-level file I/O
➢ Advanced indexing techniques

➤ Advanced Windows appearance management
➤ Project management and distribution

This is an instructor-led course that concentrates on lecture and hands-on exercises. The overall course goal is to build competency in creating advanced applications using Microsoft FoxPro 2.5. The course assumes that the programmer already possesses a basic understanding of Microsoft Windows programming concepts and wants to build on this knowledge base. It builds on material learned in previous courses.

The prerequisites for this course include the knowledge taught by course number 231. This includes an intimate familiarity with the Microsoft FoxPro command language and power tools. The student must know how to use Microsoft Windows 3.0 or later. A familiarity with a high-level programming language is good, but not required. A knowledge of event-driven programming techniques is a plus, but not required. Formal computer science training is a plus, but not absolutely required. However, such training is highly recommended.

Course length: 3 days
Course number: 230
Test number: N/A

 # Intermediate training for developers on Microsoft FoxPro 2.5

This course teaches the student how to create applications using Microsoft FoxPro 2.5. It is designed for programmers, system analysts, developers, and other support professionals. The course concentrates on the programming skills required to create applications using Microsoft FoxPro 2.5. This course provides a special emphasis on database management system skills. Upon course completion, the student can develop simple applications using Microsoft FoxPro 2.5. This includes creating menu-driven front ends and other standard Windows database application constructs. The training includes subjects like DDE, OLE, and using the utility programs that come with Microsoft FoxPro 2.5. The course topics include the following.

➤ Menu builder
➤ Control programs
➤ FoxPro and files
➤ Application event loops
➤ Data-entry screen design, controls, and architecture
➤ Input field validation
➤ Multiuser constructs, edit, add, and delete
➤ SQL select
➤ Basic report writer
➤ Enhanced data entry
➤ Array handling
➤ Screen sets

➢ Windows
➢ Browse basics
➢ Lookups and search routines
➢ Multifile constructs, data entry, SQL select, and RQBE
➢ Embedded browse
➢ Advanced Report Writer
➢ Non-SQL queries and performance
➢ Error trapping
➢ Debugging tools
➢ Context Sensitive Help
➢ Microsoft Windows Objects and applications
➢ Cross-platform issues

This is an instructor-led course that concentrates on lecture and hands-on exercises. The overall course goal is to build competency in using Microsoft FoxPro 2.5. Subgoals include the ability to create simple to intermediate-complexity FoxPro 2.5 applications.

The prerequisites for this course include a little familiarity with databases in general and FoxPro 2.5 in particular. A general knowledge of the Xbase programming language is also required. The student must possess a good knowledge of how to use Microsoft Windows. The student can meet many of the prerequisites by completing *Microsoft Windows 3.1 Step-by-Step* and *Microsoft FoxPro 2.5 Step-by-Step*. Both products are self-paced tutorials. Call (800) MSPRESS for further details on this product.

Course length: 5 days
Course number: 231
Test number: N/A

 # Advanced programming using Microsoft Access

This course teaches the student how to create applications using Microsoft Access. The course concentrates on the programming skills required to perform this task. It starts where "Introduction to Microsoft Access" (course number 233) left off. The course is designed for programmers, system analysts, developers, and other support professionals. Upon course completion, the student can develop complex applications using Microsoft Access. This includes creating menu-driven front ends, interfacing to other applications, and other standard Windows application constructs. The course concentrates on showing the student how to use both the macro and Basic programming capability of Access. The course topics include the following.

➢ Advanced forms
➢ Macros
➢ Modules (Microsoft Access Basic)

251

This is an instructor-led course that concentrates on lecture and hands-on exercises. The overall course goal is to build competency in creating advanced applications using Microsoft Access. The course assumes that the programmer already possesses a basic understanding of Microsoft Windows programming concepts and wants to build on this knowledge base. It builds on material learned in previous courses.

The prerequisites for this course include the knowledge taught by course number 233. The student must know how to use Microsoft Windows 3.0 or later. A familiarity with a high-level programming language is good, but not required. A knowledge of event-driven programming techniques is a plus, but not required. Formal computer science training is a plus, but not absolutely required. However, such training is highly recommended.

Course length: 3 days
Course number: 232
Test number: N/A

 # Introduction to Microsoft Access

This course teaches the student how to create applications using Microsoft Access. It is designed for programmers, system analysts, developers, and other support professionals. The course concentrates on the programming skills required to create applications using Microsoft Access. This course provides a special emphasis on database management system skills. Upon course completion, the student can develop simple applications using Microsoft Access. This includes creating menu-driven front ends and other standard Windows database application constructs. It does not teach either DDE or OLE concepts. The course topics include the following:

> ➢ Microsoft Access fundamentals
> ➢ Microsoft Access user interface
> ➢ Table design
> ➢ Defining relationships
> ➢ Using existing data
> ➢ Looking at data (queries)
> ➢ Reports
> ➢ Form basics

This is an instructor-led course that concentrates on lecture and hands-on exercises. The overall course goal is to build competency in using Microsoft Access. Subgoals include the ability to create very simple Access applications.

The prerequisites for this course include a little familiarity with databases in general and Access in particular. A good knowledge of how to use Microsoft Windows is also a requirement. The student can meet many of the prerequisites by completing *Microsoft Access Step-by-Step*, a self-paced tutorial. Call (800) MSPRESS for further details on this product.

Course length: 3 days
Course number: 233
Test number: N/A

 # Microsoft LAN Manager 2.2 for network administrators

This course teaches the student how to implement and support Microsoft LAN Manager 2.2. It is designed for developers, network administrators, integrators, systems and support engineers, and other support professionals. The course concentrates on the skills required to perform these tasks. Upon course completion, the student can install, optimize, customize, and support LAN Manager 2.2 with the OS/2 server edition. This includes implementing security, managing and administering network resources, allocating memory for best performance, and troubleshooting and diagnosing LAN Manager hardware and software problems. The course topics include the following.

➢ Introduction to Microsoft LAN Manager
➢ The OS/2 Server edition
➢ Installing Microsoft LAN Manager
➢ What is network administration
➢ Using user-level security
➢ LAN Manager resources
➢ Using logon security
➢ Local security
➢ Installing a printer
➢ Other security options
➢ Advanced LAN Manager features
➢ Replication
➢ Network reliability and integrity
➢ Architecture and standards
➢ Connectivity
➢ Tuning LAN Manager
➢ Troubleshooting
➢ MS-DOS memory management
➢ Installing MS-DOS LAN Manager
➢ Overview of Microsoft Windows in a network environment

This is an instructor-led course that concentrates on lecture, labs, and hands-on exercises. The overall course goal is to build competency in installing, customizing, and supporting Microsoft LAN Manager 2.2. Subgoals include the ability to troubleshoot user-related problems.

The prerequisites for this course include at least three months experience using OS/2. This means that you have more than a passing knowledge of the various configuration options that this environment offers. The student also needs

experience using a graphical user interface like the one provided by Microsoft Windows or the OS/2 Workplace Shell.

Course length: 5 days
Course number: 235
Test number: 70-10

 # Inter-Networking with Microsoft TCP/IP using Microsoft Windows NT

This course teaches the student how to install, configure, test, and manage TCP/IP using Microsoft Windows NT in local and wide area networks. It is designed for developers, integrators, systems engineers, and other support professionals. The course concentrates on the skills required to perform a variety of TCP/IP-related tasks. Upon course completion, the student can install, configure, and test Microsoft TCP/IP. The student can also define a subnet mask and IP address range for multiple TCP/IP networks, view and modify the ARP cache using the ARP utility, implement IP routing on a Windows NT-based system, configure the HOSTS file to map host names to IP addresses, configure the LMHOSTS file to map NetBIOS names to IP addresses, install and configure the Microsoft FTP server, use Microsoft TCP/IP utilities to transfer files, install and configure the Microsoft SNMP service, performance-tune Microsoft TCP/IP, and use Microsoft utilities to diagnose and solve TCP/IP-related problems. Other skills include the ability to run commands, initiate remote login sessions, and perform terminal emulation using a TCP/IP-based host.

> Introduction to TCP/IP
> IP addressing
> Subnet addressing
> Implementing IP routing on Windows NT
> IP address resolution
> Host name resolution
> NetBIOS name resolution
> Connectivity in heterogeneous environments
> Implementing the Microsoft SNMP service
> Performance tuning and optimization
> Troubleshooting Microsoft TCP/IP

This is an instructor-led course that concentrates on lectures, labs, and hands-on exercises. The overall course goal is to build competency in inter-networking with Microsoft TCP/IP using Windows NT. Subgoals include building the knowledge level required to install, configure, tune, test, maintain, and troubleshoot Microsoft TCP/IP.

The prerequisites for this course include completion of the "Supporting Microsoft Windows NT" course (number 211) or equivalent knowledge.

Course length: 3 days
Course number: 236
Test number: N/A

 Managing Microsoft Windows NT Advanced Server

This course teaches the student about the interoperability, connectivity, and fault-tolerance capabilities of Microsoft Windows NT. It is designed for developers, system administrators, and other support professionals. The course concentrates on building the knowledge level of the support professional. Upon course completion, the student will possess an in-depth knowledge of these advanced topics. The student will also possess the knowledge required to set up and configure Microsoft Windows NT Advanced Server. This includes the ability to implement, support, and administer Windows NT Advanced Server in the network environment. The course covers the following topics:

- ➢ The workgroup model
- ➢ The four Advanced Server domain models
- ➢ The single domain model
- ➢ Installing Windows NT Advanced Server
- ➢ The Windows NT Advanced Server technical overview
- ➢ Managing the domain
- ➢ Trust relationships
- ➢ Groups
- ➢ The master domain model
- ➢ The multiple master domain model
- ➢ The complete trust model
- ➢ The user environment
- ➢ Protecting server data
- ➢ Monitoring and troubleshooting a Windows NT Advanced Server
- ➢ Directory replication
- ➢ MS-DOS and Windows-based client interoperability
- ➢ The remote access service
- ➢ Macintosh connectivity (optional)
- ➢ Administration

This is an instructor-led course that concentrates on lectures and hands-on exercises. The overall course goal is to obtain an in-depth knowledge of Windows NT Advanced Server features including interoperability, connectivity, and fault-tolerance capabilities.

The prerequisites for this course include proficiency in installing and administering a network operating system. The student must also take the "Supporting Microsoft Windows NT" course (number 211) or possess equivalent knowledge.

Course length: 5 days
Course number: 237
Test number: 70-41

Advanced network administration of Microsoft LAN Manager 2.2

This course teaches the student advanced implementation and support details for Microsoft LAN Manager 2.2. It is designed for systems administrators and other support professionals who require advanced and in-depth knowledge of the interoperability, connectivity, and fault-tolerance capabilities of Microsoft LAN Manager. The course concentrates on the skills required to perform advanced administration tasks. Upon course completion, the student will understand how to tune LAN Manager file servers and MS-DOS workstations for maximum performance. The student will also know how to implement the advanced printing capabilities of LAN Manager to monitor network activity, use the vendor specific protocols that provide interoperability with Apple AppleTalk and Novell Netware, and configure and administer the LAN Manager Remote Access Server. The course topics include the following.

➤ Installing Microsoft LAN Manager
➤ Configuring the server
➤ Server tuning
➤ Workstation tuning and memory management
➤ Implementing and managing network printing
➤ Monitoring a LAN Manager workgroup network
➤ Macintosh connectivity
➤ Netware connectivity
➤ The basics of network expansion
➤ Microsoft Remote Access Server
➤ Troubleshooting

This is an instructor-led course that concentrates on lecture, labs, and hands-on exercises. The overall course goal is to build competency in advanced Microsoft LAN Manager administration and support functions. Subgoals include the ability to tune the network for maximum efficiency, connect it to other vendor networks, and troubleshoot any Microsoft LAN Manager-related problems.

The prerequisites for this course include completion of the Microsoft LAN Manager 2.1 or 2.2 for Network Administrator course or equivalent knowledge. The student must know how to install the Microsoft LAN Manager server and workstation software. In addition, the student must possess an operational understanding of basic administrative tasks like adding users and groups, creating shares for file resources and assigning permissions, adding network printers and communication devices, and installing primary and backup domain controllers. Finally, the student must possess a good understanding of OS/2. This includes using commands and the OS/2 text editor.

Course length: 3 days
Course number: 239
Test number: 70-11

Implementing a database design of Microsoft SQL Server for Windows NT

This course teaches the student how to create applications for SQL Server. It is designed for programmers, system analysts, developers, and other support professionals. The course concentrates on the programming skills required to perform this task. Upon course completion, the student can develop complex applications using SQL Server by writing Transact-SQL-code. This includes creating database devices, databases, and tables. The student will also be able to write Transact-SQL statements to perform all the normal functions required by a database management system. The course topics include the following.

➤ Data modeling
➤ Data definition
➤ Retrieving data
➤ Retrieving data—advanced topics
➤ Modifying data
➤ Indexes
➤ Views
➤ Defaults and rules
➤ Programmability
➤ Triggers
➤ Application development and open data services

This is an instructor-led course that concentrates on lecture and hands-on exercises. The overall course goal is to build competency in creating applications for SQL Server.

The prerequisites for this course include a familiarity with the relational database concepts originally presented by E.F. Codd. The student should also have some experience with SQL-Administrator or ISQL and the Microsoft Windows operating system.

Course length: 5 days
Course number: 243
Test number: N/A

Analysis and design of client-server systems

This course is designed to help a manager in charge of the design and analysis of client-server systems. It can also help the consultant in the same areas. The course does not provide application programming specifics; it is more theoretical

in nature. It concentrates on the requirements for analyzing a company's needs, then designing a system built on those needs. The only limiting factors are that this course assumes a GUI front end and relational database server. It is not product-specific.

On course completion the student will possess the knowledge required to extend an existing SDLC (system development life cycle) to include the requirements of a client server system. This includes determining the design objectives and trade-offs. The course topics include the following.

➢ Overview of development methodologies
➢ System definition
➢ Data modeling
➢ Process modeling
➢ Technology architecture
➢ Application architecture
➢ Data architecture
➢ User interface
➢ Process design
➢ Transaction design

This is an instructor-led course consisting of lectures, case studies, and workshop activities designed to help managers and consultants in charge of the analysis and design phases of a client-server system. It includes case studies that explore the considerations and technology required to implement a client-server system. The overall goal of the course is to provide managers and consultants the information they need to convert SDLCs based on conventional computing to a client-server architecture.

The prerequisites for this course include experience with an SDLC and analysis and design technique experience. This assumes that you have a better-than-average understanding of what client-server computing involves and are fully aware of the terms used within that environment. The course also requires experience in information engineering, structured methodology, and object orientation. You should also take the "New Architectures for enterprise computing" course (course number 106) or view the *Understanding New Technologies* video series (course number 295).

Course length: 3 days
Course number: 249
Test number: N/A

Performance-tuning and optimization of Microsoft SQL Server for Windows NT

This course teaches the student how to optimize and tune an SQL Server implementation running under Windows NT. It is designed for server database

owners, designers, system analysts, developers, and other support professionals. The course concentrates on the skills required to perform this task. Upon course completion, the student can tune SQL Server to achieve the best performance in a multiuser transaction processing and decision support environment. This includes diagnosing and resolving performance problems based on specific performance needs. The course topics include the following:

> ➢ Overview of performance issues
> ➢ Platform optimization
> ➢ Data storage structures
> ➢ Selecting indexes for queries
> ➢ The query optimizer overview
> ➢ Phases of query optimization
> ➢ Processing strategies of the query optimizer
> ➢ Using stored procedures
> ➢ Denormalization
> ➢ Database consistency and concurrency
> ➢ Other performance issues
> ➢ Problem analysis

This is an instructor-led course that concentrates on lectures, labs, and hands-on exercises. The overall course goal is to build competency in tuning SQL Server to run under Windows NT. Subgoals include building the knowledge level required to optimize database design, design indexes, write queries, and use various optimization tools.

The prerequisites for this course include a familiarity with the relational database concepts originally presented by E.F. Codd. You must complete the "Supporting Microsoft Windows NT" course or its equivalent, and the "Implementing a database design of Microsoft SQL Server for Windows NT" course or equivalent. The student should also know how to create devices and segments, back up and recover data, and import and export data using the Bulk Copy utility. You must have at least six months worth of Microsoft SQL Server experience, experience analyzing, designing, configuring, and tuning databases, and experience with SQL or ISQL Administrator.

Course length: 5 days
Course number: 255
Test number: N/A

 # Introduction to programming for Microsoft Windows using Microsoft Visual Basic 3.0

This course teaches the student how to create applications using Microsoft Visual Basic. It is designed for programmers, system analysts, developers, and other

support professionals. The course concentrates on the programming skills required to perform this task. Upon course completion, the student can develop simple applications using Microsoft Visual Basic. This includes creating menu-driven front ends, interfacing to other applications, and other standard Windows application constructs. The course topics include the following.

➢ Using Visual Basic
➢ Designing and building applications with Visual Basic
➢ Working with forms
➢ Laying out menus
➢ Connecting forms
➢ Using controls
➢ File browser and other controls
➢ Using data types supported by Visual Basic
➢ Writing code in Visual Basic
➢ Using conditional logic and loops
➢ Debugging code in visual basic
➢ Printing to forms and printers
➢ Using the data access control
➢ Class summary and additional features of Visual Basic

This is an instructor-led course that concentrates on lecture and hands-on exercises. The overall course goal is to build competency in creating applications using Microsoft Visual Basic. Subgoals include the ability to manage several projects at once.

The prerequisites for this course include a good familiarity with the Windows GUI and the ability to manipulate that environment. A basic computer science background is a plus, but not required. A familiarity with the Basic programming language is also a plus, but the course assumes no prior programming experience in this language.

Course length: 3 days
Course number: 273
Test number: N/A

Programming in Microsoft Visual Basic 3.0

This course teaches the student how to create applications using Microsoft Visual Basic. It starts where Introduction to Programming for Microsoft Windows Using Microsoft Visual Basic 3.0 (course number 273) left off. The course is designed for programmers, system analysts, developers, and other support professionals. The course concentrates on the programming skills required to perform this task. Upon course completion, the student can develop complex applications using Microsoft Visual Basic. This includes creating menu-driven front ends, interfacing to other applications, and other standard Windows application constructs. The

course concentrates on areas like DDE, OLE, and event-driven programming techniques. The course topics include the following.

- ➤ Review of Visual Basic
- ➤ Input validation
- ➤ Coding for mouse events
- ➤ Processing data files
- ➤ Implementing dynamic controls
- ➤ Creating dynamic menus
- ➤ Creating a Multiple Document Interface (MDI) application
- ➤ Trapping run-time errors
- ➤ Using Dynamic-Link Libraries (DLL)
- ➤ Implementing Dynamic Data Exchange (DDE)
- ➤ Object Linking and Embedding (OLE)
- ➤ Accessing data using the data control
- ➤ Accessing data—data object variables
- ➤ Adding on-line help
- ➤ Creating graphical effects

This is an instructor-led course that concentrates on lecture and hands-on exercises. The overall course goal is to build competency in creating advanced applications using Microsoft Visual Basic. The course assumes that the programmer already possesses a basic understanding of Microsoft Windows programming concepts and wants to build on this knowledge base. It builds on material learned in previous courses.

The prerequisites for this course include familiarity with a high-level programming language. The student must know how to use Microsoft Windows 3.0 or later. A knowledge of event-driven programming techniques is required. The student must possess the knowledge taught by course number 273. Formal computer science training is a plus, but not absolutely required. However, such training is highly recommended.

Course length: 5 days
Course number: 274
Test number: N/A

 # Supporting Microsoft Windows 3.1 with networks

This course teaches the student how to set up Microsoft Windows 3.1 and assist users in its use. It is designed for developers and other support professionals who need to support the product in the stand-alone, Microsoft LAN Manager, and Novell Netware environments. The course concentrates on the skills required to perform this task. Upon course completion, the student can install, optimize, customize, tune, and support Windows version 3.1. This includes product

installation over a network and a variety of other network-related topics. The course topics include the following:

➤ Introduction to Windows 3.1
➤ Examining the Windows environment
➤ Optimizing Windows
➤ Customizing Windows initialization (INI) files
➤ Running and customizing MS-DOS-based applications in Windows
➤ Fonts used by Windows
➤ Data sharing and registration editor
➤ Customizing Windows setup
➤ Troubleshooting Windows
➤ Overview of networking Windows
➤ Setting up Windows on a network
➤ Network administration with WinLogin
➤ Optimizing Windows on a network
➤ Troubleshooting Windows on a network

This is an instructor-led course that concentrates on lecture, labs, and hands-on exercises. The overall course goal is to build competency in installing, customizing, tuning, and supporting Windows 3.1. Subgoals include the ability to troubleshoot user-related problems.

The prerequisites for this course include familiarity with installing Windows 3.0 or later. Experience with Microsoft LAN Manager or Novell Netware operating system commands is a must. The student must know how to work with PC end-users in a network environment. In addition, the student must possess an operational understanding of the following topics: BIOS, memory, hard disks, types of CPUs, communication ports, printer ports, display adapters, and network hardware. Finally, the student must have a working knowledge of MS-DOS. The student can meet the MS-DOS knowledge portion of the prerequisites by completing *Microsoft MS-DOS 6 Step-by-Step*, a self-paced tutorial. Call (800) MSPRESS for further details on this product.

Course length: 5 days
Course number: 278
Test number: 70-30

Programming in Microsoft C++

This course teaches the student how to create applications using Microsoft C++. It is designed for programmers, system analysts, developers, and other support professionals who have previous Microsoft C programming experience. The course concentrates on the programming skills required to create applications using Microsoft C++. This course provides a special emphasis on object-oriented programming (OOP) techniques. Upon course completion, the student can develop applications using Microsoft C++. This includes creating menu-driven front ends and other standard application constructs. The course topics include the following.

➤ Object-Oriented Programming (OOP)
➤ Basic concepts of OOP
➤ Design methods
➤ Classes
➤ C++ features
➤ Classes and pointers
➤ Other features
➤ Inheritance
➤ Polymorphism
➤ Class libraries
➤ Moving from C to C++
➤ Advanced topics

This is an instructor-led course that concentrates on lecture and hands-on exercises. The overall course goal is to build competency in using Microsoft C++. Subgoals include the ability to describe the benefits of OOP, how to design Microsoft C++ classes, and how to write and debug Microsoft C++ programs.

The prerequisites for this course include a good knowledge of C programming. This includes the use of the following features: pointers to storage and functions, structures, control statements, storage classes, functions, arguments, type casting, object-module libraries, memory models, and preprocessor directives. A knowledge of other OOP languages like Smalltalk is good, but not required.

Course length: 5 days
Course number: 279
Test number: N/A

Programming applications for Microsoft Windows 3.1

This course teaches the student how to create applications for Microsoft Windows using C. It is designed for programmers, system analysts, developers, and other support professionals. The course concentrates on the programming skills required to perform this task. Upon course completion, the student can develop complex applications using C. This includes creating menu-driven front ends, interfacing to other applications, and other standard Windows application constructs. It also provides insights into managing data and code segments, using custom resources, implementing multitasking, implementing DLLs, optimizing the GDI, setting up and processing large print jobs, creating dynamic menus and custom dialog boxes, modifying and creating controls, implementing on-line help, and implementing a DDEML client and server. The course topics include the following.

➤ Windows-based application architecture
➤ Managing memory within a Windows-based environment
➤ Multitasking within the Windows-based environment

> Optimizing the GDI
> Handling text output
> Implementing DLLs
> Handling print jobs
> Building customizable menus
> Building help
> Building custom dialog boxes
> Modifying and creating controls
> Dynamic Data Exchange (DDE) management library

This is an instructor-led course that concentrates on lecture, lab sessions, and hands-on exercises. The overall course goal is to build competency in creating applications for Microsoft Windows.

The prerequisites for this course include successful completion of the Programming for the Microsoft Windows Environment course (number 303). The student must also possess six months programming experience in the Microsoft Windows environment. This includes creating applications that use all the standard Windows constructs including the messaging system, standard user interface objects, GDI functions and device context, and DLLs.

Course length: 4 days
Course number: 283
Test number: N/A

 # Supporting Microsoft Excel

This course teaches the student how to implement, support, and troubleshoot Microsoft Excel. It is designed for technical support specialists, developers, and other support professionals. The course concentrates on the skills required to perform these tasks in a medium-sized to large business environment. The course provides a heavy emphasis on workgroup situations. Upon course completion, the student can install and configure a workgroup implementation of Microsoft Excel. Other skills include the ability to customize the user environment, create custom templates, manage data in a variety of ways, describe how to model and analyze business scenarios, access data and construct views from multiple data sources, export and import file formats to and from other spreadsheet products, exchange data between Microsoft Excel and other applications, troubleshoot and solve common user problems, automate a series of simple actions, and educate users about potential sources of help. The course topics include the following:

> Installation
> Customizing the user environment
> Organizing data
> Data analysis
> List management
> Data access
> File exchange

➢ Presentation and output
➢ Working with other applications
➢ Automation
➢ Resources

This is an instructor-led course that concentrates on lectures, labs, and hands-on exercises. The overall course goal is to build competency in installing, configuring, and using Microsoft Excel. Subgoals include the ability to create macros and to teach users how to use the product most efficiently.

The prerequisites for this course include a familiarity with Microsoft Windows. The student should also know how to select and edit worksheet data, create and format charts, define and create names for use in formulas, create and extract records from a worksheet database, use the macro recorder, and use the Crosstab Report Wizard to access and summarize data. The student can meet many of the prerequisites by completing *Microsoft Excel Step-by-Step*, a self-paced tutorial. Call (800) MSPRESS for further details on this product.

Course length: 3 days
Course number: 284
Test number: 70-31

 # Administration of Microsoft Mail 3.2

This course teaches the student how to implement, maintain, and support Microsoft Mail version 3.2 in a PC LAN environment. It is designed for developers, systems administrators, and other support professionals. The course concentrates on the skills required to perform this task in a LAN environment. Upon course completion, the student can install, optimize, customize, and support Microsoft Mail version 3.2. This includes adding users and groups, installing multiple post offices, setting up remote users, administering program and database files, implementing a backup routine, and using the Microsoft Mail reporting features to monitor and troubleshoot the mail system. The student will also understand the Microsoft Mail 3.2 gateway options, the interconnection between a Microsoft Mail network and an AppleTalk network, and the tools available to customize the Windows-based workstation. Finally, the student will know how to extend the functionality of Microsoft Mail using MAPI. The course topics include the following:

➢ Introduction to Microsoft Mail
➢ Installing a Microsoft Mail post office
➢ Adding users and groups
➢ Running the workstations
➢ Installing multiple post offices on a single LAN
➢ Installing post offices on separate LANs
➢ Directory issues for multiple post offices
➢ Setting up remote users
➢ Message flow, database structure, and data compression

- ➢ Monitoring and troubleshooting the mail system
- ➢ An overview of gateways
- ➢ The Microsoft Mail connection: connecting Microsoft Mail for PC networks and AppleTalk networks
- ➢ Customizing the Microsoft Mail workstation for Windows

This is an instructor-led course that concentrates on lecture, labs, and hands-on exercises. The overall course goal is to build competency in installing, customizing, and supporting Microsoft Mail version 3.2. Subgoals include the ability to troubleshoot user-related problems.

The prerequisites for this course include a good understanding of LAN concepts. The student must know how to work with PC end-users. In addition, the student must know how to perform basic maintenance on a LAN. Installation and configuration skills are highly recommended, but not required for this course.

Course length: 3 days
Course number: 285
Test number: 70-35

 # New features of Microsoft SQL Server for Windows NT for system administrators

This course teaches the student how to implement an SQL Server solution that runs under Microsoft Windows NT. It is designed for programmers, system analysts, developers, and other support professionals. The course assumes that the students already know how to use SQL Server under OS/2. It concentrates on the programming skills required to perform this task. Upon course completion, the student can install SQL Server for Windows NT. This includes creating database devices, databases, and tables. The student will also be able to manage user accounts and permissions, import and export data using the Bulk Copy utility, manage remote servers and logons, troubleshoot system problems, and set server, database, and configuration options to fine-tune performance. The course topics include the following.

- ➢ Installing SQL Server
- ➢ SQL Server integration with the Windows NT environment
- ➢ System administration tools
- ➢ Managing storage
- ➢ Backup and recovery
- ➢ Managing user accounts
- ➢ Monitoring SQL server activity
- ➢ Fine-tuning
- ➢ Data import and export
- ➢ Diagnosing system problems
- ➢ Extended stored procedures

This is an instructor-led course that concentrates on lecture, labs, demos, and hands-on exercises. The overall course goal is to build competency in administering SQL Server running under Windows NT.

The prerequisites for this course include a familiarity with the relational database concepts originally presented by E.F. Codd. This course assumes that the students already possess the knowledge taught in the "Microsoft SQL Server 4.2 system administration" course (number 214). The student must take the "Supporting Microsoft Windows NT" course (number 211) or have equivalent knowledge. In addition, the student must have experience using the Microsoft Windows operating system, have a knowledge of networking concepts like sharing and accessing network resources, and possess a basic knowledge of SQL syntax. The student can meet the Microsoft Windows prerequisites by completing *Microsoft Windows 3.1 Step-by-Step*, a self-paced tutorial. Call (800) MSPRESS for further details on this product.

Course length: 2 days
Course number: 286
Test numbers: 70-22 and 70-23

Application development using Microsoft Word for Windows

This course teaches the student how to create applications using Microsoft Word for Windows. It is designed for programmers, system analysts, developers, and other support professionals. The course concentrates on the programming skills required to perform this task. Upon course completion, the student can develop complex applications using Microsoft Word for Windows. This includes creating menu-driven front ends, interfacing to other applications, and other standard Windows application constructs. The course topics include the following.

> ➤ Developing applications using Microsoft Word
> ➤ Word basic development environment
> ➤ Word basic syntax, variables, and input
> ➤ Arrays, looping, and control
> ➤ User-defined functions, subroutines, and debugging
> ➤ Dialog boxes for user input
> ➤ Fields
> ➤ Building Word basic solutions
> ➤ Dynamic Data Exchange (DDE)
> ➤ Dynamic Link Libraries (DDLs)

This is an instructor-led course that concentrates on lecture and hands-on exercises. The overall course goal is to build competency in creating applications around the Word for Windows word processor.

The prerequisites for this course include a good familiarity with word processors in general, and Word for Windows in particular. The student must know how to create and maintain complex documents using a word processor. This includes boilerplate documents and mail merge. A basic computer science background is a plus, but not required. The student can meet many of the prerequisites by completing *Microsoft Word for Windows Step-by-Step*, a self-paced tutorial. Call (800) MSPRESS for further details on this product.

Course length: 4 days
Course number: 287
Test number: N/A

 # Windows-based programming using the Microsoft Foundation Class Library 2.0

This course teaches the student how to create advanced applications using the MFC Library 2.0 and Microsoft Visual Workbench. It is designed for programmers, system analysts, developers, and other support professionals who already know how to program using C++. The course concentrates on the programming skills required to create applications for Microsoft Windows. Upon course completion, the student can develop Microsoft Windows applications using the MFC Library 2.0 and Microsoft Visual Workbench. This includes creating menu-driven front ends and other standard Windows database application constructs. It does not teach either DDE or OLE concepts. The course topics include the following:

- Microsoft Foundation Class (MFC) overview
- Developing Windows-based programs using Microsoft Visual C++
- The structure of an MFC 2.0/Windows-based application
- Event-driven programming
- The AFX document/view architecture
- Menus and commands
- Simple dialog boxes
- Starting the class application
- Graphic output
- Getting user input
- Command routing in MFC
- Data storage
- Enhancing dialog boxes
- Adding support for VBX controls
- Selecting objects
- Data-entry programs
- Memory management
- Handling text
- Clipboard support
- Controlling graphics

This is an instructor-led course that concentrates on lecture and hands-on exercises. It also provides some lab time to hone the student's programming skills. The overall course goal is to build competency in using the MFC Library 2.0 and Microsoft Visual Workbench. Subgoals include the ability to use VBX controls within applications.

The prerequisites for this course include familiarity with C++ programming. This includes a thorough understanding of the following concepts: abstraction, encapsulation, inheritance, and polymorphism. The student should also understand the associate C++ syntax. A good knowledge of how to use Microsoft Windows is also a requirement.

Course length: 5 days
Course number: 288
Test number: N/A

Programming for the Microsoft Windows environment

This course teaches the student how to create Windows applications using Microsoft C. It is designed for programmers, system analysts, developers, and other support professionals. The course concentrates on the programming skills required to create Windows-based applications using Microsoft C. This course provides a special emphasis on the Windows API. Upon course completion, the student can develop Windows-based applications using Microsoft C. This includes creating menu-driven front ends and other standard application constructs. The course topics include the following.

➢ Overview of Windows
➢ Creating an executable file
➢ Debugging
➢ Implementing menus and accelerators
➢ Text management
➢ Creating a simple text entry system
➢ Enhancing a text entry system
➢ Working with multiple windows
➢ Dialog boxes
➢ Dynamic link libraries
➢ Mouse input
➢ Graphical device interface
➢ Profile files

This is an instructor-led course that concentrates on lecture, lab work, and hands-on exercises. The overall course goal is to build competency in creating Windows-based applications. Subgoals include the ability to use the Windows messaging system and memory management system.

The prerequisites for this course include at least six months programming experience with Microsoft C applications. The student may meet this requirement by attending the "Programming in Microsoft C" course (number 155). This means that the student should know how to compile and link an application. It also means that the student knows how to use C constructs, including the switch statement and pointers. A familiarity with MS-DOS and Windows is also required. The student can meet many of the prerequisites by completing *Microsoft MS-DOS 6 Step-by-Step* and *Microsoft Windows Step-by-Step*. You can purchase these self-paced tutorials by calling (800) MSPRESS and getting further details on these products.

Course length: 5 days
Course number: 303
Test number: N/A

 # Introduction to client-server technologies

This two-day course introduces managers to the components of client-server technology. It helps them build the knowledge base required to work in this new area of computing. This includes understanding the benefits, trade-offs and requirements of client-server computing. Upon course completion the student can describe what client-server computing means: its benefits, trade-offs, and its requirements. This includes a knowledge of component selection and integration. The course topics include the following.

➤ Client-server technologies overview
➤ Building blocks of a client-server system
➤ Foundation components
➤ Client-server application components
➤ Putting it all together: integration, communication, and connectivity
➤ Taking the next step

This is an instructor-led course consisting of lectures only. The goal is to increase the knowledge level of the management of your company. This is not a programmer-level course.

The prerequisites for this course include a familiarity with the corporate information services environment. You should also have a good understanding of computers and data processing. This means that you will need at least a fundamental understanding of client-server basics to gain the most from this course. A very basic knowledge of networks and operating systems is also helpful.

Course length: 2 days
Course number: 304
Test number: N/A

Implementing Microsoft Mail 3.2

This course teaches the student how to design mail systems, develop and execute mail implementation plans, perform general administration, install mail systems, troubleshoot mail systems, and connect Microsoft Mail into the enterprise via gateways. It is designed for system engineers, developers, and other support professionals. The course concentrates on the skills required to plan, install, configure, and support Microsoft Mail version 3.2. Upon course completion the student can describe Microsoft Mail architecture, plan a Microsoft Mail system, install and configure multiple Microsoft Mail post offices, install a Microsoft Windows-based client, describe how a mail message flows through the system, perform administration activities, configure direct and indirect routing, and set up and troubleshoot directory synchronization. In addition, the student can explain the database structure used by Microsoft Mail, describe the Microsoft Mail gateway architecture, know when to use File Format API (FFAPI) and Messaging API (MAPI), install and perform general administration on Microsoft Schedule+, and diagnose and solve common mail-related problems. The course topics include the following.

> ➤ Module 1: Introduction to Microsoft Mail
> ➤ Module 2: Installing a Microsoft Mail post office
> ➤ Module 3: Mail administration
> ➤ Module 4: Schedule+
> ➤ Module 5: Working with multiple post offices
> ➤ Module 6: Directory synchronization
> ➤ Module 7: Database structure
> ➤ Module 8: Setting up remote clients
> ➤ Module 9: Extending Mail
> ➤ Module 10: Microsoft Mail gateways

This is an instructor-led course that concentrates on lecture, lab work, and hands-on exercises. The overall course goal is to build competency in implementing and administrating a Microsoft Mail setup.

The prerequisites for this course include knowledge of a mail system. The student must also possess a general knowledge of LAN administration. This includes the ability to log on to the file server and the ability to create, share, and use network resources.

Course length: 5 days
Course number: 341
Test number: 70-37

D

Sample test questions

Throughout this book you receive many tips and insights on how to prepare for the certification exams. The chapters also include in-depth information about course outlines, how to attend the courses, and detailed information about which courses are necessary to help you obtain your certification. You should also know what the questions will look like to fully prepare for the exams.

This appendix introduces you to the types of questions you will see when you take the certification exams. These questions help you prepare for the exams by showing you what to expect on the actual exam. The appendix does not contain any of the questions on the actual exam, so memorizing them will help you very little.

There is one section for each major test in this appendix. I did not include questions for some of the supplementary exams. Each section starts with a brief paragraph containing some test-taking tips to help you pass the exam. It also discusses a few of the traps that you may want to look for. After each "tips and traps" paragraph is a series of questions. Read each question carefully, then write your answer on a scrap piece of paper. You will find the correct answers to each set of test questions at the end of this appendix.

Here are a few general test-taking tips that work for all the exams. Make sure you watch for them when you take your sample exam.

❶ Always read the question completely. Once you understand the question, read all the answers. Never choose an answer until you read all of the available answers.

❷ Watch out for the word "not" in the question. Small words make a great deal of difference when it comes to answering a question. Read every word in the question carefully. Microsoft will provide an answer in the question that is correct if you fail to read these small words.

❸ You may run into a question that seems ambiguous or poorly worded. Take the time to reread the question until you understand it. Never rush yourself. If all else fails, try each answer in turn and see if it answers the question. In most cases you will find one answer that provides the best response to a question.

❹ In some cases you will find a question that has two correct answers. Always answer with the Microsoft way of performing the task when you run into this situation. One answer is correct; the other answer is more correct. Always choose the best answer to the question.

❺ Remember, there are some cases where you may see more than one right answer on the test. Always choose all the right answers for the question. Looking in the lower left corner of the test display may provide you with a clue as to whether the question requires one or multiple answers.

Microsoft Windows 3.1

The Windows 3.1 exam will ask you questions about every aspect of Windows itself. This means that you won't need to answer questions about any applications you run under Windows 3.1, but you will need to know about the utility programs that come with Windows 3.1. For example, the exam may ask you questions about Program Manager, but it is unlikely that you will see any questions about Windows Paint. Make sure you know the contents of your Windows User Guide before you take this test.

1. What does the WIN.INI file contain?
   a. The default color settings for all your Windows applications.
   b. Application-specific setup information.
   c. Any programs you want to run when Windows starts.
   d. A list of fonts installed for your Windows setup.

2. Which Dynamic Link Library (DLL) handles the user functions under Windows?
   a. HEAP.EXE
   b. USER.EXE
   c. VSHARE.386
   d. COMMDLG.DLL

3. You cannot run Windows under versions of DOS ___.
   a. 3.0 and above
   b. 3.0 and below
   c. 4.01 and above
   d. 3.1 and above

4. Microsoft Windows comes with what type of soft fonts?
   a. Adobe
   b. Bitstream
   c. TrueType
   d. Raster

5. What type of machines does Enhanced Mode support?
   a. 80386
   b. 8088
   c. 80286
   d. Pentium

6. The DOS=HIGH setting in CONFIG.SYS allows you to ___.
   a. Reset the amount of expanded memory that DOS provides.
   b. Load your device driver in the UMB.
   c. Load DOS in the UMB.
   d. Load DOS into the HMA.

7. Using the 32-bit Access setting will allow you to ___.
   a. Run your applications faster.
   b. Get better disk performance.
   c. Increase the available memory pool.
   d. Load your data quicker.

8. Why would you want to create a local copy of Windows instead of using a shared network copy?
   a. To use up the user's hard disk space.
   b. To improve performance.
   c. To free network resources.
   d. To keep the user busy.

9. The PIF editor provides for what types of video memory?
   a. EGA
   b. VGA
   c. Virtual
   d. High Graphics

10. The Ports option in the Control Panel allows you to change what settings?
    a. COM1 and COM2
    b. All serial ports.
    c. All parallel ports.
    d. All video ports.

11. You use Windows in Standard mode with what processor?
    a. 8088
    b. 80286
    c. 80386
    d. 80486

12. The VSHARE.386 drive replaces what DOS TSR?
    a. SHARE.SYS
    b. SHARE.EXE
    c. SHARE.COM
    d. VSHARE.EXE

13. A DLL is a(n) ___.
    a. Application loaded as needed by another application program.
    b. Executable code loaded by another application program.
    c. A library of executable routines loaded by Windows.
    d. Executable code loaded by applications or the operating system.

14. The .GRP files contain ___.
    a. Folder definitions used by PROGMAN.EXE.
    b. Group definitions used by PROGMAN.EXE.
    c. A series of icons used by PROGMAN.EXE.
    d. Nothing important.

15. Windows allows multithreaded application development.
    a. True
    b. False

16. The version of Paintbrush supplied with Windows 3.1 supports which of the following graphics formats?
    a. BMP
    b. DIB
    c. PCX
    d. MSP

17. The System Resources percentage referred to in the About Box of Program Manager refers to ___.
    a. The amount of CPU cycles left for other applications.
    b. The total amount of extended memory available.
    c. The amount of hard disk space left for swap file expansion.
    d. The smaller of two 64K memory areas used to store data objects like icons.

18. The COMMDLG.DLL file provides a standardized set of dialog boxes the user can access from any application that uses them.
    a. True
    b. False

19. The FILE port in the Printer Control Panel allows you to send ___.
    a. Unformatted output to a file instead of the printer.
    b. Formatted output to a file instead of the printer.
    c. Output with printer control characters to a file instead of the printer.
    d. Preformatted documents from a file directly to the printer.

20. You can start applications from File Manager by ___.
    a. double clicking on the executable filename.
    b. double clicking on any data filename.
    c. single clicking on the executable filename.
    d. double clicking on any associated data filename.

Microsoft Windows NT 3.1 installation and support

The Windows NT 3.1 exam will ask you questions about every aspect of Windows NT itself. This means that you won't need to answer questions about any applications you run under Windows NT 3.1, but you will need to know about the utility programs that come with Windows NT 3.1. For example, the exam may ask you questions about Program Manager, but it is unlikely that you will see any questions about Windows Paint. You will also want to know about the networking capabilities of Windows NT. This is a very important aspect of this operating system. Make sure you know the contents of all your Windows NT manuals before you take this test.

1. Windows NT can read which of the following file systems?
   a. HPFS
   b. FAT
   c. NTFS
   d. All of the above

2. Which group has the least amount of privileges on a standard system?
   a. Administrator
   b. Guest
   c. Power user
   d. None of the above

3. Windows NT supports distributed processing.
   a. True
   b. False

4. Which processor(s) can you use to run Windows NT?
   a. Motorola 680x0
   b. Intel 80386 and above
   c. MIPS
   d. Alpha AXP

5. Windows NT will automatically shut down during a power failure if ___.
   a. The UPS provides the proper interface connection.
   b. The UPS automatically shuts down.
   c. You key in the proper password.
   d. The UPS has a serial port connection.

6. Windows NT supports which type of tape backup device?
   a. ¼" Tape
   b. 4 Millimeter DAT
   c. QIC-40/80
   d. None of the above

7. What is the minimum and maximum number of stripe sets that you can create?
   a. 2 minimum and 16 maximum
   b. 5 minimum and 32 maximum
   c. 5 minimum and 16 maximum
   d. 2 minimum and 32 maximum

8. Windows NT can run which of the following types of OS/2 applications:
   a. 1.0 and 2.1 Presentation Manager
   b. 2.1 Presentation Manager Only
   c. 1.0 Character Mode Only
   d. 2.1 FAPI and 2.1 Presentation Manager

9. The Server option in the Control Panel allows you to view the following information:
   a. Number of users remotely connected to the computer.
   b. Number of shared resources opened on the computer.
   c. Number of file locks on open resources.
   d. Number of opened named pipes.

10. The acronym NSI stands for:
    a. Null Server Integration
    b. National Service Inc.
    c. Name Service Interface
    d. Null Service Interface

11. Windows NT provides support for which of the following NICs?
    a. Ethernet
    b. ArcNET
    c. Token Ring
    d. All of the above
    e. None of the above

12. You can reboot your computer by pressing Ctrl-Alt-Del at the Windows NT login dialog.
    a. True
    b. False

13. The Properties button on the Print Manager toolbar allows you to ___.
    a. View information about the selected print job.
    b. Connect with a shared network printer.
    c. Stop printing on the selected printer.
    d. View or change the characteristics of the selected printer.

14. When using OLE, the difference between an embedded and a linked object is ___.
    a. The embedded object must appear on the local hard drive.
    b. The application which created the embedded object must appear on the local hard drive.
    c. A linked object automatically updates itself to match the current state of the original file.
    d. An embedded object automatically updates itself to match the current state of the original file.

15. Windows NT users need to worry about the level of available system resources like Windows 3.1 users do.
    a. True
    b. False

16. You can run POSIX applications that are written to the ___ standard under Windows NT.
    a. IEEE 1002.0
    b. IEEE 1002.1
    c. IEEE 1003.0
    d. IEEE 1003.1

17. The ___ directory contains the AUTOEXEC.NT and CONFIG.NT used to run DOS applications.
    a. C:\
    b. \WINNT\SYSTEM
    c. \WINNT\SYSTEM32
    d. \USERS

18. Windows NT reserves the ___ filename extension for the ___ application.
    a. TRM, Terminal
    b. CRD, Cardfile
    c. INI, Write
    d. INI, Notepad
    e. TXT, Notepad

19. You can change the desktop font characteristics by modifying ___ entries in the ___ folder in the ___ document window using REGEDT32.
    a. IconTitle, Desktop, HKEY_CURRENT_USER
    b. IconTitle, Desktop, HKEY_LOCAL_MACHINE
    c. ScreenStyle, Desktop, HKEY_LOCAL_MACHINE
    d. ScreenStyle, International, HKEY_CURRENT_USER
    e. IconTitle, International, HKEY_CURRENT_USER

20. Windows NT multitasking options include ___.
    a. Optimal foreground application response time.
    b. Best foreground application response time.
    c. Foreground and background applications equally responsive.
    d. Foreground application more responsive than background.

⇨ Microsoft Mail for PC Networks 3.2—Desktop

Microsoft Mail is used in a variety of environments. This test will measure your knowledge of Microsoft Mail, not the environments that it runs under. This is an important consideration for the test taker, because it is nearly impossible to memorize all the information required to take the environmental context of

Microsoft Mail into account. The Desktop exam will look close at the actual use of Microsoft Mail. It will also test your ability to use Microsoft Mail in a LAN—most likely the workgroup environment rather than a WAN or multiple-server environment. As usual, make sure you study your Microsoft Mail manuals in detail before taking the exam.

1. The acronym MTA stands for ___.
   a. Minimum Transfer Access
   b. Migratory Timing Aid
   c. Message Transfer Agent
   d. Mail Transfer Agent

2. The ServerPath=drive:\directory entry appears in what section of MSMAIL.INI?
   a. [Microsoft Mail]
   b. [Custom Commands]
   c. [Server]
   d. It doesn't appear in this file.

3. The default name for the administrator message file is___.
   a. MSMAIL.MSG
   b. MSMAIL.MMF
   c. ADMIN.MSG
   d. ADMIN.MMF

4. To remove the work group post office, you ___.
   a. Press the Remove Post Office button in the Post Office Manager.
   b. Delete the WGPO directory tree.
   c. Erase all the Microsoft Mail DLLs in the SYSTEM directory.
   d. Delete the WPGO entries in the Custom Commands section of MSMAIL.INI.

5. The Shared Folders dialog box provides the following information.
   a. Number of folders.
   b. Total messages by folders.
   c. Number of returned messages.
   d. Bytes used by messages.

6. The post office Manager allows you to ___.
   a. Compress shared folders.
   b. Move your WGPO.
   c. Add and remove users.
   d. Delete your WGPO.

7. The TZ option of all computers must match the ___ computer to ensure directory synchronization works correctly.
   a. MTA
   b. Dispatch
   c. Administrative
   d. None of the above

8. You should create the following number of post offices for each workgroup.
   a. 1
   b. 2
   c. 1 for each user
   d. As many as you need

9. What task does EXTERNAL.EXE perform?
   a. Exports messages to other formats.
   b. Imports messages from other formats.
   c. Transfers messages between post offices.
   d. Provides gateway services.

10. You use a gateway to transfer messages to a foreign mail system.
    a. True
    b. False

11. Mail requires which of the following pieces of information when creating a new account?
    a. Department, Name, Mailbox
    b. Name, Mailbox, Password
    c. Name, Department, Password
    d. Name, Department, Office

12. The maximum length of most account fields is ___.
    a. 32 characters
    b. 64 characters
    c. 128 characters
    d. 256 characters

13. The default workgroup password is ___.
    a. MASTER
    b. ADMINISTRATOR
    c. PASSWORD
    d. There is no default password.

14. Mail provides the following features: ___.
    a. Folders to organize your messages.
    b. Automatic translation into other email packages.
    c. An address book for storing other users' email information.
    d. The ability to embed objects in a message.

15. Your new mail messages always appear in the ___ folder.
    a. Deleted mail
    b. Sent mail
    c. New mail
    d. Inbox

Microsoft Windows NT Advanced Server

The Windows NT Advanced Server 3.1 exam will ask you questions about every aspect of Windows NT Advanced Server; it will not concentrate very much on Windows NT. This means that you won't need to answer questions about any applications you run under Windows NT 3.1, but you may need to know about the utility programs that come with Windows NT 3.1. The exam will concentrate heavily on the networking aspects of Windows NT Advanced Server. For example, the exam will probably ask you about network security, but it is unlikely that you will see any questions about Program Manager. Make sure you know the contents of all your Windows NT and Windows NT Advanced Server manuals before you take this test.

1. Windows NT Advanced Server forces you to create an emergency repair disk.
   a. True
   b. False

2. The RAS software shipped with Windows NT Advanced Server will support how many sessions?
   a. 8
   b. 16
   c. 32
   d. 64

3. Assume that you are the administrator for three domains in your department. Users from the MANAGEMENT domain need access to the files in the ACCOUNT and RESEARCH domains. Users in the ACCOUNT domain also require access to the RESEARCH domain. How would you set this up?
   a. Establish one-way trust relationships in which:
      MANAGEMENT trusts RESEARCH
      MANAGEMENT trusts ACCOUNT
      ACCOUNT trusts RESEARCH
   b. Establish one-way trust relationships in which:
      RESEARCH trusts MANAGEMENT
      RESEARCH trusts ACCOUNT
      ACCOUNT trusts MANAGEMENT
   c. Establish two-way trust relationships in which:
      MANAGEMENT trusts RESEARCH
      MANAGEMENT trusts ACCOUNT
      ACCOUNT trusts RESEARCH
   d. Establish two-way trust relationships in which:
      RESEARCH trusts MANAGEMENT
      RESEARCH trusts ACCOUNT
      ACCOUNT trusts MANAGEMENT

4. What is the system default profile?
   a. A configuration file used for all 32-bit applications.
   b. The configuration provided for the GUEST user.
   c. The configuration in force when no one is logged in.
   d. There is no system default profile.

5. What is one way to improve security on your network?
   a. Disable the GUEST account on all domains.
   b. Impose stiff penalties for lazy users.
   c. Install locks on all the PCs.
   d. Remove the keyboard from the server.

6. You establish a one-way trust relationship where SALES trusts ACCOUNT. A user from ACCOUNT wants to access files in a shared directory in SALES. What else do you need to do to grant access?
   a. Nothing; the user already has access.
   b. Grant the user access to the shared directory.
   c. Establish a two-way trust relationship where SALES trusts ACCOUNT.
   d. The user must log in from a different workstation.

7. You are a user in the SALES domain where the following trusts are in force:
   SALES domain trusts ACCOUNT domain
   SALES domain has a two-way trust with ART
   RESEARCH domain has a two-way trust with SALES
   MFG domain trusts SALES domain

   Which domains can you access?
   a. ACCOUNT
   b. RESEARCH
   c. SALES
   d. ART
   e. MFG

8. You can simplify network administration by using master domain model for the following reasons.
   a. Simplified resource management.
   b. The master domain model only complicates matters.
   c. Network administrators can exercise total network control.
   d. All user accounts can reside in one centralized location.

9. Disk mirroring ___.
   a. Replicates the data from one disk to another.
   b. Uses disk resources efficiently.
   c. Reduces network reliability.
   d. Causes irreversible file damage.

10. Each server in the network requires a UPS because ___.
    a. The UPS companies need more money.
    b. Each server requires a UPS to obtain power failure notification.
    c. One UPS can only service one server.
    d. Using separate UPSs improves system reliability.

11. Windows NT provides support for which of the following NICs?
    a. Ethernet
    b. ArcNET
    c. Token Ring
    d. All of the above
    e. None of the above

12. You can reboot your computer by pressing Ctrl-Alt-Del at the Windows NT login dialog.
    a. True
    b. False

13. The Properties button on the Print Manager toolbar allows you to ___.
    a. View information about the selected print job.
    b. Connect with a shared network printer.
    c. Stop printing on the selected printer.
    d. View or change the characteristics of the selected printer.

14. When using OLE, the difference between an embedded and a linked object is ___.
    a. The embedded object must appear on the local hard drive.
    b. The application which created the embedded object must appear on the local hard drive.
    c. A linked object automatically updates itself to match the current state of the original file.
    d. An embedded object automatically updates itself to match the current state of the original file.

15. Windows NT users need to worry about the level of available system resources like Windows 3.1 users do.
    a. True
    b. False

16. You can run POSIX applications that are written to the ___ standard under Windows NT.
    a. IEEE 1002.0
    b. IEEE 1002.1
    c. IEEE 1003.0
    d. IEEE 1003.1

17. The ___ directory contains the AUTOEXEC.NT and CONFIG.NT used to run DOS applications.
    a. C:\
    b. \WINNT\SYSTEM
    c. \WINNT\SYSTEM32
    d. \USERS

18. Windows NT reserves the ___ filename extension for the ___ application.
    a. TRM, Terminal
    b. CRD, Cardfile
    c. INI, Write
    d. INI, Notepad
    e. TXT, Notepad

19. You can change the desktop font characteristics by modifying ___ entries in the ___ folder in the ___ document window using REGEDT32.
    a. IconTitle, Desktop, HKEY_CURRENT_USER
    b. IconTitle, Desktop, HKEY_LOCAL_MACHINE
    c. ScreenStyle, Desktop, HKEY_LOCAL_MACHINE
    d. ScreenStyle, International, HKEY_CURRENT_USER
    e. IconTitle, International, HKEY_CURRENT_USER

20. Windows NT multitasking options include ___.
    a. Optimal foreground application response time.
    b. Best foreground application response time.
    c. Foreground and background applications equally responsive.
    d. Foreground application more responsive than background.

⇨ Microsoft Windows for Workgroups 3.11

The Windows for Workgroups exam will ask you questions about every aspect of Windows itself. This means that you won't need to answer questions about any applications you run under Windows for Workgroups, but you will need to know about the utility programs that come with Windows for Workgroups. For example, the exam may ask you questions about Program Manager, but it is unlikely that you will see any questions about Windows Paint. Make sure you know the contents of your Windows User Guide before you take this test.

1. Which special workgroup-related utilities does Windows for Workgroups provide that standard Windows does not?
   a. Microsoft Mail
   b. Paintbrush
   c. Program Manager
   d. Schedule+

2. You will find the printer setups in the ___ section of WIN.INI.
   a. [Printers]
   b. [Windows]
   c. [Ports]
   d. [Desktop]

3. Which entries will you find in SYSTEM.INI when 32-bit access is enabled?
   a. device=*int13
   b. device=*access
   c. device=*wdctrl
   d. 32BitDiskAccess=ON

4. What entry in AUTOEXEC.BAT would load a TSR high?
   a. DEVICEHIGH=FILENAME.EXT
   b. FILENAME.EXT /LH
   c. LOADHIGH FILENAME.EXT
   d. UMB FILENAME.EXT

5. Which PIF settings affect application execution speed?
   a. KB Required
   b. Detect Idle Time
   c. Foreground Priority
   d. Background Priority

6. The SETUP.INF file contains ___.
   a. All your standard setup options.
   b. Special setup options for your hardware.
   c. Most of your setup options.
   d. All setup options except network options.

7. Windows for Workgroups supports Netware Lite.
   a. True
   b. False

8. Token Ring patch cables come in ___ lengths.
   a. 8, 30, 60, and 120 foot
   b. 8, 30, 75, and 150 foot
   c. 8, 16, 32, and 64 foot
   d. 15, 30, 45, and 60 foot

9. The maximum distance between a network node and a passive hub when using ArcNET is ___.
   a. 50 feet
   b. 75 feet
   c. 100 feet
   d. 125 feet

10. What Windows for Workgroups network-related drivers do you need to add to CONFIG.SYS?
    a. DRIVERS.SYS
    b. PROTMAN.DOS
    c. WORKGRP.SYS
    d. NETDRV.SYS

11. You use Windows in Standard mode with what processor?
    a. 8088
    b. 80286
    c. 80386
    d. 80486

12. The VSHARE.386 drive replaces what DOS TSR?
    a. SHARE.SYS
    b. SHARE.EXE
    c. SHARE.COM
    d. VSHARE.EXE

13. A DLL is a(n) ___.
    a. Application loaded as needed by another application program.
    b. Executable code loaded by another application program.
    c. A library of executable routines loaded by Windows.
    d. Executable code loaded by applications or the operating system.

14. The .GRP files contain ___.
    a. Folder definitions used by PROGMAN.EXE.
    b. Group definitions used by PROGMAN.EXE.
    c. A series of icons used by PROGMAN.EXE.
    d. Nothing important.

15. Windows allows multithreaded application development.
    a. True
    b. False

16. The version of Paintbrush supplied with Windows 3.1 supports which of the following graphics formats?
    a. BMP
    b. DIB
    c. PCX
    d. MSP

17. The System Resources percentage referred to in the About Box of Program Manager refers to ___.
    a. The amount of CPU cycles left for other applications.
    b. The total amount of extended memory available.
    c. The amount of hard disk space left for swap file expansion.
    d. The smaller of two 64K memory areas used to store data objects like icons.

18. The COMMDLG.DLL file provides a standardized set of dialog boxes the user can access from any application that uses them.
    a. True
    b. False

19. The FILE port in the Printer Control Panel allows you to send ___.
   a. Unformatted output to a file instead of the printer.
   b. Formatted output to a file instead of the printer.
   c. Output with printer control characters to a file instead of the printer.
   d. Preformatted documents from a file directly to the printer.

20. You can start applications from File Manager by ___.
   a. Double clicking on the executable filename.
   b. Double clicking on any data filename.
   c. Single clicking on the executable filename.
   d. Double clicking on any associated data filename.

 # Microsoft Mail for PC Networks 3.2—Enterprise

Microsoft Mail is used in a variety of environments. This test will measure your knowledge of Microsoft Mail, not the environments that it runs under. This is an important consideration for the test taker, because it is nearly impossible to memorize all the information required to take the environmental context of Microsoft Mail into account. The test will take a detailed look at various connectivity features of Microsoft Mail in addition to the usual installation and configuration issues. It will also test your knowledge about Microsoft Mail in a variety of network situations, including WANs. Make sure you spend the time required to study your Microsoft Mail manuals. Pay close attention to the material in the administrator's guide. You will also want to spend some time working with Schedule+, because the exam spends some time with this product as well.

1. Which of the following gateways does Microsoft Mail support?
   a. PROFS OV/VM
   b. X.400
   c. SMTP
   d. FAX

2. Schedule+ requires ___ per user for calendar storage space.
   a. 110K
   b. 120K
   c. 130K
   d. 140K

3. Where does Schedule+ store the user calendar information?
   a. CAL subdirectory
   b. SYSTEM subdirectory
   c. MAIL subdirectory
   d. TEMP subdirectory

4. Microsoft ships Microsoft Mail gateway packages with both hardware and software.
   a. True
   b. False

5. What is the minimum FILES= setting you should use for Microsoft Mail?
   a. 45
   b. 55
   c. 65
   d. 75

6. To use Microsoft Mail with a Netware Network, you need to ___.
   a. Create a directory where you want the WGPO to appear.
   b. Grant full trustee rights to this directory.
   c. Make the directory read-only.
   d. Use File Manager to map a drive letter to the WGPO directory.

7. You compress the shared folders by ___.
   a. Pressing the Compress button in the Shared Folders dialog box of the Post Office Manager.
   b. Using a utility program to reorganize the disk.
   c. Removing excess space by using a utility like PKZIP.
   d. Pressing the OK button in the Details dialog box of the Post Office Manager.

8. You must ___ before you can create an administrator account.
   a. Add users to the post office.
   b. Create a WGPO directory on a local or network drive.
   c. Change CONFIG.SYS to contain the path of Microsoft Mail.
   d. Create a new work group post office.

9. A WPGO requires the following amounts of disk space.
   a. 320K for the post office and 16K for each user mailbox.
   b. 360K for the post office and 16K for each user mailbox.
   c. 320K for the post office and 32K for each user mailbox.
   d. 360K for the post office and 32K for each user mailbox.

10. Schedule+ provides the following forms of data protection:
   a. Encryption only
   b. Password protection only
   c. Both encryption and password protection
   d. It does not provide any form of protection.

11. To improve network mail security you should ___.
   a. Force the user to change their password from the default.
   b. Make the shared network directory read-only.
   c. Remove the deleted folder.
   d. All of the above.

12. What folder types does Microsoft Mail support?
    a. Public
    b. Private
    c. Local
    d. Shared

13. Compressing a folder ___.
    a. Makes the messages shorter.
    b. Reduces the time required to access messages.
    c. Increases the number of messages the folder can hold.
    d. Recovers hard disk space used by deleted messages.

14. Which appointment types does Schedule+ support?
    a. Normal
    b. Tentative
    c. Recurring
    d. Private
    e. All of the above

15. Schedule+ allows the user to set access privileges for their calendars.
    a. True
    b. False

 # Microsoft SQL Server 4.2 database administration for OS/2

The Microsoft SQL Server 4.2 database administration for OS/2 exam tests your expertise in administering this product. It is an operating system-specific test. This means that you can expect to see some operating system questions mixed in with the standard SQL server questions. As a result, it pays to study your operating system manuals in addition to the SQL Server manuals before you take the exam. You will also want to study the works of E.F. Codd. This exam tests your knowledge of relational theory in addition to the practical knowledge required to administer SQL Server.

1. You can grant ___ permissions to SQL Server Users.
    a. Table
    b. Directory
    c. Column
    d. Command

2. SQL Server supports ___ processing.
    a. Reaction
    b. Proactive
    c. Transaction
    d. Correspondence

3. The Object Manager helps you create scripts to generate your database schema.
    a. True
    b. False

4. A null value is the same as ___.
    a. Providing a 0 or a blank string.
    b. No value at all.
    c. Saying you are unsure and need help.
    d. Asking the system to remove the previous value.

5. Which referential integrity devices does SQL Server support?
    a. Primary keys
    b. Foreign keys
    c. Passwords
    d. Encryption

6. Which clients does SQL Server support?
    a. IBM OS/2 Version 1.2
    b. Apple Macintosh
    c. VMS
    d. Windows Version 3.0

7. You can retrieve a list of tables in a database from the ___ table.
    a. Sysusages
    b. Sysdatabases
    c. Systables
    d. Sysobjects

8. The Service Manager utility allows you to ___ SQL Server.
    a. Reactivate
    b. Start, stop, and pause
    c. Start and stop
    d. Deactivate and reactivate

9. The SQL statement "SELECT date, time, event FROM newstips WHERE event = 'murder'" would ___.
    a. Retrieve the date, time, and event columns from the newstips table. It would only include rows where the event was a murder.
    b. Retrieve the newstips columns from the date, time, and event tables. It would only include rows where the event was a murder.
    c. Remove rows from the newstips table where the event was a murder and the date and event columns contained NULL values.
    d. Retrieve the date and time columns from the newstips table. It would only include rows where the event was a murder.

10. SQL Server supports the___ file system(s).
    a. NTFS
    b. UNIX
    c. FAT
    d. HPFS

Microsoft SQL Server 4.2 database implementation

The Microsoft SQL Server 4.2 database implementation exam tests your expertise in using this product. This is not an operating system-specific test; it evaluates your ability to use SQL Server to create a fully functional database application. Make sure you study all the SQL Server manuals before you take this exam. Concentrate your efforts on the Transact SQL and Language Reference manuals. You will also want to study the works of E.F. Codd. This exam tests your knowledge of relational theory in addition to the practical knowledge required to administer SQL Server.

1. Which statement will commit your data transaction?
   a. Rollback transaction
   b. End transaction
   c. Cancel transaction
   d. Quit transaction

2. You cannot update multiple tables through a view.
   a. True
   b. False

3. A clustered index allows you to retrieve ___.
   a. A single row.
   b. Multiple rows with noncontiguous key values.
   c. Multiple rows with contiguous key values.
   d. None of the above.

4. A one-to-many relationship is where ___.
   a. Many entries in table A relate to a single entry in table B.
   b. One entry in table A relates to a single entry in table B.
   c. One entry in table A relates to many entries in table B.
   d. Many entries in table A relate to many entries in table B.

5. The Windows NT version of SQL Server allows access to ___ of memory.
   a. 1MB
   b. 2MB
   c. 1GB
   d. 2GB

6. What is meant by the term "deadly embrace"?
   a. Two users want access to the same data at the same time and each has a lock on one part of the data.
   b. A transaction requires so many CPU cycles that there is no way to complete it.
   c. One or more SQL statements violated referential integrity and cause damage to the database.
   d. A virus placed the computer in an uncertain state, causing damage to the database.

7. The SQL statement "SELECT date, time, event FROM newstips WHERE event = 'murder'" would ___.
   a. Retrieve the date, time, and event columns from the newstips table. It would only include rows where the event was a murder.
   b. Retrieve the newstips columns from the date, time, and event tables. It would only include rows where the event was a murder.
   c. Remove rows from the newstips table where the event was a murder and the date and event columns contained NULL values.
   d. Retrieve the date and time columns from the newstips table. It would only include rows where the event was a murder.

8. Given a table named SALES with columns DATE, CUSTOMER, TOTAL, and COMMENT, how would you create a view containing only the DATE, CUSTOMER, and TOTAL column data for sales over $1,000?
   a. Create view no_comment(DATE, CUSTOMER, TOTAL) as select DATE, CUSTOMER, TOTAL, COMMENT from SALES;
   b. Create view no_comment(DATE, CUSTOMER, TOTAL) as select DATE, CUSTOMER, TOTAL from SALES;
   c. Create view no_comment(DATE, CUSTOMER, TOTAL) as select DATE, CUSTOMER, TOTAL from SALES where SALES.TOTAL > 1,000;
   d. Create view no_comment(DATE, CUSTOMER, TOTAL) as select DATE, CUSTOMER, TOTAL from SALES where TOTAL >= 1,000;

9. A foreign key must reference a ___ in another table.
   a. Similar value
   b. Primary key
   c. Unique reference
   d. Foreign key

10. SQL Server protects your database from damage by providing ___.
    a. Instant processing
    b. Rollback capability
    c. Automated damage control
    d. System and database logs

→ Microsoft SQL Server 4.2 database administration for Windows NT

The Microsoft SQL Server 4.2 database administration for Windows NT exam tests your expertise in administering this product. It is an operating system-specific test. This means that you can expect to see some operating system questions mixed in with the standard SQL Server questions. As a result, it pays to study your operating system manuals in addition to the SQL Server manuals before you take the exam. You will also want to study the works of E.F. Codd. This exam tests your knowledge of relational theory in addition to the practical knowledge required to administer SQL Server.

1. SQL Server supports the ___ file system(s).
   a. NTFS
   b. UNIX
   c. FAT
   d. HPFS

2. You can use the following networks with SQL Server.
   a. IBM LAN Server
   b. Microsoft LAN Manager
   c. Novell Netware
   d. TCP/IP-based Networks

3. The SQL statement "SELECT date, time, event FROM newstips WHERE
   event = 'murder'" would ___.
   a. Retrieve the date, time, and event columns from the newstips table. It would
      only include rows where the event was a murder.
   b. Retrieve the newstips columns from the date, time, and event tables. It would
      only include rows where the event was a murder.
   c. Remove rows from the newstips table where the event was a murder and the
      date and event columns contained NULL values.
   d. Retrieve the date and time columns from the newstips table. It would only
      include rows where the event was a murder.

4. A primary key must provide a ___ for each row in the table.
   a. Similar value
   b. Password
   c. Unique reference
   d. Set of mandatory input columns

5. SQL Server protects your database from damage by providing ___.
   a. Instant Processing
   b. Rollback Capability
   c. Automated Damage Control
   d. System and Database Logs

6. Windows NT allows you to provide filenames that are ___ characters long.
   a. 8
   b. 128
   c. 254
   d. 255

7. Gateways allows you to ___.
   a. Access data on foreign computer systems
   b. Access the OS/2 version of SQL Server
   c. Open your SQL Server database
   d. Configure your SQL Server database

8. You can retrieve a list of tables in a database from the ___ table.
   a. Sysusages
   b. Sysdatabases
   c. Systables
   d. Sysobjects

9. You can grant ___ permissions to SQL Server Users.
   a. Table
   b. Directory
   c. Column
   d. Command

10. You can use the Windows NT Performance Monitor to ___.
    a. Check the reliability of your implementation.
    b. Check the speed of your implementation.
    c. Check the integrity of your implementation.
    d. Improve the speed of your implementation.

Microsoft Windows 3.1 answers

1. a, b, c, d	11. b, c, d
2. b	12. b
3. b	13. d
4. c	14. a
5. a, d	15. b
6. d	16. a, b, c, d
7. a, b, d	17. d
8. b, c	18. a
9. d	19. c
10. b	20. a, d

Microsoft Windows NT 3.1 installation and support answers

1. d	11. a, c
2. b	12. b
3. a	13. d
4. b, c, d	14. b, c
5. a	15. b
6. b, c	16. d
7. d	17. c
8. c	18. a, b, ,d, e
9. a, b, c, d	19. a
10. c	20. b, c, d

Microsoft Mail for PC Networks 3.2—desktop answers

1. c	9. c
2. a	10. a
3. b	11. b
4. b, d	12. a
5. a, b, d	13. c
6. a, c	14. a, c, d
7. c	15. d
8. a	

Microsoft Windows NT Advanced Server 3.1 answers

1. b	11. a, c
2. d	12. b
3. b	13. d
4. c	14. b, c
5. a	15. b
6. b	16. d
7. b, c, d, e	17. c
8. a, d	18. a, b, d, e
9. a	19. a
10. b, d	20. b, c, d

Microsoft Windows for Workgroups 3.11 answers

1. a, d	11. b, c, d
2. b	12. b
3. a, c, d	13. d
4. c	14. a
5. c, d	15. b
6. a	16. a, b, c, d
7. b	17. d
8. b	18. a
9. c	19. c
10. b, c	20. a, d

⇨ Microsoft Mail for PC Networks 3.2—Enterprise answers

1. a, b, c, d	9. b
2. c	10. c
3. a	11. a
4. b	12. b, d
5. d	13. d
6. a, b, d	14. e
7. a	15. a
8. b, d	

⇨ Microsoft SQL Server 4.2 database administration for OS/2 answers

1. a, c, d	6. b, c
2. c	7. d
3. a	8. b
4. b	9. a
5. a, b	10. c, d

⇨ Microsoft SQL Server 4.2 database implementation answers

1. b	6. a
2. b	7. a
3. a, c	8. c
4. c	9. b
5. d	10. b, d

⇨ Microsoft SQL Server 4.2 database administration for Windows NT answers

1. a, c, d	6. d
2. a, b, c, d	7. a
3. a	8. d
4. c	9. a, c, d
5. b, d	10. b

Index

Other Bestsellers
of Related Interest

Novell Certification Handbook
—*John Mueller, CNE and Robert WIlliams, CNE, CNI*
A one-stop source of essential information for network administrators, engineers, and instructors who want to obtain Novell certification or, having already acquired it, use it to the best advantage in an increasingly competitive job market.

0-8306-4555-1 $24.95 Paper
0-8306-4554-3 $39.95 Hard

Windows NT: The Complete Reference
—*Allen L. Wyatt*
This outstanding resource is ideal for all users and covers the full range of Windows NT commands, functions, and features, from installing the program and using basic commands to handling advanced operations such as multi-tasking, networking, and security issues.

0-07-881832-X $29.95 Paper

Excel for Windows Made Easy, Fourth Edition
—*Martin S. Matthews*
Hands-on examples, clearly-written instructions, and well-chosen exercises boost skills in the three major components of Excel: worksheets, databases, and charts.

0-07-881973-3 $24.95 Paper

Excel for Windows: The Complete Reference, Second Edition
—*Martin S. Matthews and Stephanie Seymour*
Every user will want this comprehensive desktop reference that answers Excel questions. With the reference arranged alphabetically and formatted with thumb tabs like an encyclopedia, answers to all questions are guaranteed.

0-07-881975-X $34.95 Paper

NT Programming Handbook

Herbert Schildt

This fast-paced, far-reaching volume gives experienced programmers detailed, ground-up coverage of the entire application development process under Windows NT.

0-07-811873-7   **$29.95 Paper**

How to Order

 Call 1-800-822-8158
24 hours a day,
7 days a week
in U.S. and Canada

 Mail this coupon to:
McGraw-Hill, Inc.
Blue Ridge Summit, PA
17294-0840

 Fax your order to:
717-794-5291

 EMAIL
70007.1531@COMPUSERVE.COM
COMPUSERVE: GO MH

Thank you for your order!

EASY ORDER FORM—
SATISFACTION GUARANTEED

Ship to:

Name _____

Address _____

City/State/Zip _____

Daytime Telephone No. _____

ITEM NO.	QUANTITY	AMT.

Method of Payment:

☐ Check or money order
   enclosed (payable to
   McGraw-Hill)

☐ [American Express Cards]   ☐ VISA

☐ MasterCard   ☐ DISCOVER

Shipping & Handling charge from chart below	
Subtotal	
Please add applicable state & local sales tax	
TOTAL	

Account No. ☐☐☐☐☐☐☐☐☐☐☐☐☐☐

Signature _____ Exp. Date _____
Order invalid without signature

**In a hurry? Call 1-800-822-8158 anytime,
day or night, or visit your local bookstore.**

Code = BC44ZNA

Shipping and Handling Charges

Order Amount	Within U.S.	Outside U.S.
Less than $15	$3.45	$5.25
$15.00 - $24.99	$3.95	$5.95
$25.00 - $49.99	$4.95	$6.95
$50.00 - and up	$5.95	$7.95